Charles Dickens on the Screen

The Film, Television, and Video Adaptations

Michael Pointer

Consulting Editor: Anthony Slide

The Scarecrow Press, Inc.
Lanham, Md., and London

SCARECROW PRESS, INC.

Published in the United States of America
by Scarecrow Press, Inc.
4720 Boston Way
Lanham, Maryland 20706

4 Pleydell Gardens, Folkestone
Kent CT20 2DN, England

Copyright © 1996 by Michael Pointer

All rights reserved. No part of this publication may be reproduced,
stored in a retrieval system, or transmitted in any form or by any
means, electronic, mechanical, photocopying, recording, or otherwise,
without the prior permission of the publisher.

British Cataloguing-in-Publication Information Available

Library of Congress Cataloging-in-Publication Data

Pointer, Michael.
Charles Dickens on the screen : the film, television, and video adaptations / Michael Pointer ; consulting editor, Anthony Slide.
p. cm.
Includes bibliographical references and index.
1. Dickens, Charles, 1812-1870—Film and video adaptations. 2. English fiction—Film and video adaptations. I. Title.
PR4575.P65   1996   791.43'75—dc20   94-49372

ISBN 0-8108-2960-6 (cloth : alk. paper)

™ The paper used in this publication meets the minimum requirements of
American National Standard for Information Sciences—Permanence of
Paper for Printed Library Materials, ANSI Z39.48–1984.
Manufactured in the United States of America.

Contents

Introduction   v

Acknowledgments   vii

1 Dramatizing Dickens   1
2 The Wizardry of Boz   7
3 Pictures From Everywhere   25
4 Condensing Dickens   37
5 Dickens With Dialogue   49
6 In a Tradition of Quality   55
7 A Social Chorus   65
8 A Companion Picture   73
9 Reconstructing Dickens   83
10 Television Triumphs   91
11 Television Torments   99
12 The Great Inimitable   105

Catalog of Film, Television, and Video Productions   115
   Abbreviations   116
   Cinema Films   117
   Television and Video Productions   145

Bibliography   195

Index   199

About the Author

Introduction

> When television, the cinema or even the theatre adapt a distinguished novel for their own purpose they are liable to subtract more than they add... The conclusion to be drawn, and it is a vital one, is that literature has an inviolable nature of its own. But that does not mean that there is no merit in these endeavours to adapt literature for another medium.
>
> *The Times*, reviewing
> *A Tale of Two Cities*, April 24, 1965

The name Charles Dickens appears to carry two distinct associations in the minds of most people. There is Dickens, the so-called inventor of Christmas, all stagecoaches, holly, jollity, and punch bowls, and there is the word *Dickensian,* which has become a synonym for the conditions of squalor and deprivation in mid-Victorian England which Dickens campaigned so hard to rectify. These two aspects have been exploited in dramatizations for both the cinema and television; more frequently the former. In fact, it has become customary on both British and American television for something by Dickens to be transmitted at Christmas, even though sometimes the TV play or old movie has nothing to do with Christmas.

Charles Dickens is one of the authors most adapted for the screen, although such a claim requires some qualification and explanation. There have probably been more Sherlock Holmes films, for example, but not all taken from Conan Doyle's works. There have probably been more films with other famous fictional characters, with the same reservation. But there have been no *series* of films and sequels built on particular Dickens characters; no *Son of Oliver Twist,* no *Martin Chuzzlewit Rides Again,* no *Brides of David Copperfield,* not even *Abbot and Costello Meet Edwin Drood.* Only once on television has a sequel to a Dickens novel been attempted.

Dickens has not been treated like any mere writer of fiction whose books can be distorted and altered beyond measure if a large enough sum is paid for the film rights, or if, as has always been the case with Dickens films, the works are in the public domain. On the contrary, Dickens's works form part of that corpus of classic literature that is so well-known and loved that filmmakers and dramatists tamper with them at their peril. In a way, they have become almost sacrosanct and are sometimes treated with a veneration unsuited to their real literary worth.

Nonetheless, there have been widely differing presentations of Dickens's stories on the cinema and television screens of the world. This book is an attempt to survey and record as many of those productions as it is possible to trace. The range includes silent films, sound films, color films, television plays and films, comic versions and parodies, plunderings for TV sitcoms, animated films, musicals, and videos. Through them all, there runs a common thread—the magical gift of characters and stories created by the great, inimitable Charles Dickens.

Acknowledgments

A book of this nature can never be accomplished without the assistance and cooperation of a large number of people, and I am deeply grateful for the help, interest, and encouragement I have received from so many performers, historians, enthusiasts, and custodians of archives.

Jean Alderman of the National Film and Sound Archive, Canberra, Australia; Terence Alexander; John Arnatt; Ronnie Barker; Dr. Aldo Bernadini; Rob Blackmore of the State Library of Victoria, Australia; Peter Blau; Richard Briers; Roy Castle; Dolores Devesa of the Filmoteca Española; Geoffrey Donaldson; Marguerite Engberg; Alan Gevinson of the American Film Institute; Valerie Hobson; Dinsdale Landen; Paul Lemieux of the National Archive of Canada; Barrie MacDonald of the Independent Television Commission; Wolf Mankowitz; Teresa Moreno of Radiotelevision Española; Sheridan Morley; Helnut Morsbach of the Staatliches Filmarchiv of the former DDR, Berlin; Bill Parker of Thames TV; Dr. David Parker, Curator of Dickens House; Steve Race; Anthony Slide; Pat Stewart of the National Library of Australia; Jane Wyatt.

Special thanks are due to Larry James Gianakos, chronicler supreme of American TV drama, for his generous assistance, and to Q. David Bowers for kindly providing much information from his exhaustive *Thanhouser Films: An Encyclopaedia and History*.

Finally, the never-failing cooperation and help of the personnel of the British Film Institute Library and Viewing Service is very greatly appreciated.

1

Dramatizing Dickens

> Dickens's nearness to the characteristics of cinema in method, style and especially viewpoint and exposition, is indeed amazing.
>
> Sergei Eisenstein

Few writers have achieved a degree of popularity and success that has continued for more than a century after their deaths. Charles Dickens is exceptional in the way his novels appeal to many young readers of today, as well as to their parents and grandparents.

In part that is due to the style in which Dickens wrote, which does not seem to date, like that of many of his contemporaries. But it is much more than mere freshness of writing that maintains Dickens's appeal. Charles Dickens was fond of claiming that he had "the common touch," and almost everything he wrote revealed his awareness of the social conditions around him. Through the medium of his essays, stories, and novels, he was constantly drawing attention to appalling injustices and inadequacies of much of the social system of the times. His own impoverished childhood left an indelible impression on him, and his experiences as a newspaper reporter confirmed his resolution to campaign for change and improvement. At the same time, those experiences gave him the opportunity to study closely a multitude of persons from all classes of multilayered Victorian society, and his quick, retentive brain enabled him to people his stories with them, with seemingly little effort.

As a great creative artist, Dickens made his serious social messages more widely known by enclosing them within the context of his stories to make them more palatable, although he risked a mixed reception at the time of first publication. Keith Fielding has pointed out that "the causes for contemporary disapproval of his novels were due to class-prejudice and a dislike of social criticism rather than purely critical considerations."

Although Charles Dickens has the reputation of having remained fresh and modern in his writing, this is due less to his written style than to the astonishing characterization in his books that has proved so attractive to cinema and television. Dickens's sheer skill, vitality, and high spirits enabled him to fill his sprawling novels with a gigantic gallery of memorable heroes, heroines, eccentrics, and villains—a gallery that includes many of the best-known characters in the world's fiction—Oliver Twist, Mr. Pickwick, Micawber, Scrooge (a name now virtually part of the English language). There seems to be no end to the favorites one can pick and, in many instances, they cry out to be impersonated.

Among the first to realize this was probably Charles Dickens himself. In addition to his prodigious tasks of novel writing and magazine editing, he found time to perform in a number of amateur stage productions which, in at least one instance, included a dramatization of one of his own stories. Dickens had, in fact, always wanted to be an actor. It was a childhood ambition that he confided to his biographer, John Forster, one that never left him. Apparent throughout his stories is his taste for lurid, melodramatic incidents. John Ruskin observed that as a novelist, Dickens was "essentially a stage manager, and used everything for effect on the pit." His daughter Mamie described how he gestured and grimaced in front of a mirror, living the roles of his characters as he wrote his stories. During the latter years of his life, he turned more and more to performing public readings from his own books, in versions that were carefully edited from the original texts to produce the highest dramatic effect.

At the same time, other writers had perceived the dramatic possibilities in the stories and characters whose fame was well established by the phenomenal success of Dickens' works. During his lifetime, Dickens was plagued by unauthorized plays that traded on his name and his stories. One impetuous producer even staged a dramatic version of *The Old Curiosity Shop* before the final monthly installments had appeared and before it was known whether or not Little Nell was going to die. Since those days, there has been an unbroken succession of dramatizations of Dickens's famous stories, from stage plays and dramatic monologues to motion pictures, radio plays, musicals, and television plays. Such is the astounding pull of his characters and stories that, although we are now familiar with many of the plots and personalities, we are still drawn to see the latest versions. As G. K. Chesterton pointed out, one rereads a detective novel because one has forgotten the plot, but a Dickens novel because one has remembered the plot. It was also Chesterton who observed that the man in the street knows the stories of Dickens, even though he has never read them. Surely that must be because of the many dramatizations of his works.

In Victorian times, stage versions of Dickens's most successful books were legion, but from the end of the nineteenth century, the live theater began to decline and was gradually usurped by the upstart entertainment medium of the kinematograph. With innumerable daily performances, the moving-picture show became a voracious devourer of stories, and at a very early stage in the development of motion pictures, filmmakers began their unending search for new material. Many English and non-English classics were already in the public domain—not that such considerations weighed too heavily on the movie pioneers—but more importantly, they provided well-known titles that carried the near certainty of popularity and success. More important still was the respectability attached to famous literature, especially as the pure novelty aspect of moving pictures wore off and the low standing of the medium persisted. At a time when films were under heavy attack, particularly from churchmen, as being pernicious influences of evil, and fairground picture-shows were defensively claiming to be "refined and moral, pleasing to ladies," a few reels of would-be culture proved to be an enormous asset.

The theatricality of much of Dickens's writing makes it attractive for a dramatist. The stories have often been adapted by extracting episodes or sections from what are actually massive and unmanageable compendia of Victorian life and manners on many levels of the social scale. While these episodes can often be made dramatically workable, they are sometimes difficult to assemble into coherent plots.

The severest critics of any dramatizations invariably complain that the play or film does not stick closely to the book, and that it omits certain incidents or characters. Such an outlook is too literal and simplistic, for clearly there is no practical way a dramatist can overcome such fundamental objections, save by having someone stand on the stage or before the camera and recite every word in the book. The plain fact, usually overlooked or ignored in these objections, is that the playwright or filmmaker is engaged in translating the story into a totally different medium, and within that medium, different rules apply as to form and content.

The form of a motion picture requires a story to be advanced in an easily comprehensible manner, for there is no opportunity to go back and reread a few pages, to return and savor again the delights of a particularly enjoyable passage, or to make oneself more familiar with the development of the plot. Limitations of time and space necessitate the early and swift delineation of characters as well as the compression of a book into an acceptable length. The latter limitation inevitably means sacrificing a number of incidents and characters. Nevertheless, provided the end result is a good dramatic piece that captures and conveys the real spirit of the original, such amputations are frequently justified.

Where a novelist can afford to spend several pages describing the thoughts of a character and his mental responses to a particular set of circumstances, a film has to abbreviate such matters and portray many of them visually, using the subtleties of camera angle, frame composition, sound effects, music, and cutting. All such aids need to be skillfully incorporated in the screenplay. In some instances, there are features of the author's treatment of a story that prove to be almost unfilmable and test the skill of the adaptor.

As we know in considerable detail from his correspondence, Charles Dickens took great pains to ensure that the illustrations to his stories were produced as he wanted them. We can accept that the depiction of most of the characters in the original printings of his novels is very close to what Dickens envisaged. Those illustrations have been reproduced in so many editions that the appearance of Pickwick, Sikes, Fagin, Micawber and all the others is widely known. If we are unfamiliar with this great tradition of Dickens illustrations and read the novels in editions with no pictures, our impressions of the characters are formed by our own imaginations. Either way, dramatizations may cause deep disappointment by their depiction of well-remembered persons from the stories.

As far as adaptation for television is concerned, the experience of the cinema had to be learned afresh. Television was originally handled as an offshoot of radio, and it took some time for radio techniques to be discarded. Sound broadcasting had developed to an extremely high standard by the 1950s, and many radio adaptations of classics had been exceptionally good, while still leaving the visual aspect of the drama to the listener's imagination.

In the early days of television, the severe limitations of live plays yielded rather stiff, uncomfortable drama that was frequently the result of writers having to construct their work to suit the confines of the studios, for filmed inserts of exterior scenes were rare and difficult to match to live transmission. Although some plays were made on film, TV drama only really began to develop away from that inflexibility with the introduction of videotape recording. Videotape enabled the adaptor to become a screenwriter with all the visual resources of the cinema. However, the writer needs to understand the intimacy and immediacy of television. In the cinema, there is always a sense of occasion. The picturegoer has made a deliberate effort to attend and, since the audience is some distance from the screen, looking up at a presentation which is larger than life, there is considerable glamour involved. Television, on the other hand, brings its drama closer to the individual viewer, who is usually looking down at a scene in which practically everything appears much smaller than life and entails acting and dramatic writing at a less intense level. Also, TV is watched in a far more casual way by viewers who have been exposed to years of overindulgence in entertainment and overexposed to the many grim realities repeatedly shown in news and documentary programs. Drama on television is not merely a scaled-down movie; attention has to be focused more on the actors and less on the vistas. The very proximity of the TV set demands this distinction, and in Dickens's books, it is the characters on whom the attention is focused for much of the time.

Like the cinema, TV has devoured so much material so quickly that there is a constant search for new subjects for its satiated audiences. One effect of this perpetual need to fill screen time has been the development of the television serial. The lengthy novels of Charles Dickens lend themselves to this form of adaptation, whereas attempted condensations for conventional feature-film versions of some of the same novels have been much less successful. A good example is *Nicholas Nickleby*, which has rarely been filmed, since there is just too much of it and too many fascinating characters who must either be omitted or reduced to mere walk-ons. When made into a serial for TV, however, *Nicholas Nickleby* retained most of its amiable eccentrics and many of the various episodes of the story. Indeed, the episodic structure of most of Dickens's novels, written for the most part in monthly installments, makes serial dramatization an attractive and acceptable approach.

It can be argued that the writing by installments of Dickens's books had a detrimental effect on the construction of the plots. Trevor Blount commented, "As an improvisor, able to shift direction to correct falling sales, he has few equals: no one is more aware of his audience." That audience, of course, was the reading audience, as opposed to a television-viewing audience waiting at the most a mere week rather than a month for the next installment. *They* may be able to detect more readily the turns and changes to which Blount alludes, or they may be sufficiently detached, emotionally and critically, not to let it trouble them. The skill of the adaptor plays a large part in such instances.

Structure and characterization are not in themselves sufficient to ensure satisfactory adaptation, and although most of Dickens's novels have now been dramatized for the screen, not all have been successful. Sometimes this was because the book did not lend itself to dramatization, but mostly it seems to have been the adaptation that was poor.

The task of the dramatist is not merely transforming material that is meant to be read into material meant to be performed, difficult though that may be. It is to create a drama that is good in its own medium and, above all, faithful to the original author's intentions.

2

The Wizardry of Boz

Dickens's novels do not necessarily make good film plays. There is so much material in them, and it is so closely interwoven that it is really difficult to boil it down within the scope of a single film. The only thing to do is to take some central incident, devote one's attention exclusively to it, and ruthlessly cut away everything that does not actually appertain to that one phase of the story.

The Times March 1, 1920

Charles Dickens was one of the first authors to have his work used by moving pictures. In New York, at the incredibly early date of 1897, the American Mutoscope Company made *Death of Nancy Sykes*, a depiction of the brutal incident in the novel *Oliver Twist* where Bill Sikes kills his woman partner, believing she has betrayed him.

Nancy Sykes was not Sikes as written by Dickens, and was not Sikes anyway. An unmarried woman cohabiting with a man was not an acceptable feature of the drama in those days, and for many years afterwards. The small scene was a record of the thrilling dramatic sketch that was given by Charles Ross and Mabel Fenton in vaudeville and burlesque houses, and marks them as the first recorded performers in the first recorded piece from Dickens on the screen, made by one of the first film-producing firms. The company soon changed its title to American Mutoscope & Biograph Co, and later still became known as just Biograph, a now-famous name among the pioneers of early American cinema. This brief film, a mere snippet from a novel, showed how the cinema would adopt the great characters from Dickens through more than 130 films.

The following year in England, British movie pioneer R. W. Paul made *Mr. Bumble the Beadle*, lasting approximately 45 seconds. This demonstrated Paul's confidence that the public would be familiar enough with the story of *Oliver Twist* to recognize Bumble's name or know enough about workhouses to understand what a beadle was. The film showed a beadle courting a workhouse matron.

Robert W. Paul was a movie pioneer whose importance has been somewhat neglected by historians, partly because of his retirement as early as 1910 to concentrate on the development and production of photographic equipment. That was when many of the early filmmakers were just beginning to get into their stride. Paul had been the first Englishman to present a projected film show in Britain before a paying audience, so he can rightly be counted as a founder of the industry. His technical achievements were not always matched by an imaginative choice of subjects, but while many of his competitors were busily churning out variations on Watering the Gardener, Trains Entering Stations, and poor imitations of Georges Méliès, Paul produced a few original ideas, including fragments from several of the classics, among them three of the earliest Dickens films to be made. In 1901, three years after *Mr. Bumble the Beadle*, he also produced *Mr. Pickwick's Christmas at Wardles* and *Scrooge; or Marley's Ghost*.

Mr. Pickwick's Christmas at Wardles was only 140 feet long (approximately 1-1/2 minutes), about the average length for Paul's pictures at that time. *Scrooge* was an altogether more ambitious undertaking, and was marked by Paul taking an unprecedented 1-1/2 columns of advertising space in the entertainment periodical *The Era*. Thanks to that extraordinary action, which Paul appears never to have repeated, we have been left with what amounts to a copy of an exceedingly early film scenario. It is reproduced in full here:

Description of the Film

"Scrooge; or Marley's Ghost" founded on Dickens's "Christmas Carol," in twelve tableaux, dissolving and otherwise, changing from one to another to form consecutive series, and introducing about thirty actors, with special scenery and novel effects.

Tableau I
Christmas Eve at Scrooge and Marley's

Following the announcement of the title of the film the curtain rolls up, disclosing the office of Scrooge with the name of his dead partner Marley still upon the door. His ill-paid clerk Bob Cratchit is vainly endeavoring to keep himself warm, when Scrooge enters evidently in a bad temper at the prospect of having to pay Cratchit for a day's idleness on the morrow. After Scrooge has seated himself to his work, Bob proposes to put some coal on the fire, but Scrooge is enraged at the idea of such waste and sends Bob back to his desk, where he wraps himself in an enormous comforter, and gives rise to much laughter in his comical endeavors to warm his hands at the flame of his solitary candle. Scrooge's nephew Fred calls and endeavors to persuade Scrooge to have his Christmas dinner with him on the morrow, but the old man will have none of it, and in spite of Fred's endeavors to ingratiate himself by offering the old man a pinch of snuff he is rudely hustled off, not however before giving Bob a few pleasant words and a small remembrance. The next visitor, who is collecting subscriptions for a Christmas dinner for the poor, meets with no better reception, and after Bob has received a severe scolding and instructions not to be late in the morning, he is sent off home without even "A merry Christmas" or a present. The old curmudgeon puts out the light and retires, locking the office door, when the scene rolls up, disclosing

Tableau II
The Street Door of Scrooge's House

As the old man is unlocking the door the knocker gradually changes into the face of Marley, which appears to be speaking words of warning to him. Scrooge starts back affrighted, but looking again he perceives that it was only a fancy, and so makes bold to enter his house. Again the scene rolls down and rises upon

Tableau III
Scrooge's Bedroom

He enters, still suffering from the shock to his nerves, and starts at the slightest sound. Throwing on a dressing gown and night cap, he draws close the window curtains and seats himself by the fire, where a basin of gruel is ready for him. He gradually dozes off and sleeps uneasily in the chair for a few moments. He awakes with a start at the violent ringing of the bells. Looking round he sees gradually appearing through the curtains the ghost of Marley, from which he retreats in terror, but he is forced to gaze upon the visions which Marley presents in the darkened portion of the room. These visions appear gradually, then fade away. They show two visions of Christmases Past.

Tableau IV
Scrooge Sees Himself as a Boy at His Lessons

His sister comes quietly behind him and claps her hands over his eyes; he jumps up with start, and they embrace affectionately. She, looking over his shoulder, takes the slate from him and they go off hand in hand. The next vision being

Tableau V
Scrooge as a Young Man Parting From His Sweetheart

He explains to her that he loves not her, but gold, and that their engagement must be broken off. She hands him his ring, and leaves him as the vision fades from Scrooge's sight.

Tableau VI
During the Appearance of the Visions

Scrooge is in terror and begs the ghost to desist. He cowers before Marley, who steps back and gradually fades from his sight. Scrooge is left shivering with terror as the picture dissolves to

Tableau VII
The Flight of Father Time

Carrying Scrooge from the past to the present is shown in a short effect film, this again changing to two visions of Christmas Present.

Tableau VIII
Cratchit and His Family at Their Christmas Dinner

Unobserved by them, Scrooge's spirit watches the merry and bustling scene in the poor home of his clerk, whose large family of young children are eagerly helping their mother to prepare the spread and waiting for the eldest daughter, Martha the young dressmaker, to come home from her work. She appears, all aglow with hurrying through the frosty air, and kisses them all round, not forgetting Tiny Tim the cripple boy, whom she embraces, affectionately. The youngsters tell her to hide, as Father is coming. Bob comes in just as his wife is bringing in the goose, and his first question is for Martha, his regret at not seeing her being evident. Amid great glee on the part of the children he drags her out from her hiding place beneath the table, and picking up Tiny Tim with his crutch, he carries him to his place at the table, while the youngsters crowd round for their share in the wonderful goose. Before commencing, however, Bob has a toast to propose, and the glasses are filled but as he says the words "To Mr Scrooge" his wife puts down her glass. Nevertheless, he persuades her to join in the toast, even Tiny Tim struggling up on his crutch, so that one can almost read the words on his lips "To Mr Scrooge and God bless us all!" as the scene gradually changes to

Tableau IX
The Home of Scrooge's Nephew Fred

In somewhat more comfortable surroundings his nephew is seated at dessert with his wife and children. He also has a toast to propose to which Scrooge, though unseen by them, is seen eagerly listening; and he is visibly affected when he hears those whom he has treated so badly heartily drinking the health of "Uncle

Scrooge." He is again hurried off by Father Time, and in the next two scenes are shown two short versions of the Christmas That Might Be. The first of these is

Tableau X

The Graveyard

Hither he is led by the spirit of Marley, and is so moved by terror and by the lessons that he has already received that it is with difficulty that the ghost is able to induce him to look at the solitary gravestone. When he does so, he sees on it his own name, and he is left, prostrated by fear and remorse, as his vision dissolves and takes further form in another scene.

Tableau XI

The Death of Tiny Tim

In Bob's old room a far different scene is taking place to the one previously depicted. The poor child lies on a rough couch, tended by his mother, while the girl Martha is seated at the little table, helpless with grief, and scarcely able to rise when the mother tells her that the poor cripple's spirit has flown. While Mrs. Cratchit is tenderly covering the face of the dead child the father hurries in with a bottle of medicine, which he is hastily unwrapping but he is stopped by a gesture of his wife, which tells him that all is over. Scrooge, whose phantom form is still unobserved, is moved to distress as the curtain rolls down upon the vision of the Christmas that might have been, had his niggardly spirit not already given place to a resolve to make amends. The result of Scrooge's dream in changing his character is fully shown in the lively and comical picture following.

Tableau XII

Christmas Morning at Scrooge's

Freed from the terrors of the night, and his whole nature changed, the old man bounds into his room, and the first thing he does is to change the date in the almanac to December 25th. He then stands thinking as to what he can do to make people happy and determines to send Bob a handsome Christmas present. He goes to the door and calls in a boy; while he is shouting for the boy the charity collector, who appeared in the first scene, passes the door and to his great surprise is dragged into the room and Scrooge with the utmost glee subscribes an evidently large amount. But Scrooge will not part with him until he has sent for a bottle of wine. The urchin who comes to Scrooge's call is told to fetch a goose, vegetables, etc. and "lots of them." These are brought in and stowed away beneath Scrooge's desk, waiting Bob Cratchit, who hurries in with a woebegone expression and gets a comical scolding for being late. But Scrooge is evidently unable to keep up the farce, and rushing to the boy's basket loads Bob up with both arms full of good things, finally flinging the goose over Bob's shoulder, sticking a bottle of wine in his pocket, and piling a bag on top of all. Bob's amazement and delight at the sudden change are wonderfully funny, his expressive face being contorted by emotion. As he is being hurried out home, he runs into Scrooge's nephew Fred, who is no less astonished at such an unusual sight. Scrooge insists on everyone taking a glass of wine with him and the merry scene concludes with Bob loaded up to the eyes with his gifts, of which he is unable to leave go, having a glass of wine poured down his throat by the exultant Scrooge. As the film runs out the following words flash successively across the screen, "A Merry Christmas and a Happy New Year."

It is quite clear from the above detailed summary that the film followed almost exactly the stage dramatization of the story *A Christmas Carol*, as sketched out by Seymour Hicks, written by J. C. Buckstone, and first performed earlier the same year under the title *Scrooge*.

Paul's *Scrooge* is variously recorded as being 600 or 620 feet, which was an exceptional length in 1901. No doubt the length was largely determined by the nature of the stage performance on which the film was based, and Paul's publicity made much of the fact that *Scrooge* was "as presented on Tuesday, Nov. 26th, at Sandringham before their Majesties the King and Queen, the Prince and Princess of Wales and distinguished company. *Scrooge* was chosen by His Majesty as the first theatrical representation to be produced before him since his accession, thus giving further proof, if such were needed, of its perennial freshness and interest for all classes."

The question obviously arises as to whether the company that performed for Robert Paul ("about thirty actors" claimed the advertizement) was the same one that performed for King Edward VII. One can only assert that it may well have been, for early filmmakers were fond of filming stage companies in their current productions, when they could be persuaded to collaborate. The costumes, and sometimes the scenery, were already available, and a popular and successful title always helped sell cinema seats. The actors. on the other hand, were not so keen for their personal names to be used. The members of what they chose to regard as the legitimate theater looked with disdain on the "galloping tintypes," as some of them called the movies, and to acknowledge participation in such a cheap and trivial entertainment was like admitting to performing in a fairground.

If, in fact, the company *was* the same, the Scrooge of the play and the film was Seymour Hicks, who appeared and reappeared in the role well into the 1930s. Unfortunately, he makes no reference to the film in his published reminiscences. His wife, actress Ellaline Terriss, recounts the play's performance at Sandringham in her memoirs, and states that Hicks later made a film from the play, but that could refer to either of the film versions made by Hicks in 1913 and 1935. Writing in 1958, the brief Animatograph film of 1901 could well have been overlooked. (A curious omission from Miss Terriss's memoirs is any mention of the career of her brother Tom, who also played Scrooge on the stage and became involved with numerous other Dickens dramatizations.)

While publicizing *Scrooge* so well, R. W. Paul scarcely advertised his Pickwick film at all, and so very little is known about it, but all three films suggest that there existed a widespread knowledge of Dickens's most popular works. That knowledge was supported by the great stage successes of numerous touring companies performing various Dickens stories at that period. In addition, there were at the turn of the century performers whose acts comprised impersonations of various celebrated literary characters and, needless to say, many of the characters were from Dickens. One actor who was performing such extracts at the time of Paul's first Dickens film and went on to make a specialty of Dickens characters was Bransby Williams, whose activities in Dickens dramatizations lasted for almost 60 years, ending with appearances on television.

The little group of four pictures by American Mutoscope and R. W. Paul blazed a trail of popularity and success that ensured that there has never been a very lengthy period without a new Dickens movie appearing somewhere in the world. Television seems to have followed suit and evolved a somewhat similar pattern of adaptations.

R. W. Paul's films were followed in 1903 by *Dotheboys Hall; or Nicholas Nickleby,* made in England by the Gaumont company and distributed in America as *Nicholas Nickleby* by the American Mutoscope & Biograph Company. Thanks to the Library of Congress having received paper contact prints of many early movies for copyright registration, this Gaumont film based on *Nicholas Nickleby* has survived, painstakingly restored frame by frame to a viewable film. The 90-year-old picture opens with a calm schoolroom scene of a class being taught by Nicholas. Smike enters, and then the ruffianly Squeers. Mrs. Squeers follows with a bowl and spoon, and doses the pupils. Squeers drags out Smike in a threatening manner, and Nicholas attempts to restrain him. Squeers beats Smike, so Nicholas beats Squeers, to the joy of the class and the consternation of Mrs. Squeers. Nicholas takes his coat and hat to leave, and Smike begs to go, too. Nicholas takes Smike with him as Mrs. Squeers comforts Squeers, who is still on the floor. The film ends with the classroom in uproar. All this is accomplished in approximately 2-1/2 minutes, filmed from a single camera position. The pantomiming of the unknown performers conveys all the above activity extremely well, and the film is a highly creditable and entertaining extract from the novel, as well as being the oldest surviving movie from Dickens.

In 1904, another pioneer British filmmaker, James Williamson, made *Gabriel Grub the Surly Sexton,* based on a chapter from *The Pickwick Papers.* The story of Gabriel Grub really has nothing to do with the narrative of *The Pickwick Papers,* being merely an interlude in that book. In common with many authors of his time, Charles Dickens was given to holding up the action of a novel while one of the characters recounts a ghost story or some harrowing reminiscence, and probably the only serious flaw in *The Pickwick Papers* is the frequency with which that happens. Williamson's film of *Gabriel Grub* appears to be a rare example of one of those interludes being filmed, and is particularly interesting in that the episode is really a forerunner of *A Christmas Carol*, and Grub himself is a clearly recognizable prototype of Ebenezer Scrooge.

By 1906, the idea of using Dickens for film stories really seemed to catch on among filmmakers, for four new titles arrived to compete with the earlier ones, which were still in circulation. In France, Gaumont produced *Oliver Twist*, while in the United States the Vitagraph Company made *The Modern Oliver Twist; or, The Life of a Pickpocket*, in which the rudiments of the novel were used in a 1906 setting. Both these films arrived in Britain at the same time (March 1906), and the first advertisements for the Vitagraph film were headed with the warning, "Do not confuse the following subject with one of similar title announced last week." The modernization was an odd treatment of the subject by Vitagraph, which was already making a specialty of adaptations of various classics of world literature (and in fact made a conventional version of *Oliver Twist* only three years later).

The Gaumont and Vitagraph versions of 1906 seem to have made good renderings of *Oliver Twist*. Gaumont started with the celebrated scene of Oliver asking for more, and their summary reads as follows.

Scene 1 Oliver asks for more.
2 He runs away from the workhouse.
3 Oliver's meeting with the Artful Dodger.
4 Fagin's Den. Lessons in thieving.
5 Bill Sikes. The Burglary at Mr. Brownlow's. Oliver is caught.
6 Sikes's Room. Nancy. Fagin shadows the girl.
7 At the bridge. Nancy discloses the plot against Oliver. Fagin in hiding.
8 The murder of Nancy. Sikes's dash for freedom.
9 Pursuit and death of Sikes.
10 Fagin in his cell. The Hangman's noose. Oliver's recompense.

Evidently Gaumont was not afraid of the task that faces all adapters—boiling the story down to essentials without too much interference with the main story line. The Vitagraph version is recorded in a more detailed synopsis revealing that, apart from being in a modernized setting, the story dispenses with the workhouse episodes altogether and becomes more of a crime melodrama.

Scene No. 1

Homeless

Oliver Twist, a poor little orphan, has run away from a charitable institution where he has been ill-treated, and is picked up by the Artful Dodger, a young scamp, who is a member of a gang of thieves.

Scene No 2

The Thieves' Den

We see old Fagin, the Jew who teaches boys to become criminals, anxiously awaiting the return of some of his "scholars." Soon some of the boys arrive and hand him watches, handkerchiefs, and other stolen goods. The Artful Dodger then arrives and introduces little Oliver. Old Fagin welcomes the newcomer, and teaches him the new game of "Find the Watch" in which Oliver is unconsciously taught to pick pockets. The familiar characters of Bill Sikes and Nancy arrive in Fagin's den, and then Bill Sikes and the boys take little Oliver with them to initiate him into the profession of pocket-picking.

Scene No. 3

Oliver Finds a Home

The well-known figure of Mr. Brownlow is seen walking down the street. He stops at a news-stand, and while buying a paper the Artful Dodger, with Oliver Twist and another of Fagin's boys, approach and deftly steal Mr. Brownlow's watch and run swiftly down the street. Mr. Brownlow discovers the theft, and calling a policeman they start in chase of the pickpockets, down the street, over fences, and around corners. Finally the bigger boys leave Oliver and he, being exhausted, crouches down behind some barrels, where he is discovered by the pursuing crowd. One of the policemen takes him roughly by the arm, but kind-hearted Mr.

Brownlow intervenes, and picking little Oliver up in his arms, carries him home.

Scene No. 4

Recaptured

We see Oliver in his new home, well clothed and fed, and looking very happy. Old Mr. Brownlow goes off to business, leaving Oliver to amuse himself. Suddenly the door is cautiously opened, and the hideous face and burly figure of Bill Sikes appears. Poor little Oliver is terrified and tries to run away, but Sikes, quickly placing a hand over the boy's mouth, starts to drag him from the room. The butler, hearing the noise, rushes in. He is knocked senseless, and Bill Sikes drags the boy back to Fagin's den.

Scene No. 5

The Robbery

In Fagin's den we see the return of Bill Sikes and Oliver. The thieves plan to rob Mr. Brownlow's house by forcing Oliver to climb through a small window and open the door for them. They terrify the poor boy with threats until he consents to aid them. Nancy Sikes overhears the plan, and after the thieves have left, taking Oliver with them, she stealthily follows them, intending to warn Mr. Brownlow. Next we see the burglars breaking into the house, Oliver being put through the window. The butler awakens, rushes hurriedly downstairs, and seeing a figure in the semi-darkness, shoots at it. When the lights are turned up and the rest of the household aroused, they find to their astonishment and grief that poor little Oliver is the "burglar." This entire scene is very effective and dramatic. Nancy Sikes arrives, but finds she is too late. The police follow her when she leaves, and thus track her and the other criminals to Fagin's den.

Scene No. 6

Retribution

Bill Sikes and Toby Crackit rush into Fagin's den and tell him of their ill-luck. Bill asks where Nancy is, and Fagin describes how she followed them to the scene of the robbery. Bill suspects treachery on her part, and at that moment she enters. He accuses her, and although she denies having betrayed them, Bill disbelieves her, and in a moment of rage brutally chokes her. He drags the inanimate body from the room. Suddenly the doors and windows of the den are battered in, and the police, swarming in, overpower the criminals. The closing scene is very dramatic. While Bill Sikes, Fagin and the other thieves are held in the grip of the police, poor Nancy painfully drags herself into the room, and pointing an accusing finger at Fagin, falls dead at their feet.

It should be borne in mind that the Gaumont and Vitagraph films each accomplished the story in approximately eight to nine minutes. In spite of this drastic abbreviation, each managed to convey the essence of the story and rightly concentrated on key elements of the relatively short dramatic situations into which this and other Dickens novels are cast.

Given the rapidly increasing popularity of moving pictures, the success of the Vitagraph and Gaumont 1906 films of *Oliver Twist* was probably predictable, even though each was in direct competition with the other, and Gaumont went on to make two further Dickens films in the same year. *Dolly Varden* was extracted from some of the romantic part of the book *Barnaby Rudge* and was made in England at Gaumont's London studio. The synopsis was brief.

> Dolly, disguised as a man, elopes with her lover, and is followed by her irate father, who is afterwards held up by a highwayman, and eventually rescued by his daughter and her lover. Exciting finish. The vehicle used in this picture is the original state carriage of His Late Royal Highness the Duke of Cambridge.

Gaumont also appears to have been responsible in 1906 for the first Dickens sound film with *Little Nell*, an excerpt from *The Old Curiosity Shop*. It was one of a series of "Chronophone" films made by Gaumont, which had accompanying sound from a gramophone. There were several sound-on-disc systems for "talking" pictures at that time. They relied on pressure for the amplification of a wind-up gramophone to suit a cinema hall, using compressed air or, in the case of the Chronophone, acetylene gas. The length of the film was generally restricted to the running time of one 78rpm disc, about 4 minutes, and the Chronophone series seems largely to have been confined to performances of songs, which makes *Little Nell* more outstanding. According to a Gaumont advertizement, it was given "by Mr. Thomas Nye from the Surrey Theater and all the principal theaters in Great Britain, assisted by several well-known artists," so it seems there was a form of performance given, and not merely a recitation or monologue. The advertizement boasted of "Absolute synchronism (under operator's control)" but we may imagine that it was not always achieved.

The year 1908 saw two more new Dickens films—the first film of *A Tale of Two Cities*, made by the Selig company, and *A Christmas Carol*, made by the Essanay company—each one reel long. To judge from the pictures on Selig's publicity leaflet, the adaptation was a bold attempt to depict the revolutionary frenzy that pervades much of the story. "The greatest drama ever staged" (according to the leaflet) was for Selig a rare encounter with a famous book.

So it was also for Essanay and their film of *A Christmas Carol*. The American company Essanay (S & A, or Spoor and Anderson) was chiefly successful because of its long series of cowboy films featuring Broncho Billy, played by the second of the partners, G. M. Anderson, but occasionally they ventured into the realm of celebrated literature. Essanay's only other attempt at Dickens was the first movie version of *The Old Curiosity Shop*, in 1909.

Meanwhile Vitagraph, who had been busily producing a number of films based on well-known books and stories, must have had second thoughts about the subject of *Oliver Twist*. In 1909, they released a conventional, unmodernized version, with "Miss Elita Proctor Otis as Nancy Sykes" identified on one of the intertitles. In this film, Nancy is assailed by Bill Sykes off camera, but struggles back into shot for a prolonged operatic-type death scene. Vitagraph may well have been prompted to this remake by the increased activity in the field of Dickens films, for in that year, beside the Essanay *Old Curiosity Shop*, appeared the first film versions of *The Mystery of Edwin Drood*, made by Gaumont in Britain, and *The Cricket on the Hearth*, made by D. W. Griffith for Biograph. The build-up of Dickens films continued in 1910 with five more films, and in 1911 with another nine, by which time it was obvious that the imminent centenary of Charles Dickens's birth, to be celebrated in 1912, had not been overlooked by the movie makers.

A record of Gaumont's *The Mystery of Edwin Drood* has survived in a synopsis printed in a trade paper, from which it is clear that a commendable condensation of the story was made, to fit into something like 10 or 12 minutes of film. Many of the synopses of films published in the entertainment periodicals of the time were reproduced verbatim from those supplied by the film companies themselves, and they are sometimes the only data available as to the content of movies that no longer exist.

The grave lack of recorded information on films made in the first decade of this century makes any survey of Dickens films of the period seem little more than a catalog of titles and dates, but even with that sparse amount of data, certain patterns are discernible. Aside from being the first Dickens book to be used on film, *Oliver Twist* had already shown itself to be the most popular title, with no fewer than six version by 1910, followed by *A Christmas Carol* with four. Now filmed some 22 times, *A Christmas Carol*, the affecting, emotional tale of a flinty heart softened to kindness, has always been one of the most popular of all Dickens's works, and probably one of the best-known books in world literature. The story of *Oliver Twist*, the waif whose adventures take him from the workhouse to a rich living by way of a thieves' kitchen and through a series of amazing coincidences, has similarly had constant appeal for the public, and has yielded 25 films. In the cinema, those two Dickens stories are easily the most frequently filmed, for no other Dickens tale reaches halfway to those totals.

The contrasts between the two books are quite marked. In *Oliver Twist*, there is plenty of action, while in *A Christmas Carol* there is very little. *Oliver Twist*, being a lengthy novel, is bulging with characters, whereas the cast in *A Christmas Carol* is relatively limited, and there are no scenes of violence, crime, or cruelty in that book. Of course, both stories rely on the thick coatings of sentimentality Charles Dickens was able to use in his works with such telling effect, but in the case of *A Christmas Carol*, when the sentimentality is stripped away, there is virtually no plot left. *Oliver Twist*, on the other hand, contains all the intricacies of a full-scale Dickens novel, with subplots and parallel action abounding. Apparently size has not troubled the adapters very much. *Oliver Twist* can be compressed without too much harm, and it seems that *A Christmas Carol* is capable of adjustment to an unlimited range of lengths and treatments, especially when we look at television's appropriations.

Probably the most eminent director of silent films to make a Dickens movie was the legendary D. W. Griffith, whose whole film technique and story-telling methods have been compared with Dickens's narrative methods. No less an authority than the great Russian director Sergei Eisenstein has contributed to this consideration with his essay "Dickens, Griffith and the film today," in which he points out how cinematic in style Dickens's writing can be shown to be. The opening words of the story *The Cricket on the Hearth*, "The kettle began it..." are given by Eisenstein as an example of how Dickens opened with a close-up, before drawing back and revealing more of the scene. "Dickens' nearness of the characteristics of cinema in method, style and especially in viewpoint and exposition is indeed amazing," wrote Eisenstein, whose essay deserves some consideration, even though it suffers from the usual Russian fault of heavily elaborated reiterations.

> As soon as we recognize the kettle as a typical close-up, we exclaim "Why didn't we notice it before!" Of course this is the purest Griffith. How often we've seen such a close-up at the beginning of an episode, a sequence, or a whole film by him... Atmosphere always and everywhere is one of the most expressive means of revealing the inner world and ethical countenance of the characters themselves. We can recognize this particular method of Dickens in Griffith's inimitable bit characters who seem to have run straight from life on to the screen... Occasionally these unforgettable figures actually walked into Griffith's films almost directly from the street.

Although *The Cricket on the Hearth* of 1909 was Griffith's only film directly based on a Dickens story, his indebtedness to Dickens can also be seen in *True Heart Susie*, which includes a partial reworking of *David Copperfield,* and particularly in *Orphans of the Storm*. With this latter film, Edward Wagenknecht considered that Griffith "here made his most direct and important use of the writer who had been the major influence upon his artistic life...Like Dickens, Griffith approved of the French Revolution but deplored its excesses." *Orphans of the Storm,* beautifully made and excitingly directed and acted, is a key film in Griffith's work. It was actually based on an old melodrama entitled *The Two Orphans,* and Griffith added the setting of the French Revolution in a manner that evoked the atmosphere and background of *A Tale of Two Cities* so powerfully that at times one feels the film *must* be from Dickens, whereas in fact only one small incident in the film is taken directly from Dickens's book.

While Griffith has been credited over the years with many innovations in filmmaking which are now known to have been devised or initiated by others, he was really responsible for using those innovations to elevate the motion picture with a narrative flow and a story-telling technique similar to the methods of Charles Dickens, although that seems to have been little understood at the time. Griffith's wife, Linda Arvidson, writing in 1925, recounted a direct reference to the great author.

> When Mr. Griffith suggested a scene showing Annie Lee waiting for her husband's return to be followed by a scene of Enoch (Arden) cast away on a desert island, it was altogether too distracting. "How can you tell a story jumping about like that? The people won't know what it's about." "Well," said Mr. Griffith, "doesn't Dickens write that way?" "Yes, but that's Dickens; that's novel writing, that's different."

Like Dickens, David Griffith often made use of children as a channel for social comment and, also like Dickens, it was for his social comment that Griffith was heavily criticized during his most productive years. Alistair Cooke, commented more sharply on the resemblances in 1938.

"Griffith might explain that he got the idea of the flashback and much of his lighting from Dickens, but most people would be content to believe he got them from a mawkish imagination (which might be, of course, in that instance, the same thing)."

Alistair Cooke seems not to have changed his views about silent film dramatizations, for in his book *Masterpieces* (1982), while praising more recent television adaptations of classic literature, he cannot resist a jibe. "Dickens is a ready favorite of directors and writers eager to transfer 'the classics' to the screen. Even before the sound film, at least ten of his novels had been made into silent films. A silent Dickens? It is as much of a contradiction as a talkative statue."

One wonders whether Cooke cares much at all for silent films, for while one is bound to recognize the limitations imposed by the absence of dialogue, his rather sweeping condemnation appears to ignore all the visual accomplishments and techniques of the silent picture. All literature is changed by the transfer from the printed page to the screen, with or without audible dialogue.

3

Pictures from Everywhere

Dickens is just full of pitfalls for the film maker. The desire to bring in all that appeals to a lover of Dickens is fatal, for it begets confusion and bewilderment.

W. Stephen Bush
The Moving Picture World, 1912

In 1910, the Edison company, began what became an irregular series of one-reel films consisting of episodes or extracts from various Dickens stories. After the first, the oft-repeated *A Christmas Carol*, Edison produced a string of six films that did not use the original Dickens titles. *Love and the Law*, from *David Copperfield*, and *A Yorkshire School*, from *Nicholas Nickleby*, were issued in 1910, and in 1911 *How Bella Was Won* and *Eugene Wrayburn*, both from *Our Mutual Friend*, as well as *Mr. Pickwick's Predicament* (no problem in identification there) and *Dolly Varden*, from *Barnaby Rudge*. The changes in title may have been because the films were only excerpts, but they were well publicized as being from Dickens and, within their limitations of length, were all very well made little dramas. Edison's 1910 *Carol* was a particularly lively and well filmed adaptation, with very good trick photography in the ghost scenes. Especially striking was the biblical phraseology of an intertitle that read, "The ghost of Marley, who was like unto Scrooge, warns him of his punishment hereafter unless he becomes a different man."

Many exhibitors genuinely believed that their audiences would not tolerate films of more than one reel, or about 10 to 12 minutes duration. Moreover, those entrepreneurs who had set up moving picture shows in empty shops and other vacant premises were reluctant to make changes in their arrangements for getting rich quickly, and anything that might have proved unacceptable to the audiences of the day, and thus disrupted the steady flow of cash into the till, was definitely not wanted. In underestimating the taste of audiences, the distributors seem to have changed very little, right up to the present day, for it has mostly been the filmmakers who have forced the developments in their products which eventually the exhibitors have accepted. In this respect, the changes in style and approach in the presentation of Dickens on the screen have followed the corresponding changes in filmmaking through the decades.

By 1911, some filmmakers had realized the necessity of longer films to enable them to do justice to both original and adapted stories, and the Vitagraph Company showed how well it could be done with their three reel adaptation of *A Tale of Two Cities*. Vitagraph, one of the first, best, and longest-lived of the early American companies, contributed greatly to the establishment and development of the movie industry and was then at the height of its fame, both in America and Europe. With productions such as *A Tale of Two Cities*, they set a standard that other companies struggled to emulate. Even so, Vitagraph remained cautious and released the film in three separate parts. The trade magazine *The Moving Picture World* urged exhibitors to show the three parts together, a suggestion that may have persuaded Vitagraph to issue its next three-reel picture, made later the same year, as a complete film.

A Tale of Two Cities was made at the spacious Vitagraph studio in Flatbush, Brooklyn, which enabled the scope and sweep of the novel to be well depicted. It featured two performers whose names were becoming well-known to the cinema-going public Florence Turner (the Vitagraph Girl, the first of what became known as "film stars") as Lucie Manette, and the handsome leading man who often played opposite her in Vitagraph films — Maurice Costello in a fine performance as Sydney Carton. The resemblance of Leo Delaney (Charles Darnay) to Costello was close enough to be convincing.

The film was a prestige presentation, boldly staged, imaginatively directed, lavishly costumed, and utilizing just about the entire Vitagraph stock company in the large cast. James Morrison, in his first film part, played the brother of the peasant girl abducted by the Marquis St. Evremonde, who kills the brother. In an interview with Kevin Brownlow in 1964, Morrison recounted how, once dead, he was obliged to lie on the floor of the set for 3 hours, because it was not then the practice to move the camera between scenes. Norma Talmadge played the seamstress who goes to the guillotine with Carton, and John Bunny had a small part as a jailer, but it was Charles Kent as Dr. Manette who gave a most moving demonstration of the strength of silent film acting, in his slow, gradual recognition of his daughter Lucie after his release from years in the Bastille.

A Tale of Two Cities was a deservedly enormous success for Vitagraph and was reissued in 1913. Irrespective of any other attributes of that film, it had a far-reaching effect on one young man named Rex Ingram, who went on to direct such outstanding films of the 1920s as *The Four Horsemen of the Apocalypse, The Prisoner of Zenda, Scaramouche,* and *The Garden of Allah.* In 1922, Ingram wrote:

> In 1913, when I was studying drawings and sculpture at the Yale School of Fine Arts, a motion picture play, founded upon Charles Dickens' famous story *A Tale of Two Cities,* came to New Haven. It followed in the wake of many cut and dried one-reel subjects, and while this picture was necessarily full of imperfections, common to all pioneer films, it marked a tremendous step ahead in the making of them...I left the theatre greatly impressed; absolutely convinced that it would be through the medium of the film play, to the production of which the laws that govern the fine arts had been applied, that a universal understanding and appreciation of art finally would be reached. I brought several friends of mine, most of them either students of the art school, or members of the Yale Dramatic Association, the following day to see this picture, which had been made by the Vitagraph Company of America, and each and every one of them was as much impressed as I. All of us thereupon decided to enter the motion picture field. After leaving New Haven, I lost track entirely of the other members of the party.

Like Robert Paul of England, American Edwin Thanhouser is another pioneer filmmaker who is now little remembered, because he retired from the industry in the early years. Yet his contribution to the earliest decades of American movies was important to the industry in general—in particular his many adaptations of well-known books had great and deserved success. Thanhouser's career and films were in some ways similar to those of another pioneer —Cecil Hepworth of England. Each man produced a batch of Dickens films that were outstanding presentations. Thanhouser began in 1911 with a one-reel version of *The Old Curiosity Shop*, followed by an adaptation of *David Copperfield* made in three reels and, like the Vitagraph *A Tale of Two Cities*, issued in three separate parts. Thanhouser's three reels were made as three distinct films, released in three consecutive weeks, with three different titles, *The Early Life of David Copperfield*, *Little Emily and David Copperfield*, and *The Loves of David Copperfield*.

Unlike the Vitagraph film, Thanhouser's *David Copperfield* was clearly only an interim stage toward a multi-reel picture, but the following year he produced a two-reel *Nicholas Nickleby* (releasing a full list of the cast, a rarity in those days), and in 1913 a two-reel *Little Dorrit*. This last film was released after Edwin Thanhouser left the Thanhouser Company, which he had founded in 1908.

There is an extensive portion of the novel *Martin Chuzzlewit* in which young Martin travels to and in America. Here Charles Dickens cuts loose with a collection of wounding satires on American life that the Americans of the time believed he usually reserved for the bad old ways of mid-Victorian England. Following closely behind his equally critical book *American Notes*, this 1845 novel was a profound shock to the American press and public and antagonized them to an enormous extent. They felt betrayed by the young man they had lionized on his visit to their country only three years earlier.

With such antipathy toward the book in America, the real surprise is that the only two film versions of *Martin Chuzzlewit* ever made have both come from the United States. When the Edison film of the story was produced in 1912, seventy years after the book's first appearance, trade paper critic Louis Reeves Harrison was unable to refrain from uncomfortable references to the book, calling it "the least understood of his works," and averring "the novel is no favorite of mine." Indeed, the import of Harrison's review in *The Moving Picture World* is that the Edison film company managed to reveal the true heart and drama of the story Dickens was struggling to present.

The Edison film, which was in three reels, appears to have been a conscientiously made adaptation, with the scenes aptly staged and the actors chosen and costumed to resemble the characters in the original illustrations by Phiz. Judging from the sparse information available, the screenplay reduced the American interlude of the story. In a shrewd move, Edison launched the film in England three months before releasing it in the United States, and the company's American publicists were able to quote liberally from the highly favorable reception given the film by the British press and public.

Since 1912 marked the centenary of his birth, there was a predictably large crop of Dickens films that year. The movie industry was moving well into multi-reel pictures by then, which made production and distribution times somewhat more extended. Consequently, some companies that did not start in sufficient time (or awoke very late to the event) did not get their films out until 1913. The occasion ended up with no fewer than 20 films released in those two years, including the first film versions of the already mentioned *Martin Chuzzlewit* and *Little Dorrit*, as well as the only films of the two Mrs. Lirriper stories and one of the Boz pieces.

Great publicity was given to the first appearance on the screen of the famous American actor Nat C. Goodwin, who had achieved great success on the stage as Fagin in J. Comyn Carr's play *Oliver Twist*. Goodwin had completed a run of the play at the New Amsterdam and Empire Theaters in New York on Saturday, May 4, 1912. On the following Monday, May 6, he moved straight into the Crystal studio in the Bronx, to commence the filming of the play, together with his dog, who repeated its role as the cur belonging to Bill Sikes. The enterprising young man who had negotiated the deal for the film was H. A. Spanuth. At the time he declared

> We are not going to try to cram *Oliver Twist* into two reels or three reels. If it takes four reels to do it right, then the production will be four reels long. If it requires five reels, five reels it shall be. Or six, or seven for that matter. We do not intend to allow this picture to look as though it had come out of a sausage machine, as some recent Dickens productions have given the idea. It has been the fad lately to film the works of Dickens as special releases and jam them into two thousand feet by hydraulic pressure. The results have not been satisfactory. They have not been such as would enhance any great regard to Dickens in people who have never known him, much less with those who do know him. A short production of any of Dickens' plays enables the producer to touch only the high spots. Most of the charm of Dickens is thereby lost, and sadly missed by the beholder if he happens to be a lover of Dickens. In producing this drama we do not only have a standard work of fiction but we have an artist of great renown in the leading role, surrounded by a well-trained set of principals who have just made it a Broadway success. How stupid, therefore, it

would be of us to ruin it by cramping it into the confines of an arbitrary number of feet.

Spanuth's film recorded most of the action of the play and was then edited down to five reels, making it the longest Dickens film at that time. It was frequently shown in major American cities with an accompanying lecture, and the whole presentation was very successful. Much was made of the fact that an important stage actor such as Goodwin was appearing in a filmed play, which might encourage others to follow suit. But like many players of the period, Goodwin was either embarrassed by appearing in movies or merely regarded the film as trivial; he makes no reference to it in his memoirs. Marie Doro, the actress who had played Oliver to Goodwin's Fagin on the stage, was replaced in the film by Vinnie Burns, but Miss Doro's opportunity came four years later, when Jesse L. Lasky made another film version of the same story in 1916.

Meanwhile, in England, Cecil Hepworth launched his first Dickens film in 1912, yet another *Oliver Twist*, four reels in length. It is plain that 1912 marked a greatly increasing confidence in the production of longer films. Hepworth was something of a misfit in the film world. A sensitive and cultured man, he was finally overwhelmed by the business manipulations of the industry, but during his 20 years as a filmmaker, he was responsible for a considerable body of work made with enormous charm and artistry. His very early film *Rescued by Rover* became a small classic, celebrated for the skill and economy of its visual story-telling.

Hepworth's success did not even continue to the end of the silent era, for after the World War I during which the British film industry was severely curtailed, many companies failed to survive. In the harsh commercial field of that recession, Hepworth staggered and finally fell. His importance to this survey is a group of five well-made and faithful Dickens films. Hepworth was conscious of the need for preserving the spirit of the original, and the well-known characters were portrayed by Hepworth's regular team of actors, few of whom were bothered about becoming stars. In Dickens adaptations, there is little room for star performances, since the multiplicity of characters makes them unnecessary and undesirable. The best results are generally obtained by close ensemble playing, as many of the most recent dramatizations have demonstrated.

Hepworth deliberately selected the majority of his film subjects for their English characteristics, as he explained in his autobiography. He went on to reminisce about some of his Dickens films.

> A less artistic but commercially more important venture was *Oliver Twist*. My father was a popular lecturer when I was a youngster and one of my greatest joys was to go with him and work his "Dissolving Views" for him. His most successful lecture was The Footprints of Charles Dickens in which I gloried, and heard over and over again. As a result I read every book that Dickens wrote and got myself thoroughly saturated with him. So when Thomas Bentley presented himself to me as a "great Dickens character impersonator and scholar" my heart naturally warmed to him and I was readily receptive when he offered to make a Dickens film for me. In the end he made several, but I think *Oliver Twist* was the first and its length was nearly four thousand feet. It may not have been outstandingly good but it was very successful and it marked the beginning not only of a Dickens series but also of a long range of increasingly important pictures from other novels and plays.

Thomas Bentley had, in fact, appeared on the variety stage in both Britain and Australia, giving studies of Dickens characters, very much like Bransby Williams. In 1912, before approaching Cecil Hepworth, he had performed some of these studies on sites referred to in the novels, in a short British film called *Leaves from the Books of Charles Dickens*.

Hepworth went on to describe the making of *David Copperfield* in 1913—the first British eight-reel feature film.

> Bentley certainly loved his Dickens and there is no gainsaying the fact that he turned out a great deal of very good work which redounded considerably to his credit and also to ours. He was a rum chap but I found him very pleasant to work with. He went to Dover among many other places in the making of this film. When he came back he told me that he had found the very house that Dickens had described. I remember the joyful glee with which he recounted how he had managed to secure *in the picture* the fascia board upon it saying that it was "the house immortalized by Dickens as the house of Miss Betsey Trotwood." I do not think he ever understood why I received this news with so little enthusiasm...There came to see me at this time a wonderful little boy with masses of curly hair and a most angelic expression. He was a delightful child with the name of Reggie Sheffield...He brought with him a slightly older boy, an awkward fellow named Noel Coward who I disliked immediately...Reggie Sheffield,

under the film name of Eric Desmond, was cast for the part of the young Copperfield in the early part of the film, but direction failed there, for he too often looked at the camera or the producer when he was spoken to...

Seeing this particular film more than seventy years after its first showing, one cannot allow Hepworth's opinion of Eric Desmond's performance to pass unchallenged. The portrayal of David Copperfield as a boy is a daunting task, and Desmond provided a good depiction of that character on the screen, one that contrasts favorably with the heavy overacting of some of the adult performers. Perhaps that was because many of the older film actors of the time had spent most of their careers on the stage and found it hard to adapt to the more restrained style required for the screen.

Like the book, the first part of the film is better than the rest. That is partly due to the more leisurely pace in the first part of the film, with the result that there is so much to cram in later, that titles and scene changes come much more frequently and abruptly. Bentley and Hepworth were clearly obliged to speed up the second half of the adaptation to avoid unpopular omissions from the book. In spite of its faults, the film is undeniably a milestone in translating Dickens to the screen and demonstrates in scene after scene the pictorial quality and realism for which Hepworth was renowned. It should never be forgotten that the courageous efforts of such dedicated pioneers as Thanhouser and Hepworth were the means of ensuring that adaptations of celebrated literature for the cinema were taken seriously and accorded the merit and respect they eventually achieved.

The Moving Picture World devoted a three-quarter-page review to *David Copperfield,* and acknowledged that "Hepworth has set a high standard in this production and has fairly disproved the oft-repeated charge that the British producer could not make a good motion picture." Rather more surprising is the same reviewer's apparent unfamiliarity with a cinematic device of some long standing.

> One noticeable innovation is the method of dissolving one scene into the next following, and into the titles. There is none of that chopping off of scenes abruptly that is so destructive to illusion. The Hepworth idea is a great improvement and adds much to the pleasure of looking at motion pictures. American producers might adopt it to advantage.

The dominant theme of the book *The Pickwick Papers* is the betrayal of innocence, for Mr. Pickwick is innocence personified. The whole book is a gradual progression from his state of innocent belief in a good world to an eventual realization that evil abounds and may not be easily overcome. Mr. Pickwick is a simple person, against whom all the other richly drawn characters operate. They are all shown against the background of Mr. Pickwick's goodness and naivety, both the spongers, like Jingle and Job Trotter, and the protectors, like Sam Weller and Mr. Wardle. Pickwick is almost invariably the passive ingredient in any of the extraordinary incidents.

Although *The Pickwick Papers* is padded with various interludes of macabre and harrowing tales that hark back to the Gothic Horrors, these are easily omitted in adaptation, and the book breaks down into a number of key episodes, some of which are among the best-known scenes in Dickens's writings: Bardell versus Pickwick; scenes at Dingley Dell; the Shooting Party; Mr. Pickwick at the Ladies Seminary. These short, self-contained sequences were extremely handy for early filmmakers, who were limited both by their apparatus and the conventions of the time.

Many of the reproductions of Pickwick on the screen have selected a few incidents dealing with the fun and games of the story and disregarded the darker side of the tale. That is typical of the way the cinema extracted all possible attractiveness from Dickens and frequently glossed over or ignored completely the great social awareness that Dickens displayed in all his books. In so many of his works there are representations of prison scenes that appalled him, as well as frequent depictions of grinding poverty and abject misery. When such topics could not be avoided, the cinema often treated them in a romantic or "genteel" way. They were problems to be simplified and disposed of quickly, being regarded as lacking in entertainment value. The term *Dickensian* was often a synonym for the quaint and the charming, and a 100 percent safe subject for films.

The Edison company made *Mr. Pickwick's Predicament*, a one reel depiction of the Bardell versus Pickwick episode, in 1912. The picture was well up to the high standards of the other Edison films from Dickens. In Britain, the same adventure was one of two incidents from the book used in 1913 as "Clarendon Speaking

Pictures," which were not talkies at all, but merely dramatizations intended to accompany stage reciters.

The more important use of Pickwick, also in 1913, was by the Vitagraph Company of America, which had already made three one-reelers based on some of Dickens's shorter pieces during the previous twelve months, and whose 1911 *A Tale of Two Cities*, one of their finest productions, was reissued in 1913. Encouraged by the response to those films, the company spread itself over three reels of *The Pickwick Papers*. Some of the filming was carried out in England during a visit by John Bunny, Vitagraph's tubby star of many comic short films, who had apparently long wanted to play Mr. Pickwick. Unfortunately, Bunny's heavy features and often gloomy expression did not really convey the idea of a benign benefactor. Both the planning and distribution of this film seem to have been haphazard, the former probably due to pandering to the whims of the principal actor. Each reel was taken from a different episode in the book—Honourable Event, The Westgate Seminary, and The Shooting Party—and while the first two reels were issued together, the third was not released until six months later. The studio was suffering from Bunny's delusions of grandeur, brought on by the unexpected adulation he had received on his trip to Europe, so completion of the film was no doubt difficult.

In between the British releases of the two parts of Vitagraph's *The Pickwick Papers* came a British-made *Scrooge*, with Seymour Hicks in the title role, a film of 2-1/2 reels length. This was based on the production of J. C. Buckstone's play then being performed at the Coliseum Theatre in London, and the film actually had Buckstone in the cast. "Mr. Seymour Hicks has played the part of Scrooge for so long," wrote a reviewer in *The Bioscope*, "and has found it such a favorite with the public, that there can be little doubt as to its success when introduced to the larger public of the picture theaters." Certainly the Zenith Company traded on the stage reputation, for the opening title included the words "As played by Seymour Hicks for over 2000 performances." The film actually began with Dickens in his library at Gads Hill, a view of his birthplace in Portsmouth, and then Dickens in his library suddenly being inspired to pen the words "A Christmas Carol." Unfortunately, the fact is that Gads Hill only became available for purchase by Dickens some 12 years after the Carol was published; but it probably looked impressive in 1913.

Apart from Scrooge being very raggy and unkempt, the film was an uneven adaptation, with curious deviations from the story. In one instance a woman carrying a baby enters the office and pleads with Scrooge, who rebuffs her. She is helped by Bob Cratchit, who is much neater in appearance than his master. "The poor help the poor" explains a sanctimonious subtitle. An affluent character named Middlemark is seen at his doorway giving "relief to the poor," with the help of his servant. His resources exhausted, Middlemark is seen as the representative of the Guardians of the Poor, and is spurned by Scrooge. Economy in set making meant that Scrooge dwells in his office, where the ghost of Marley, minus chains, visits him and shows him scenes of his school days and his sweetheart. The trick photography was good here, but the continuity in the film was at times a little erratic, with Scrooge appearing at a window that is sometimes on the ground floor and sometimes on the floor above. Many elements of the original story were present, but overall, the film did not do it justice.

4

Condensing Dickens

> The effort to condense a Dickens novel into three reels of moving pictures is sure to rob the story of much of its charm. There are hundreds of little character touches that must necessarily be left out of a condensed version of Dickens that are sadly missed by the great majority.
>
> *The Moving Picture World*, June 1912.

Plagiarism has been an occupational hazard among filmmakers ever since the movies began, and 1914 turned out to be no exception, with two versions of *The Chimes* (not filmed before or since) and two of *The Cricket on the Hearth*. Cecil Hepworth's film of *The Chimes*, made as usual at his Walton-on-Thames studio, was 2-1/2 reels, and was written and directed by Thomas Bentley. In America, Herbert Blaché produced a version twice that length, which seems a little strange, since the story is not all that long. Blaché's film was written and directed by Tom Terriss, brother-in-law of Seymour Hicks. Terriss had appeared on the stage in several productions of Dickens stories, including a portrayal of Scrooge in a one-act piece in 1911 which he developed into a three-act play in 1912, and he had appeared in the same role in America. The apparent imitation of Hicks's immensely successful presentation was probably not welcomed by the Hicks family in the United Kingdom, and relations would not have been helped by a spurious claim in the American cinema press that Terriss had "played Scrooge before the King and Queen of England by special command at Sandringham Palace (sic) and scored more than one success with the part in London."

The two 1914 films of *The Cricket on the Hearth*, each two reels long, were made in the United States by the Flying A and Biograph companies. Biograph's purpose in remaking a story they had already had filmed by D. W. Griffith in 1909 is unclear.

The flow of Dickens films diminished as their length increased, despite the enormous demand for movies of all types during World War I. Of course, many of the earlier films remained in circulation.

Tom Terriss's film of *The Mystery of Edwin Drood*, made for Blaché in 1914, seems to have been influenced by some established Hollywood clichés, as it contained both a prison scene and a dramatic chase sequence. When it was distributed in Britain by the Ideal Film Renting Company, which offered prizes for the best criticism of the ending of the story (or for an alternative ending), a contributor to the Dickens Fellowship magazine *The Dickensian* poured scorn on the production.

> The thing's wrong all through....Wrong period to start with. Coaching instead of early railway. Wrong dresses. Wrong scenes, or right scenes mixed up wrong. Wrong numbers, wrong vaults, wrong weirs, wrong hags, wrong Grewgious, Mrs. Tope a comic landlady, and no Durdles at all, wrong people marry wrong people, wrong, wrong, wrong, every road. Call it a Dickens play, why it's a Dickens nightmare!

The year 1915 saw the release of a Russian version of *The Cricket on the Hearth*. Considering the Russians' fondness for the works of Charles Dickens and their oft-repeated assertions that the bad conditions described by Dickens still prevailed in twentieth-century Britain, it is surprising to find that no other Russian film has been based on his books. Thomas Bentley's fifth and final Dickens film for Hepworth (and in Hepworth's view his best) was a spectacular 5-1/2 reel *Barnaby Rudge*, made on a grand scale, with 1,500 extras reenacting the historical Gordon Riots incorporated by Dickens in his story. These took place in large sections of old London of the 1780s faithfully reproduced in a meadow near the Hepworth studio. "It is a wonderful piece of stage architecture," reported *The Bioscope*, "complete in every detail, and the illusion of solid realism, when viewed from the proper aspect, is quite perfect." Hepworth himself pointed out that the sets had to be strong enough to withstand the rough treatment which must hang upon scenes of disorder and struggle. Part of the ambitious set-up was a replica of old Newgate prison which in the story is destroyed by fire, so that the prisoners may be rescued....Like all the stories of Charles Dickens this is far too complicated to tell clearly in any reasonable length, and it is to the credit of (Bentley) that he managed to make it understandable within the limits of a film of not undue extent.

Thomas Bentley's successes with his Dickens films for Hepworth had not gone unnoticed, and he was invited to join the Universal Film Company in America. He resisted crossing the Atlantic and instead worked for Universal's European arm—Trans-Atlantic—for whom he directed their first British-made film. It was the first screen version of *Hard Times*, in four reels.

Serious attempts to transfer famous books to film sooner or later invite serious attempts at criticism, and Bentley's *Hard Times* did not escape the views of the newly emerging breed of film critics.

Some of the worst evils of Lancashire life prevalent in Dickens' time have now been remedied, and perhaps Mr. Bentley was right in toning down these elements of the story. At any rate, the sense of bitterness and indignation and biting satire left by the book has almost entirely disappeared in the film. (*Kinematograph Monthly Film Report*, October 1915, quoted by Rachael Low.)

The truth was that cinemagoers were not concerned with seeing the realism of social inequality. There was a war on, and they went to movies to be entertained. As was the case with many adaptations from serious literature, the sense of moral indignation in the original work was still being diminished in the condensation, often to the point of exclusion. This has been the fate of Dickens, as of many other authors, for a large part of the cinema's history.

The waiflike Marie Doro, one-time protegée of the great American actor William Gillette, and adored from a respectful distance by the very young Charles Chaplin when he played Billy in Gillette's stage play *Sherlock Holmes* in 1905, had missed the chance of playing Oliver Twist on the screen when Nat Goodwin's play was filmed in 1912. But she made up for her lost opportunity when Jesse Lasky made yet another film of the ever-popular story in 1916. "Miss Doro, white and fragile as a snowdrop, depicts the unwelcome and unloved child, who with big questioning eyes wonders that so much misery should fall to the lot of one small orphan," wrote Agnes Camp in *Motion Picture News*. "Miss Doro's acting is exceptionally good in Oliver's long tramp, after his escape from the coal cellar, when footsore, his tired little legs give way under him and he sinks down by a milestone." The murder of Nancy was regarded by some contemporary critics as particularly shocking and "too realistic to be wholesome." Similar views were expressed nearly fifty years later, when the scene was first presented on BBC television.

The only other Dickens film in 1916 was Rupert Julian's *The Right to be Happy*, a retitled 5 reel adaptation of *A Christmas Carol* in which Julian played the role of Scrooge, as well as director.

It was not until 1917 that the first films were made of *Great Expectations* and *Dombey and Son*. The former was a 5 reel American production by Paramount that featured Mary Pickford's brother Jack as the grown-up Pip. It appears to have been well received in the United States, where *Variety* wrote

> There is one thing certain about this feature; if the average picture house manager will make enough fuss about the authorship of the picture story, he will be assured of the attendance of patronage of a type that will be unusual and augment his usual picture followers.

The implication seems to be that in 1917, readers of Dickens were not likely to be filmgoers, which was perhaps only half true or less.

On the other hand *Dombey and Son*, a 7-reel British film with Lillian Braithwaite as Edith Dombey, was reduced to 5 reels when it was released in the United States two years after its United Kingdom debut, and suffered severe criticism. "All too evident is the fact that this is an importation," said *Variety*.

> Worst of all, an English importation. They haven't the sunlight or the mastery of lighting in the island kingdom that is necessary to excellent photography. What is more, the English haven't motion picture skill....This particular picture, poorly photographed throughout, hasn't a close-up in it....The acting too, was so melodramatic that the audience tittered, and exhibitors, making careful selections, should bear that fact well in mind.

The scenario writer of the film, Eliot Stannard, had already incurred the wrath of many in Britain by setting the story in 1917, with all the characters in modern dress.

In 1917, Frank Lloyd wrote the third film version of *A Tale of Two Cities*, which he directed for William Fox's burgeoning film corporation. It was a well-deserved success and the first big triumph of Lloyd's career after four years in moving pictures. In particular, his handling of the crowd scenes in the storming of the Bastille attracted glowing tributes, and praise was justly given to the remarkable double-exposure scenes in which William Farnum as Sydney Carton encounters and eventually saves William Farnum as Charles Darnay. The picture was widely regarded as one of the finest films of 1917.

In the same year, a 4-reel *Little Dorrit* was released under the Dutch title *Klein Doortje*. Although shot in the Fern Andra-Atelier studio in Berlin, the film was set in Holland. Film historian Geoffrey Donaldson has suggested the following explanation.

> In 1917 Germany and England were at war. A film made in that year with an English setting would never have passed the German censor (and would probably have been booed from the screen by patriotic German audiences). By giving the Dickens story a Dutch setting, the director or producer was able to tell exactly the same story without offending the German censor or the German cinema-going public. Furthermore, the picturesque Dutch costumes would give the film something "exotic" and simultaneously let German audiences know that the story was taking place in a foreign country. The title KLEIN DOORTJE is grammatically correct and the same in both German and Dutch. If the story is supposed to take place in Holland the heroine must, of course, have a Dutch name. Hence '"Doortje," an abbreviation of Theodora.

In 1917, the first film burlesque of a Dickens theme appeared in *Oliver Twisted*, the work of English comedians Fred and Joe Evans, who made a vast number of spoofs of well-known stories and genres in the busy days of the silents.

Perhaps even more than *Nicholas Nickleby*, the complexities of the novel *Bleak House*, its very size and quantity of characters and subplots, make it unsuitable for a dramatic adaptation worthy of the original. In the preamble to the British silent film version of 1920, the producers acknowledged that the novel was complex and crammed with characters, and made clear that their selection of a basic story line covered only the unravelling of Lady Dedlock's past by the lawyer Tulkinghorne and Mr. Guppy. Clever casting offered Bertha Gellardi as Esther Summerson, for she passed most believably as the daughter of Constance Collier's Lady Dedlock. The film was the usual competent achievement that one expected from director Maurice Elvey: relatively brisk in narration and visually satisfying. The bulk of the action took place indoors, emphasizing the claustrophobic atmosphere of so much of the story, while the few exterior scenes were shot in fascinating surroundings that were still abundant in Britain in 1920. The shrinking of the story to a film of about 80 minutes meant the elimination of all the digressions, subplots, and minor characters, and the reduction of John Jarndyce to a relative cipher. The case of Jarndyce and Jarndyce appears only as a name on a deed box, and the word *Chancery* is not mentioned. In its way, the film was a good example of the early cinema's inability to cope with a book like *Bleak House*. In fact, it was only attempted once more, in 1923, and there has been no talkie version.

Richard Oswald, a famous German director and writer, mainly of silent films, tackled many bold and controversial topics in his productions, and was celebrated for his social conscience. It was not surprising that when he made a film of *Oliver Twist* in 6 reels in 1920, entitled *Die Geheimnisse von London (Secrets of London),* it depicted quite fearlessly the monotony and cruelty of workhouse and orphanage life and the poverty and wretchedness allied to the criminal underworld. The film was set in 1920 and, while it adhered fairly closely to the original story line, it had a boy actor who looked far too plump and well cared for to be a believable workhouse orphan.

Oliver Twist Jr. (Fox 1921) was another version with an up-to-date setting, located in America and apparently introducing romance for Oliver as an adolescent.

> In this modernized version of the familiar story, Oliver's mother, cast off by her family for marrying against their wishes, dies in childbirth, leaving only a locket as a clue to his identity, and the child is brought up in a New York orphanage. Aged 17, Oliver is persuaded to run away by Monks, who promises him a good home but he falls in with a gang of thieves headed by Fagin. They discover the whereabouts of the boy's wealthy grandfather, James Harrison, but during a robbery attempt Oliver is shot and found on the ground by Ruth Norris, who befriends him. After

learning his identity, he finds happiness with Ruth. (*AFI Catalogue.*)

Variety was scornful. "The thing was not worth doing in the first place, and to make it complete (it) has been done badly."

In an attempt to recapture some of the international business lost to the American film industry as a result of World War I, the legendary Nordisk company of Denmark produced a batch of four feature-length Dickens films in the early 1920s: *Our Mutual Friend* (the only feature film version), *Great Expectations, David Copperfield,* and *Little Dorrit.* They were among the most distinguished works of director A. W. Sandberg, aided by what was described as "editorial supervision" by the eminent English Dickensian B. W. Matz, and were distributed in Britain and America as well as Europe.

Great Expectations (1921) was a very good presentation of the story, excellently lit and photographed in some carefully devised settings. A first-class interior of Miss Havisham's house was particularly noteworthy, although Joe Gargery's cottage appeared exceedingly roomy for a humble blacksmith. The acting was well restrained, and the whole film demonstrated how advanced the Scandinavian filmmakers were before the coming of sound. The boy and man Pip were well matched in appearance, but unfortunately were the least natural in their acting. The girl and woman Estella, equally well matched, were much more convincing, the girl being particularly good at conveying by gesture and pose the spoiled and disdainful Estella.

Emil Helsengreen (once a fearsome Professor Moriarty on the stage) was really fine as Magwitch, big and rough without being overly melodramatic, while Peter Nielsen's Orlick was suitably fierce and repulsive, especially in the scene in which Pip is bound by Orlick and saved from death in the nick of time by Herbert Pocket. The film suffered from excessively wordy intertitles, which was probably an indication of Sandberg's inexperience in visual story-telling under the pressure of condensing the plot into a reasonable feature film length. Even so, the fiery death of Miss Havisham (partly achieved by painting flames on the individual prints of the film) was a bold and frightening dramatic high spot, and at such times Sandberg was content to leave the scene to tell the story.

In 1922, Sandberg's *David Copperfield* showed a distinct improvement in his film technique and, although the intertitles were still rather wordy, they advanced the story, which was quite a thorough adaptation of the novel. The main omissions were David's experiences at school and the Peggotty family, other than Peggotty herself. An unusual addition was a brief epilogue showing David Copperfield transformed into Charles Dickens, sitting in the garden with his family, plus Betsey Trotwood and Mr. Dick.

Martin Herzberg, who had played the boy Pip the year before, this time played the boy David. While still overdramatic, he gave a better performance, particularly in scenes with the beautiful Margarethe Schlegel, who played David's mother. For the American release of both films, Herzberg was renamed Buddy Martin and compared favorably with Jackie Coogan. Peter Malberg's portrayal of Mr. Dick was delightfully skillful without being ridiculous, and Sandberg's wife Karina Bell was a suitably spoiled, childish Dora. But the most enjoyable performance came from Frederick Jensen, stealing scene after scene as possibly the best silent-film Micawber. The entire film was made with loving care for both the story and the characters, and again showed the fine standard of composition and photography achieved by the Scandinavians well before the end of the silent era.

Also in the prolific 1920s came a well-cast but poorly condensed British *Little Dorrit*, a not very satisfactory French *The Cricket on the Hearth*, and a superior *The Old Curiosity Shop* from the vastly experienced Thomas Bentley, who was then working with producer George Pearson for the Welsh-Pearson company. "As a film director he had great patience," wrote Pearson, "and a keen sense of characterization in its most intimate detail." The screenplay was written by the film critic of *The Daily Telegraph*, G. A. Atkinson. Not only did Bentley accomplish an impressive film, but the presentation when the film was shown at the Alhambra, Leicester Square, was exemplary. On the stage, three players, appearing as travellers in the setting of a village inn, discussed the works of Charles Dickens. As one of them began relating the story of Little Nell, the lights dimmed, the curtains parted, and the film began.

"Mr. Thomas Bentley, as a film producer, deserves the grateful thanks of all Dickensians," observed *The Times* in 1921.

Condensing Dickens 45

> In picture after picture he has succeeded in re-creating the immortals who pass through the author's pages, and a new public which does not read Dickens has been given an opportunity of making the acquaintance of Barnaby Rudge, of David Copperfield, of Micawber, of Quilp, of Little Nell and her grandfather, and of scores of others who are not of an age but for all time. Now Mr. Bentley, enthusiastic Dickensian that he is, has taken on the hardest task of all to give in the scope of a single film a comprehensive idea of the strange adventures of Mr. Pickwick.

The Times correspondent was reporting on the filming that was then being completed at Elstree, and he clearly understood that Bentley's aim was "to tell a story which will appeal to those who have not read the book and which will, at any rate, contain no glaring omissions to rend the hearts of the enthusiasts."

Bentley's *Pickwick*, his eighth film from a Dickens novel, had a very strong cast that included, as Mr. Pickwick, Frederick Volpe, who had previously played the part on the stage at the Coliseum Theatre, London, in the Dickens Centenary celebrations that had been organized by Seymour Hicks to raise funds for certain descendants of Charles Dickens. As well as Mary Brough as Mrs. Bardell, the film also had the ubiquitous Bransby Williams in a memorable portrayal of Serjeant Buzfuz, Ernest Thesiger as Jingle, and Athene Seyler as the hapless Rachel Wardle. A month after the above production report, *The Times* gave the film an excellent review, and commented:

> The whole-hearted Dickensian may complain that considerable liberties have been taken with the text, but most of these can probably be justified on the score of expediency....There are enough instances of "improving" Dickens in this film to turn grey the hair of the pedantic, but the result of this sacrilege practically justifies it. Probably it is better to produce a good film that does not faithfully follow the original than an accurate transcript of the book which is not a satisfactory film.

Jackie Coogan, the child actor who shot to stardom in Chaplin's film *The Kid* in 1920, became much sought after by other film producers and was an obvious choice for important juvenile leads. While he was an appropriate Tom Sawyer or Huckleberry Finn, his suitability as an Oliver Twist may well be questioned. But after Coogan's previous triumphs (three box-office hits in two years), the success of his appearance as Oliver Twist was guaranteed, as producer Sol Lesser recollected:

> For *Oliver Twist* the man I thought most capable of doing it was Frank Lloyd, an English director. He was a Dickens scholar and had stage-directed it in England. In addition, he had an outstanding record as a motion picture director in Hollywood. He and I agreed to independently go through the book to see which of the many incidents should be retained for the picture. By lucky coincidence we selected identical material. Lloyd suggested that it was just a question of inserting the scenes in proper continuity and full detail. This he did and in a matter of four weeks we were on the floor producing it. We assembled a magnificent cast. It took about six weeks to make the picture. The publicity established it as a road show, and we got excellent percentage terms from first-run theatres throughout the country. The cost was justified. It paid off handsomely in England and throughout the world...I never realized the value of old negatives. The business manager came to me and asked "Are you going to make any more prints of *Oliver Twist*?" "No," I said. "Can I destroy the negative? I need the vault space!" I told him "Sure, go ahead, it's dead." I had no sense then that it was an art form. The revivals of the old pictures make me just about the most surprised man in the world.

At the time of the film's presentation in England, a blatant publicity event was arranged whereby Coogan gave a donation to the Foundling Hospital in London, where the first English showing of the film was given. Sadly, the print of this version of *Oliver Twist*, which had been presented to the Dickens Fellowship in 1922, was rediscovered in 1973 and found to be largely damaged beyond repair. "All things considered," observed the New York *Times* at the time of the film's debut, "they've done a good job, an excellent job, with Dickens in the picturized *Oliver Twist* which is destined to keep the house full, if the crowds that packed the place yesterday mean anything. But whether it is Mr. Dickens or little Jackie Coogan that is drawing them in is, of course, a question." The Fagin in this film was that remarkable disguise artist Lon Chaney, whose appearance in the role was certainly bizarre. It is reported that on Chaney's first visit to the set in make-up, the nine-year-old Coogan ran away, screaming in fright. Yet Chaney appeared not to be fully within the range of the part, which is a much more difficult role than is often supposed. Frank Lloyd's direction contained some interesting touches, but as the New York *Times* hinted, the picture was mainly a showcase for Coogan.

Last and longest of all the silent Dickens films was *The Only Way*, made by British director Herbert Wilcox in 1925. For 25 years, Sir John Martin Harvey had enjoyed enormous success on the stage with an adaptation of *A Tale of Two Cities* under the above title, and Wilcox finally persuaded Harvey to appear before the camera in what had become very much Harvey's own play. Herbert Wilcox had only started his own film company a few months earlier, yet he made *The Only Way* for £24,000—a relatively high figure for British films of that era. The result was rather slow and ponderous, but because of the tremendous prestige of both Harvey and the stage play, the film was a great commercial success in Britain and America, causing Harvey to bring a lawsuit against Wilcox for increased remuneration!

The Only Way brought to a spectacular close the immense run of silent Dickens films, for Wilcox had indulged in gigantic sets and huge crowds, which he handled to advantage in opening up what was in large part a filmed stage play substantially based on a Dickens novel, rather than an adaptation directly from the book. As Jeffrey Richards justly wrote of Wilcox, "His work was never less than highly professional and in the best of taste, the two qualities he most prized."

5

Dickens With Dialogue

> Dickens' dialogue at its most idiomatic is often suitable for the screen; but when it becomes affected, wordy, and sentimental, its faults seem exaggerated in the mouth of an actor observed at such close range at the moment of speaking.
>
> Roger Manvell, 1965

Bransby Williams had one of the longest careers, if not *the* longest, as an impersonator of characters from famous fiction. He first established himself as an imitator of popular actors in their great roles, and in 1897 he commenced his celebrated "studies" of Charles Dickens's characters. His large repertoire included Micawber, Peggotty, Uriah Heep, Bill Sikes, Fagin, Pecksniff, Chadband, Sydney Carton, Grandfather Trent, and many others. These impressions were performed on the stages of Victorian music halls, and he was sufficiently well-known to be commanded to appear before King Edward VII at Sandringham in 1903. He also toured in various Dickens plays and, in 1923, appeared in *David Copperfield* at the Lyceum Theatre, London, doubling as Micawber and Peggotty as well as producing the play. Having acted various Dickens roles in plays and films, he ended his career in the 1950s by giving some of the same impersonations in numerous television appearances when he was over eighty. His first appearance on the screen in a Dickens part was in the silent film of *Hard Times* in 1915, as Gradgrind. He also played Buzfuz in the 1921 film of *Pickwick*. His rich style was doubtless suited to the silent screen, but he also had the unique distinction of performing in the first two genuine sound films from Dickens, made by British Sound Film Productions in 1928.

In the first film, Bransby Williams gave his impersonation of Grandfather Smallweed from *Bleak House*, and in the second he portrayed the perpetually popular *Scrooge*. Discounting the early sound-on-disc film by Gaumont in 1906, these were the first true talking pictures based on Dickens with the sound-on-film process, each 9 minutes long. In a sense, it was a return to pioneering days, for many cinema owners were slow to embark on the considerable expense of equipping their premises for sound, and so filmmakers proceeded cautiously in producing talkies that initially would only have a limited distribution. Yet small, enterprising companies were keen to enter this new field, even if their resources only ran to shorter items.

In Britain another six years elapsed before a feature-length Dickens sound film was produced. Meanwhile, in the United States, Paramount made the first full-length Dickens talkie—*Rich Man's Folly*—in 1931. Perhaps better described as a near-Dickens talkie, it was set in modern America and claimed to be "suggested" by the novel *Dombey and Son*. Certainly the film followed the main theme of the book. George Bancroft, well-known for tough gangster roles, played Brock Trumbull, a rough, domineering shipbuilder whose business of Trumbull & Son is his sole motivation. As with the Dickens original, his wife dies, his son dies, and his daughter is rejected by her ruthless father and his second wife. The similarity to *Dombey and Son* came no closer. Mordaunt Hall, in a review headed "A Mighty Failure" in the New York *Times*, wrote, "Part of this picture is maudlin, part is annoying and most of it is hopelessly illogical."

After this apparent lapse from good box-office appeal, the first talking version of *Oliver Twist* was released in 1933, made at he Monogram studios, where the staple product was westerns, serials, and low-budget thrillers. Although primarily a source of B pictures, Monogram was occasionally capable of producing first features but this adaptation was barely adequate for its time. In New York and elsewhere, the film had to compete with the immense successes of *King Kong* and *42nd Street*. Understandably, it had a very lukewarm reception. Irving Pichel's Fagin was too well-spoken and insufficiently forbidding to be really convincing, although the New York *Times* did describe the Bill Sikes of William Boyd as "a thorough-going account of the murderous burglar." Dickie Moore as Oliver was plump and winsome, totally unbelievable as a child raised in a workhouse. "Young Moore's performance is mechanical and unyielding," said *Variety*. "It is almost possible to follow the coaching of the director in some scenes." The film survived to be reissued in Britain in 1947, in an apparent attempt to steal the thunder of the David Lean version, then nearing completion.

In 1934, Universal Pictures presented the first of a pair of Dickens films—*Great Expectations*—a story only filmed twice as a silent, each time as a feature. The Universal version was a well-photographed feature, but never reached any level of outstanding quality. Neither the scriptwriter nor the director (Gladys Unger and Stuart Walker) seemed to understand how important it is with Dickens to present the characters generously and well, at the expense of simplifying and condensing the plot.

The young English actress Valerie Hobson was taken to Hollywood to play Estella opposite the Pip of former silent star Phillips Holmes, but the role was then given to Jane Wyatt. It was Jane Wyatt's second film. "I loved playing Estella," she wrote.

> I auditioned for the part with another girl, who was also at Universal studio. She was English and beautiful and I was sure I didn't have a chance...Valerie was so good-looking, handsome actually, that I imagine she looked older than I did and wouldn't have been right for the young Estella. In the English production they used two girls for Estella and she fitted right in.

Valerie Hobson was, in fact, six years younger than Jane Wyatt, but the role went to Wyatt anyway, and Hobson was recast as Biddy, a part eventually cut from the final print.

Phillips Holmes's Pip was very wooden, and scarcely looked like a gentleman. On the other hand, Alan Hale as Joe Gargery actually looked like a blacksmith. Francis L. Sullivan's lawyer Jaggers was a persuasive trial run for his later Jaggers, and just about the only confident performance in the film, for most of the Americans in the cast were so busy trying to sound English that they forgot about acting. As for Georgie Breakston as the boy Pip, he should have been throttled in the graveyard by Magwitch right at the outset. The New York *Times* compared this film with a British production that had just preceded it.

> The first of the series of Dickens sound films shown here came from a British studio, British International. *The Old Curiosity Shop*

was the story selected, and a company of capable artists, headed by Ben Webster, was gathered together by Thomas Bentley, who directed, and who is an ardent student of the author. Mr. Bentley and his cast have caught the Dickensian atmosphere most successfully, but the development of the story is more in keeping with the slow-moving days of the stage coach than with the rapid motion of this era of airplanes...Almost synchronously with the trade showing of *Curiosity Shop* came the London presentation of the American version of *Great Expectations*, done by Universal. Despite Carl Laemmle's announcement on program that the latter picture comes to the screen with the real Dickens flavour untouched, *Great Expectations* compares unfavorably with *The Old Curiosity Shop*, for in the American picture more of an effort has been made to bring the story into conformity with present-day requirements of alert audiences than Mr. Bentley attempted in his leisurely fashion... Charles Dickens's stories have, of course, long been recognized by amateur critics of British film production as providing the kind of wholly and truly English subject and scenario which the millions of cinemagoers of this country were waiting for.

Thomas Bentley was a Dickensian from the Edwardian era of theatrical supremacy. He had gained much experience during 20 years of filmmaking, and his adaptations were firmly based on the slower-moving methods and manners of the Victorian and Edwardian stage. This, his last Dickens film and his third of that particular story, was also his best. *The Old Curiosity Shop*, the first British feature-length Dickens talkie, was one of a host of creditable products of British studios in the 1930s, many of which were obscured by the massive Hollywood output and are now being recognized for their real worth. "BIP's version of *The Old Curiosity Shop*," wrote John Betjeman, "contained some shots which were the best Dickensian scenes yet reproduced, particularly that of the old village church in the closing scene. This had the quality of a three-dimensional Cruikshank drawing." As the New York *Times* noted, Bentley's film had the benefit of an excellent cast, headed by the venerable Ben Webster as probably the best-ever Grandfather Trent, and Hay Petrie, who gave a splendidly robust performance as a particularly malevolent Quilp. Amy Veness was perfectly cast as Mrs. Jarley, and Elaine Benson's Nell, becoming noticeably shabbier and feebler as the film progressed, was extremely good, in spite of the exquisite elocution which also plagued Mrs. Quilp and Kit. With outstandingly good sets and decor, the whole production was a fitting conclusion to Bentley's distinguished Dickensian career.

Of course, the New York *Times* was right on two matters: Americans have long been fond of English costume dramas and still are, either in the cinema or on TV. By 1935, cinema audiences *had* become more sophisticated and expected to see films of ever-improving quality.

6

In a Tradition of Quality

> Whenever the motion-picture industry creates an outstanding piece of work like *David Copperfield*, it points with pride to the wonderful effect this picture will have on the youth of the country. When the same industry puts forth a gangster story, it takes great pains to explain that the youth of the country is in no way affected by what it sees on the screen.
>
> William de Mille, 1935

David O. Selznick appeared to regard himself as a self-appointed converter of literature for the cinema, and was probably responsible for more successful screen adaptations than any other film producer, including the unforgettable *Gone With the Wind*. His triumphs in that field began with *Little Women*, made at RKO in 1933, shortly after which he moved to M-G-M and began work on one of his favorite subjects—*David Copperfield*. He felt that the opposition he encountered to filming *David Copperfield* was based on the fact that classics and costume pictures had been out of favor in the industry for some time and that although the film could not possibly be a star vehicle, it would be very costly to make.

Of course, Selznick not only enjoyed, but actually seemed to thrive on, the internal politics and maneuvering of the big studios, and he proceeded with *David Copperfield* despite the obstacles placed in his way by Louis B. Mayer. Although Mayer, who ran the gigantic M-G-M studio, was Selznick's father-in-law, there was little affection between them. In fact, Selznick left the studio not long after *David Copperfield* had been released. Selznick recalled that one of his most difficult experiences while at M-G-M was casting that film. Louis B. Mayer wanted Jackie Cooper for the title role, but both Selznick and his director, George Cukor, refused.

> We won our point, Cukor reported, and found Freddie Bartholomew, who was perfect except that he had a British schoolboy's *noblesse oblige* and it was terribly difficult to make him cry. It's a pity that in the book David Copperfield grows up to be such a bore, a typical young Victorian—people chided me about this when they saw the picture and said "The second half is not as good as the first." By then I'd discovered my own rule in doing adaptations. . .You must get the essence of the original, which may involve accepting some of the weaknesses. When you read *David Copperfield* you know why it's lasted. There's too much melodrama and the second half is unsatisfactory, but there's this underlying vitality and invention. For me, that determined the style of the picture. In the same way, there was the problem of re-creating Dickens characters, making them slightly grotesque, at times caricature, yet completely human—as Dickens did himself. You achieve it partly by the casting but also by deciding on the style of playing.

Between them, Selznick and Cukor assembled one of the most brilliant and satisfying casts ever to appear in a Dickens film, in a screen version of a famous book, or indeed in an M-G-M picture, and those portrayals are still regarded by many as some of the most enjoyable impersonations of Dickens characters ever put on the screen. It is difficult to do justice to the multitude of fine performances in the film without devoting a disproportionate amount of space to the topic, but certain portrayals should not be left unremarked.

The casting of W. C. Fields as Micawber was not the first choice for that part. George Cukor had selected Charles Laughton, and Selznick even considered Laughton to be the one important name in the cast. Laughton's wife, Elsa Lanchester, wrote:

> Charles quite liked the idea, so they got permission from Paramount to borrow him for the part. On the face of it, Micawber seemed to be a wonderful part for Charles. He set about the make-up, was fitted for a skin-tight suit, and had all his hair shaved off. Hugh Walpole and George Cukor saw the silent test and they and everybody else agreed that Charles just was Micawber. He himself thought he had got the walk and with the jaunty cane and top hat he appeared to be all that is associated with the character. But Charles realized when it came to speaking the lines that he had not got the necessary quality for the part. He felt that it needed a music-hall technique. He started the film, but per-

suaded David Selznick, and quite rightly, that he was not suitable for it.

George Cukor agreed that Charles Laughton looked perfect as Micawber but that he lacked the geniality. "He was the first actor I encountered who prepared to make a laughing entrance by going and doing *ha-ha* sounds for hours. But it didn't work out. We shot for a week and then he withdrew."

Even today, the choice of W. C. Fields for the role is regarded by some as daring, but his performance, although it edged toward burlesque, did what Selznick and Cukor required in capturing the spirit of Dickens's original character. They managed to restrain Fields from introducing his famous juggling routine but agreed to other bits of acting business that he suggested.

"There was a scene in which he had to sit at a desk writing," said Cukor, "and he asked me if he could have a cup of tea on the desk. When he got agitated, he dipped his pen into the teacup instead of the inkwell. Another time he was sitting on a stool and asked for a wastepaper basket so he could get his feet stuck in it." Neither of these is from Dickens, but the ideas enhance the character Dickens created.

The effectiveness of the remainder of the players is a tribute to the outstanding capabilities of both Selznick and Cukor, who had worked together on *Little Women* at RKO and were both extremely sensitive in the handling of classics on the screen. In spite of plans to shoot the picture in England, *David Copperfield* ended up being filmed at the M-G-M studio at Culver City, California, and the cliffs at Malibu Beach were used as a substitute for the White Cliffs of Dover. Selznick, who had at one stage contemplated filming the story as two separate pictures, became concerned at the finished size of the film.

> At the time I produced *David Copperfield* the average picture of importance ran seven to eight thousand feet in length.... In its first cut *Copperfield* ran over fourteen thousand feet, or almost twice the usual length of films at that time. As I was made somewhat nervous by the opinions of the experts, I asked Mr. Schenk what was the maximum length in which he thought we could release *David Copperfield*. Mr. Schenk gave me a reply which I have never forgotten and have often quoted: "What do you mean, how long can you make it," asked Mr. Schenk. "How long is it good?"

On top of the problems normally arising with a production of this magnitude, Selznick had to contend with a studio that was more than usually apathetic about the picture. He had been persuaded by Louis B. Mayer to leave RKO and join M-G-M, not because Mayer particularly wanted his son-in-law in the firm, but as a political move to strengthen Mayer's hand in dealing with Irving Thalberg. Selznick was in the customarily unpopular position of being one of the boss's family and therefore not to be trusted, helped, or encouraged.

> The opposition lasted all through the picture, and the entire studio thought I was going on my nose. Even at the preview, the executives still didn't realize what we had and pressed me with their consoling opinion that "it might do well in England." Hollywood trade papers suggested the second half be thrown away and the picture end when the story of the children ends. Not until its sensational success at the Capitol Theatre in New York did the company realize that it had one of the outstanding successes of all time. And even then it was thought it would not repeat its success throughout the country—that there might have been just enough lovers of Dickens in New York to support the run at the Capitol.

The resounding success of *David Copperfield* was fully deserved. The film enjoyed various reissues and made enormous profits for M-G-M. Its triumph was due to the combined talents of Selznick and Cukor, for by then both were well into the most creative period of their careers. The book *David Copperfield* embodies much of the anguish and hardship of Charles Dickens's own early life, and the two filmmakers were able to capture the heart of this and reproduce the *feeling* of the book in a way that made the film acceptable both to Dickens lovers and to the then-huge cinemagoing public. In this respect, they were helped by the distinguished English novelist Hugh Walpole, who also participated, as Cukor related:

> We thought Walpole would be good to write the dialogue. He didn't know anything about screen technique, but he understood Dickens and the tone that we needed. He also played a small part in the picture, the parson. His father had been a bishop in New Zealand, and Hugh was good at imitating long sermons—although when we tried to shoot close-ups he got self-conscious.

In A Tale of Two Cities, Selznick had a completely different type of subject to tackle; not that he was in any way deterred. His continuous, overwhelming enthusiasm for all his projects was much needed on this second Dickens picture, and again he achieved a conspicuous success, both with the adaptation of a Dickens novel and with the exceptional performance by Ronald Colman as Sydney Carton, which he had agreed to play, provided he did not have to be Charles Darnay as well.

The novel lacks the broad humanity of *David Copperfield* and its enormous collection of characters and eccentrics, and it was vital for the acceptance of the film by 1930s cinema audiences to camouflage the rather crude melodrama of the book. Selznick selected Sam Behrman to write the dialogue and Jack Conway to direct, to inject some vitality into the slow-moving tale. While the picture was in production, David Selznick ended his contract with M-G-M, but he stayed on for a fee to complete both this film and *Anna Karenina*, which he was also producing. The total production cost of *Two Cities* was $1 million, slightly less than that of *Copperfield*. Selznick encountered even more opposition from the studio personnel, who resented the success of *Copperfield* and the fact that he had been right about it, and when *A Tale of Two Cities* was completed, he complained bitterly to Nicholas Schenk in New York about the attitude of the studio. "Were this picture made by any other studio in the industry, the town would be agog about it....Can you imagine if it were made by Zanuck?"

Such barbs merely added to the rancor with which Selznick left M-G-M, which needed him but didn't want him. But Selznick believed he was right and had no hesitation in saying so at great length. The picture was a deserved triumph and yielded one of the best performances of Ronald Colman's acting career as the world-weary, cynical Sydney Carton—a fundamental change to Colman's normal casual style.

In *A Tale of Two Cities*, the wicked Marquis St. Evremonde was played by Basil Rathbone, with what Graham Greene once called his "dark knife-blade face and snapping mouth." That polished actor was a master of the sardonic role and had been a wonderfully cold and emotionless Murdstone in *David Copperfield*. Elizabeth Allan had been one of the few English players specially conveyed to Hollywood by M-G-M for *David Copperfield*, in which she played David's mother. She reappeared in *A Tale of Two Cities* as Lucie

Manette. Edna May Oliver also gave her regular performance as Edna May Oliver in both films, thinly disguised as Betsey Trotwood and Miss Pross respectively. Notable in smaller parts in *Two Cities* were old-timers Henry B. Walthall, once the star of Griffith's *The Birth of a Nation,* and Billy Bevan, featured in countless silent comedies. They played Dr. Manette and Jerry Cruncher.

The exciting scenes of the storming of the Bastille, directed by Val Lewton and Jacques Tourneur, were presented on a magnificent scale, characteristic of those days of the great studios and far too costly for anyone to emulate nowadays. The whole production was in the Hollywood style of the time, overlaid with customary M-G-M gloss but, as with *David Copperfield,* it succeeded in conveying the essential theme of the novel at a time when M-G-M was unexpectedly riding high with a string of filmed classics.

Both of the Selznick Dickens films provided a lot of employment for the colony of British actors residing in Hollywood. One of these, Reginald Owen, who was Stryver in *A Tale of Two Cities,* turned up later as Scrooge in M-G-M's *A Christmas Carol,* a film planned for M-G-M by Selznick but not made until several years after his departure from the studio. That delay may well have been because of the production in Britain of a film of the same story, entitled *Scrooge* and featuring Seymour Hicks in the title role. So, in the same year as the two M-G-M Dickens films, and 34 years after his Royal Command appearance, Hicks reappeared on the screen in one of his most famous characterizations, in a film that was successful both in Britain and the United States. The *New York Times* commented rather generously: "The danger of adapting so widely read an author as Dickens to the screen always has been that the mortals chosen to fill the roles will prove so much less than the characters he created out of pen, paper and genius. Happily there is no such disappointment here."

It is extremely interesting to compare the Hicks *Scrooge* of 1935 with the M-G-M *A Christmas Carol* which appeared only three years later, and this has been done at some length by Professor Paul Davis in his book *The Lives and Times of Ebenezer Scrooge,* in which he considers all versions of the story, printed and performed. Davis rightly points out that different perceptions and presentations of the *Carol* story have come about according to the times in which they have been produced, ranging from Dickens's own time, when the moral and social lessons of the tale were only too necessary, to the thoughtlessly selfish economic ideology of the 1980s.

In 1935, in the depths of the Depression, the cinema provided one of the few luxuries available to the general public, and films that gave some glimpse of hope in those dark times were popular. The plight of Scrooge's downtrodden clerk was only too familiar to audiences then. By 1935, Seymour Hicks had aged into the part of Scrooge (he was then 64) and was famous in that role after so many years performing it on the stage and in halls. It is therefore no surprise that the film is based more on the stage dramatization used by Hicks than directly on the book itself. Consequently, the emphasis of the production is on the angry, mean Scrooge that Hicks personified in the British public's mind, rather than on the methods of Scrooge's transformation and the equally important circumstances of Scrooge's nephew Fred and the multitudinous Cratchit family.

The result is the omission of Scrooge's unhappy school days and his apprenticeship with Fezziwig, and especially the gaiety in young Scrooge's life as exemplified at the Fezziwig's Ball. Thus the opportunity for pointing up the significance of the change that overcomes Scrooge is lost, and the audience is left to assume that he has always been angry and mean and is therefore strangely converted by his experiences against his nature. Such criticisms aside, the film *Scrooge* is a very well-made British movie of its time, fully deserving of the praise given to it in the New York *Times* and elsewhere. Hicks's performance was clearly that of an actor well familiar with his part and completely at home in the ably recreated atmosphere of the 1840s, splendidly aided by Donald Calthrop, the unsurpassed embodiment of Bob Cratchit.

In M-G-M's *A Christmas Carol* of 1938, on the other hand, Reginald Owen was not entirely comfortable in the role of Scrooge, although he played it with great gusto. Owen had a remarkably long career in Hollywood and was always in demand for character parts, as well as the occasional leading role. He spent 20 years at M-G-M, and in 1938 alone appeared in seven films. But in *A Christmas Carol*, in spite of a strong performance, he was, at the age of 51, trying unsuccessfully to portray a much older man. Owen's Scrooge was preoccupied by business, rather than naturally mean, although unforgivingly petty in dismissing Bob Cratchit, who was engagingly played by Gene Lockhart. It was Lockhart's misfortune to have the physical appearance of a Pickwick, rather than a shabbily treated Cratchit, and he played with unrelenting good humor in a version of the *Carol* story that was handled generally in a much more cheerful way. That was understandable, for by December 1938, when the film was released, the shadows of the Second World War were already looming, and the cinema industry was gearing itself up for its biggest output of escapist entertainment. Curiously, no more Dickens films figured in that wartime output, although the talkie versions of the 1930s were frequently reissued.

Those talkie versions included another film made in 1935, Universal Pictures' second Dickens feature—the first sound film of *The Mystery of Edwin Drood*, which was dealt with in Universal's usual brisk horror-movie style, complete with bell tower, tombs and crypts, and a rabble of easily roused citizens. One of the writers, John L. Balderston, had earlier helped write Universal's *Dracula* and *Frankenstein*. Since the novel *Edwin Drood* was left unfinished at Dickens's death, any dramatist rash enough to attempt the story must provide his own solution to the mystery, thereby risking the wrath of many Dickens lovers. On this occasion, Universal chose a relatively straightforward course and had an evil John Jasper—delightfully played by the ever-reliable Claude Rains—murder Drood and try to frame Neville Landless for the crime. The hot-tempered Landless, vigorously played by Douglass Montgomery, returns disguised as the enigmatic Datchery and finally exposes Jasper, who falls to his death from the cathedral tower in time-honored Universal fashion. Despite a number of stock formula scenes and incidents, the film did manage to convey some spirit of the novel, as far as Dickens had been able to develop it. The real strength of this rather likable film lay in its good assembly of actors. Francis L. Sullivan was a very satisfactory, if rather overweight, Reverend Septimus Crisparkle; Heather Angel played the typically sweet Dickens heroine Rosa Bud; and Valerie Hobson, in one of her last films at Universal, was Rosa's calm and reassuring friend Helena Landless, sister of Neville.

Valerie Hobson recalled:

> I remember only slightly anything about *The Mystery of Edwin Drood;* the wonderful beauty of Claude Rains' voice and strength of his personality, although he was so short in stature. My "brother" I remember as being a very unsure and temperamental

young actor and I can't remember any other films he made, although I feel sure that he did. The part of the sister, me, wasn't a very fully-drawn character; I remember being fascinated to wear very dark make-up for the first time, since brother and sister were intended to look half-caste.

In fact, the Canadian-born Douglass Montgomery made comparatively few films, and his performance in this picture was probably the least convincing of all. The film is one of the monochrome Universal pictures that frequently turn up on television.

7

A Social Chorus

> Most Dickens is really unfilmable, because his amplitude, his prodigality of invention, are both his most telling qualities and those least susceptible to transfer from the printed page. However, in this less than perfect world the temptation to try remains potent.
>
> John Russell Taylor, 1970

It was significant that the little wave of Dickens films that appeared in England immediately after the Second World War came at a time of great social upheaval in Britain. The wartime upsurge in recreational reading had introduced Dickens to new readers and reawakened interest in old readers. The excellent dramatizations of some of the novels on BBC radio had further stimulated interest. At the same time, a revived British cinema was eagerly seeking peacetime subjects to follow the many fine wartime films made by a new generation of British filmmakers. In the austere economy of the postwar era, stories in the public domain were particularly attractive.

When David Lean's *Great Expectations* (1946) flared onto the screen, closely followed by Alberto Cavalcanti's *Nicholas Nickleby* (1947) and by Lean's *Oliver Twist* (1948), a Dickens revolution appeared to be upon us. In fact, what really happened was the emergence of David Lean as a great director, with two masterpieces that are now a part of film history. In both instances, Lean played a major part in the adaptations, which were so skillfully done that many enthusiasts believed virtually nothing had been omitted from the books. Both stories were depicted with the outstanding visual skill that has rightly earned Lean a place among the world's finest film directors. Who can forget the gripping opening of *Great Expectations,* when young Pip is suddenly confronted in the graveyard by the convict Magwitch? In the cinema, the encounter left the audience as nervous as Pip himself. Then there was the eloquently shot opening of *Oliver Twist,* where Oliver's mother makes her way to the workhouse, bears her baby, and dies unwanted and unmourned. That sequence runs for some eight minutes before the first words of dialogue are spoken. David Lean wrote:

> What we were trying to do in *Great Expectations* was to create in the film that larger-than-life picture which is really most characteristic of Dickens' kind of writing. The scenes of the boy Pip lying terrified in his bedroom after a night of fear, creeping downstairs at dawn, and then stealing the food for the convict out on the moors was something Dickens wrote as if he were right inside the boy himself. We tried in the film to make the audience share Pip's fear. If we hadn't done this, we should have been faced with quite a different problem—making the audience accept what is really a pretty exaggerated piece of melodrama. They might easily have found the convicts and their fustian dialogue just funny instead of terrifying, if we had not built up the fear in the audience at the same time as we did in the boy.

Here Lean shows the same understanding as Dickens of the need to manipulate his public, albeit in a different medium, to make such high drama plausible. David Lean had not previously read *Great Expectations* but in 1939 he and Ronald Neame saw the stage adaptation of the book made by Alec Guinness, in which Guinness played Herbert Pocket and Martita Hunt was Miss Havisham (the roles they subsequently acted in the film). Lean later acknowledged that had he not seen the play, he would not have made the film. On such a slender chance rested the origin of one of the great film classics, which was nominated for five Academy Awards and received Oscars for cinematography and art direction.

One of the Oscar nominations was for the screenplay by David Lean, Ronald Neame, and Anthony Havelock-Allan. "A good 90 per cent of the words we hear are the unadulterated and unimproved words of Charles Dickens," wrote Alan Dent in an enthusiastic review.

> I dare to say that it is this plain, undeclared fact—even more than the sensitive direction, adaptation, photography, and acting—that makes this film the huge success it is.... It is Dickens, nothing but Dickens, but not the whole Dickens. Perhaps—though this is

the most concentrated of the novels—the whole was too much to expect.

In the role of storyteller, David Lean had a marked affinity with Dickens and possessed similarly exceptional craftsmanship. All the aspects of filmmaking—camerawork, editing, the sparing use of background music and sound effects—are employed with masterly skill in advancing the narrative. Probably no finer Dickens film has been made than Lean's *Great Expectations*. The cast assembled for this masterpiece included some acknowledged British stars, but none was allowed to dominate the picture. John Mills, as the adult Pip, carried the major role of the story as well as speaking the voice-over narration that Lean sensibly adopted. Jean Simmons was ideal as the young Estella, coldly obeying Miss Havisham's exhortations to break not only Pip's heart, but those of other young men; a pursuit continued with exquisite calm and polish by Valerie Hobson, who observed, "It was very much better to have two different-aged Estellas, as David Lean wisely did. And I thought when David cast me how extraordinary it was that sometimes things do go full circle and that I did get the part in the end!" Martita Hunt's Miss Havisham was seriously unnerving without being grotesque, and Bernard Miles' lovable, awkward, and gangling Joe Gargery lacked only the large physique generally associated with village blacksmiths. Francis L. Sullivan's lawyer Jaggers (played by him for Universal in 1934) was a bravura performance. A number of the many accomplished actors in this film were used again by Lean shortly afterward when he made his second Dickens film. Lean commented:

> I tried throughout the writing and filming of both *Great Expectations* and *Oliver Twist* to recapture my impressions on first reading the two stories. I imagined *Great Expectations* as a fairy tale, just not quite true, and *Oliver Twist* as a grimly realistic study of what poverty was like at that time. In writing the script, we read and re-read the novels and made a one-line summary of the actual incidents in each chapter, ignoring all conversation and descriptive matter. Any duplication or similarity of scenes was cut out. Actual scenes for the film were built up from this summary. Dickens's dialogue is perfect for the screen, and almost all of it was taken from the book. Occasionally an incident has been altered to suit the demands of the cinema. In some cases the actual sequence of events has been interchanged to make for a better balance and dramatic value. Technically I would say that *Oliver Twist* was more difficult to adapt for the screen than *Great Expec-*

tations. The main problem was that of making fantastic, larger than life characters fit into a starkly real setting.

Great Expectations depends heavily on narration and dialogue, so it is understandable that only two silent-film versions were ever attempted. By 1946, the techniques of sound motion pictures had been so well developed that the happy conjunction of film and Dickens novel reached what may well remain its peak in *Great Expectations*. To follow such an achievement must have been a daunting challenge, even to so skilled a director as David Lean, but two years later he brought forth another extraordinary essay in the genre with his remarkable *Oliver Twist*, a film equally accomplished but not quite as universally regarded as its predecessor. Much of the reason for this was the depiction of Fagin by an unrecognizable Alec Guinness in makeup and costume closely based on George Cruikshank's original illustrations. Vociferous Jewish communities and Jewish members of the entertainment industry objected to the film as being anti-Semitic. The film was not released in the United States until nearly three years after its first showing in Britain, and even then cuts reduced the part of Fagin.

This extraordinary response to a film version of a literary classic, at least the twenty-first to be made, could be regarded as a tribute to the power of Guinness's performance, which was closer to Charles Dickens's conception than many other portrayals. It seemed to have been forgotten that not only is Fagin an evil character involved in the corruption of young people and the teaching of criminals but a reflection of a type of criminal organizer and receiver that flourished in mid-Victorian London. Some Jews *were* involved in such activities then, as were members of other sects and races. The anti-Semitism that prevailed in Dickens's time was widespread and strong. Jews were frequently the object of verbal and physical attacks and remained one of the commonest objects of coarse humor for generations after Dickens. Given such a background, it is not entirely surprising that in the book Fagin is referred to as "the Jew" several hundred times. In David Lean's film, that word is never used.

Alec Guinness's remarkable performance as Fagin marked the opening of a new stage in his acting career, leading to starring roles in increasingly important productions.

Fagin was, of course, grotesque and overdrawn, like so many Dickens characters, and it was a shrewd choice to cast Robert Newton as Bill Sikes, for Newton's customary overplaying was a wonderful complement to Guinness's Fagin, and a precursor of Newton's other highly successful eye-rolling performances, such as Long John Silver. Sikes is a criminal fanatic, and Newton's style caught the crazed desperation of the psychotic burglar. David Lean's handling of Sikes's violent behavior is exemplary and, unlike the common practice of today, his brutal and murderous acts take place off the screen. As a result of Lean's consummate artistry, we are all the more horrified by Sikes's dog tearing at the door when Nancy is killed, and filled with revulsion when Sikes tries to drown the dog in the canal.

Most child performers in films look to be well-fed and cared for. John Howard Davies was a rarity, in that he really looked like a waif. His gaunt, weak-looking face helped make his appearance convincing as a child brought up in the harsh conditions of a Victorian workhouse. Unfortunately, the effect was somewhat spoiled by his voice and manners, which marked him apart from all the other products of that grim upbringing. But then, Dickens's concept of Oliver Twist does not ring true in that respect, either. Both Dickens and Lean are such skilled storytellers that this small but basic flaw is not realized until afterward, and not even then does it detract from one's satisfaction with the overall tale. Under Lean's direction, John Howard Davies's performance overcame the handicap very well. Set against this particular Oliver was the Artful Dodger of Anthony Newley, whose impudent face and confident manner yielded a Dodger that helped to launch Newley on his impudent and confident career.

In between the two Dickens films by David Lean, *Nicholas Nickleby* appeared, directed by Alberto Cavalcanti as his last film for the famous Ealing Studios. He made an exceptionally good attempt to compress that unmanageable novel into a feature film that is still the only talkie version of the story. Leaving aside the inevitable signs of massive amputations, one must acknowledge the effectiveness of the achievement, accomplished by concentrating on the main plot of the Nicklebys, Squeers, Smike, and the Brays, and affording mere tantalizing glimpses of some of the rest. Derek Bond was adequate as Nicholas, while Sally Ann Howes as Kate had the thankless task of portraying one of Dickens's standard heroines, a rather weak and helpless ninny. Sir Cedric Hardwicke was a remorseless Ralph Nickleby, finely matched by the Newman Noggs of Bernard Miles and especially the faultless Smike of Aubrey Woods. The cast was further strengthened by the inclusion of such acting stalwarts as Athene Seyler, Sybil Thorndike, Alfred Drayton, and Fay Compton, and the film was unique in being the only Ealing Studios production based on a classic of English literature. There can be little doubt that it suffered by appearing so closely to the two David Lean films, which overshadowed everything else in the genre.

The postwar burgeoning of British Dickens films came to an end with *Scrooge* in 1951 and *The Pickwick Papers* in 1952, both from the Renown company. Renown had already handled the reissue of the 1933 Monogram *Oliver Twist* in 1947, and then made these two most competent dramatizations, with excellent use of the wealth of British character actors then available. Both films were written by Noel Langley, perhaps best remembered for his adaptation of *The Wizard of Oz*. He was obviously no stranger to the fantasy required for *Scrooge* and the jollification for *Pickwick*.

Scrooge featured Alastair Sim in the title role, and that superb actor presented a gripping performance as the hard, grasping moneylender of the first part of the story. After the transformation of Scrooge, he was in his element as the gleefully mischievous, reformed Ebenezer. By contrast with the prewar M-G-M film, this *Scrooge* was a more somber affair, described by Bosley Crowther in the New York *Times* as an accurate comprehension of the agony of a shabby soul. Yet in the United States this film is shown on television practically every Christmas, and has now been treated to a colorized version, with a "wraparound" commentary by Patrick McNee, who had the small part of young Marley in the film.

The Pickwick Papers was made by the same studio in 1952. It was a warm and very enjoyable adaptation, suffering considerably from condensing and held together by the delightfully engaging Mr. Pickwick of James Hayter, supported by a suitably cocky Sam Weller, played by Harry Fowler, who repeated the role in a television series some years later. Sam's father, the coachman Tony Weller, was touchingly played in a brief appearance by George Robey, one of dozens of well-known actors appearing in what amounted to little more than an orderly procession of cameo roles. Pride of place among those went to Donald Wolfit's storming performance as Sergeant Buzfuz, while of the characters with a continuous role throughout the film, Nigel Patrick's saucy Jingle was exceptionally good. The two films were made at a time when television was just beginning to influence cinema attendances.

By the time the next Dickens feature film, *A Tale of Two Cities*, appeared in 1958, television was affecting the cinema very seriously, and the film doubtless suffered from that, as well as from comparison with the glossy Selznick version of 1935. This 1958 Rank film was also unfortunate in coming rather too late to benefit from the success of the other British Dickens films made in the immediate postwar years. The film was rather underrated at the time, yet it contained a very moving portrayal of Sydney Carton by Dirk Bogarde, full of the elegance and understatement associated with this fine actor. It was a forerunner of his many sensitive film performances.

The remainder of the casting was extremely well carried out, with the possible exception of Paul Guers, whose Charles Darnay was a complete prig throughout, which made Lucie Manette's affection for him puzzling. Rosalie Crutchley has gone on to play other bitter and vindictive women since her ferocious Mme. Defarge, and she repeated the role on television seven years later. Christopher Lee, in one of his first film roles, marked himself out for a career of evil on the screen with his coldly despicable Marquis St. Evremonde, while Dorothy Tutin as Lucie Manette was the epitome of most of Dickens's feeble heroines.

The production was able to capture the atmosphere of the period without lavish costs on the scale employed by M-G-M, the least effective aspects of the piece being the artificial bulk of the Bastille and the handling of the crowd scenes. Otherwise, Ralph Thomas's direction credited the audience with intelligence and did not waste time explaining the obvious. In particular, there were no scenes of gratuitous violence and the episodes of fighting, execution, and general unpleasantness were all handled unobjectionably.

Two years prior to this Rank film, an extract from *The Pickwick Papers* was filmed in Britain for Encyclopedia Britannica, under the title *A Charles Dickens Christmas*. This short educational piece had as Mr. Pickwick the actor Roddy Hughes, who had played Pickwick in a television film in 1955 and filled numerous other Dickens roles in films and television. Small incidents were taken chiefly from the chapter "A Good Humoured Christmas" to present a stereotyped idea of a Dickens Christmas, with neither plot nor story line. The film's one claim to distinction is that of being the first Dickens movie in color.

8

A Companion Picture

> Dickens must surely be the first literary genius to have become a popular favorite of viewers...
>
> *The Times* November 1958

The arrival of regular television services in Great Britain in 1936 did not appear to be an event of world-changing significance, although the great technical achievements were rightly admired. Television was held to be interesting and probably beneficial. In the United States it was suggested it would help in "halting the drift of farm boys to the cities," and very importantly, it would be "no menace to books."

Just over half a century later, we can see that, as far as books are concerned, television is regarded as a parasite, the cause of greater articulacy and diminished literacy, and nourishing itself on the best literature available, which includes the great classics of literature.

Curiously, the first appearance on television of a piece based on Dickens was almost incidental to that fact. Conductor and composer Albert Coates had written an opera entitled *Mr. Pickwick* and one week before its first performance at Covent Garden, the London Television Program of the BBC, broadcasting from Alexandra Palace, transmitted a 25-minute program of extracts from the opera on Friday, November 13, 1936.

Considering the extremely limited experience of anybody with television, the observations of the reviewer in *The Times* seem somewhat perceptive.

The process is wonderful enough and technical improvement advances continuously, but one may question whether such a broadcast has at present of more than a curiosity value. True, we got some idea from the minute visual image how far Mr. Coates's music suited the story therein presented, but on the other hand the distortion of values was very great.... These doll-like marionettes let forth at us immense voices, while the orchestra had to be content with a comparatively modest place in the background. Then, too, owing to the small area of vision, the drama is inevitably cramped, and one could hardly form any idea how it would appear on a large stage like that of Covent Garden. One great advantage television possesses over the cinema—it eschews the reckless and restless discontinuity of the film, and the *tempo* of music and action, at any rate as compromised in any operatic performance, is not confused with the excessive speeds of cinematographic spectacle. Here, at least, the three arts all march together in time.

Of course, that was written long before the introduction of videotape recording.

The next Dickens program on BBC television appears to have been *Characters from Bleak House*, in November 1937. Billed as a 10-minute talk by Hugh Miller, it sounds more suited to radio than TV. The first actual dramatization was *Bardell Against Pickwick*, transmitted in July 1938. It contained a selection of scenes dealing with the familiar Bardell breach-of-promise episode in the book. The intervention of war and the consequent closure of television in Britain prevented any further dramatizations that may have been contemplated.

It was not until 1946, when both peace and television had been restored, that a Dickens story reappeared—the same 1938 play, with four of the same players repeating their roles. In both 1938 and 1946, the plays were transmitted live. In 1938, that had meant performing the play twice in the same week, on Monday evening and Wednesday afternoon. The choice of only an extract from one of the books is quite understandable. In addition to very limited periods of transmission, the studio facilities at Alexandra Palace were only sufficient for very modest productions.

The 1946 BBC play had been preceded by what appears to be the first American television presentation of Dickens in December 1945, when a 30-minute amateur production of *A Christmas Carol* was transmitted by WBKB-Chicago. It was also the first TV appearance of the story that has endeared itself to television producers and audiences on both sides of the Atlantic ever since. *The Strange Christmas Dinner* (1945) introduced a mysterious stranger (Charles Dickens) who reforms a Scroogelike restaurant owner who has refused to allow his staff Christmas Day off.

In December 1946, BBC presented the *Christmas Carol* story with a ballet, with music by Vaughan Williams. In 1947, DuMont in the United States gave a conventional dramatic rendering of it, with the cadaverous John Carradine as Scrooge.

A rather more ambitious BBC adaptation of a Dickens story was *The Only Way*, transmitted live twice in February 1948. This 90-minute production was one stage removed from *A Tale of Two Cities*, being taken from the stage play, as was Herbert Wilcox's silent film. At the end of that year, the seasonal outbreak of sentimentality resumed with two televised versions of *A Christmas Carol*. NBC presented a straight dramatization, with Dennis King as Scrooge. Included was a postscript of Bing Crosby's much-heralded debut on television, singing "Silent Night" with the Mitchell Boys Choir. After that, ABC's presentation of a performance of the tale by the Rufus Rose Marionettes must have seemed rather tame.

In 1949, *The Cricket on the Hearth* was the only Dickens offering on TV, in a 30-minute film on CBS but, in 1950, *A Christmas Carol* was back, in a generous 90-minute BBC production by Bransby Williams, transmitted live on Christmas Day and repeated two days later. Bransby Williams had been playing the role of Scrooge on and off for more than 50 years. Following the success of this play, BBC ran a number of programs featuring Bransby Williams reminiscing about his long acting career and performing some of his celebrated character studies, naturally including Dickensian ones. At that time, another actor named Williams—Emlyn (no relation)—was appearing on the stage in a novel recreation of the dramatic readings as given by Charles Dickens himself. With an identical reading desk and makeup to resemble Dickens, it was as close a reversion to the author's original intentions as was practical, and was the forerunner of a number of remarkable solo performances by other famous actors. It also proved to be a great triumph in Emlyn Williams's acting career, and he continued to present the Dickens readings for more than 30 years. It was a concept that would have appealed to Bransby Williams, and excerpts from Emlyn's performance were first televised in 1951 (and on later dates), while Bransby's programs were being shown.

During 1951, a CBS production called *Marley's Ghost*, based on *A Christmas Carol* and shown in the series *Danger*, was overshadowed by the Christmas Day *Fireside Theatre* adaptation of *A Christmas Carol* on NBC. This prestigious production brought Sir Ralph Richardson from England to play a highly acclaimed Scrooge, plus Malcolm Keen as Marley's Ghost and Melville Cooper as Christmas Past. The following Christmas, NBC presented a longer version of the same story, and this time Malcolm Keen had graduated to the role of Scrooge, while Melville Cooper had moved up to Christmas Present.

In between those two NBC *Carols*, there had been a positive surge of Dickens stories on TV. CBS had presented two of the darker stories, *The Mystery of Edwin Drood* and *Hunted Down*, both with John Baragrey. NBC had *A Cricket on the Hearth* with Grace Kelly. In addition to a couple of educational programs on Dickens, the BBC had shown the first televised Dickens serial, *The Pickwick Papers*, in seven weekly installments of 30 minutes. It was a major TV drama production of its day, and was transmitted at peak viewing time on Saturday evenings. The episodic nature of that particular book makes it very suitable for adaptation, and this was the first occasion on television that a really substantial adaptation of a Dickens novel was made. It established the way television serials would prove to be the most satisfactory medium of dramatization for many of Dickens' works, although not invariably the most popular or favored, as later exceptions were to show.

While the BBC *Pickwick* serial was being shown in Britain, CBS in America was transmitting *Omnibus*, the TV cultural anthology series sponsored by the Ford Foundation. For one of those programs, Alistair Cooke had written an adaptation of that favorite episode from the same book—*The Trial of Mr. Pickwick*—which had Sir Cedric Hardwicke as the Judge and Francis L. Sullivan as the devastating prosecutor BuzFuz. Later in the *Omnibus* series, in 1953, Emlyn Williams presented one of his Dickens readings. That was followed a week later by an ambitious ABC version of *A Tale of Two Cities*, featuring Wendell Corey as Sydney Carton. In the New York *Times*, Jack Gould referred to:

> ...the much debated question of expanding the panoramic vision of the TV camera. On that score the American Broadcasting Company moved away out in front with its two part production of *A Tale of Two Cities* on the last two Sundays. On its spacious

studio lot in Hollywood the ABC network had the most impressive live crowd shots yet seen on TV. The climactic guillotine scene had a scope worthy of a Cecil B. DeMille production. Similarly, there were other outdoor street scenes replete with hordes of extras, and extremely lavish court-room settings. ABC proved that TV has barely scratched the surface in what it can do visually. Dramatically the outcome was a little different. To boil *A Tale of Two Cities* down to less than an hour's running time is not to leave much of the Dickens classic, and what emerged on the screen was an episodic and foreshortened version that could only touch a few highspots of the narrative. The production won; Dickens was lucky to show.

By the time Christmas 1953 arrived, Melville Cooper had finally reached the leading role of Scrooge in ABC's latest *Carol,* and the story itself was clearly set to appear and reappear on television almost every Christmas, even if only as a rerun of a film.

As the 1950s progressed, television in the United States and Britain became much more widely spread. The number of channels increased, and transmission times were lengthened, while cinema attendance fell correspondingly. In Britain in particular, the Queen's Coronation in 1953 was responsible for a tremendous increase in the sales and rental of television sets, with a consequent overnight jump in viewing figures and a long-term problem of finding more material to fill the expanded screen time. That problem was compounded with the advent of commercial television in Britain in 1954. Needless to say, dramatic adaptations from the world's great literature formed a significant proportion of both British TV channels. Yet when Independent Television (ITV) eventually transmitted its first Dickens offering, it played absolutely safe and used the much-adapted trial episode *Bardell Versus Pickwick,* with Donald Wolfit as prosecutor Sergeant Buzfuz, as well as three actors repeating their roles from the 1952 BBC serial of *Pickwick.* This production, made on film, was shown in the United States a year later in the series *Lilli Palmer Theatre.*

The television Dickens serial has never been attempted in the United States, although British-made serials have been shown from time to time. American TV has confined itself to one-or two-part adaptations of some of the best-known Dickens stories, together with the occasional surprise of a dramatized little-known short story. In the 1950s, NBC presented *Great Expectations,* with Roddy McDowall as Pip, and *David Copperfield,* both in two parts. CBS, on the other hand, seemed to prefer one-piece dramas and used a large number of British actors in their version of *A Tale of Two Cities* and in the first television dramatization of *Oliver Twist*. Both were 90 minutes long and lavishly produced by David Susskind. The most serious criticism seems to have been that *Oliver Twist* was not long enough ("a hasty hint of the times and a rush-hour glimpse of its people" wrote *Variety*), and that the incident of Sikes murdering Nancy was needlessly violent and objectionable. That was not to be the only time the killing of Nancy would cause trouble for television.

Back in Britain, the BBC produced an imaginative "play for Easter" entitled *The Man From the Moors*, shown on Easter Day 1955. It depicted Dickens himself visiting the North of England and encountering a cruelly run school, plainly a model for Dotheboys Hall in *Nicholas Nickleby*. Charles Dickens was played by Barry Letts, who many years later became the producer of a number of the BBC's great Dickens serials.

In September 1956, the BBC began to mark out its dominating ground for Dickens serials on television with a massive 13-episode *David Copperfield*, claiming it to be "the first time on English television that so much space had been devoted to one work." This impressive and successful serial, with Robert Hardy as the adult David, was followed in 1957 by *A Tale of Two Cities* and *Nicholas Nickleby*. By that time, the BBC had demonstrated its firm dependence on adaptations from the famous classics of literature for a very considerable proportion of its drama output. *Two Cities* was being transmitted during the same period as serials of *Kidnapped*, *Villette*, and *Vanity Fair*, while *Nickleby* coincided with *Treasure Island*. In many ways, it was a golden era of television, with the new medium attracting and holding vast audiences to the detriment of cinemas, theaters, bars, and public houses. The developing confidence and ability of British television companies in presenting convincing characters from celebrated books in realistic settings and costumes laid the foundations for the great dramatizations that have since been made and exported with enormous success.

An unusual and interesting TV production in 1958 was an opera based on *A Tale of Two Cities*, with music by Arthur Benjamin. This version, lasting two hours, had been performed first on radio by the BBC Third Programme five years earlier, but not given on the stage until 1957. The libretto was by Cedric Cliffe, who pointed out that because music always has the effect of slowing down the pace of the words, a libretto has to be much shorter than a play or film or TV script, and drastic surgery was necessary to achieve that and to simplify the time scale of the novel, which is spread over four different periods of time.

That operatic production was in addition to what had become a fairly regular cycle of Dickens serials, continuing in 1958 with *Our Mutual Friend*, transmitted on Friday evenings, followed in 1959 by *Great Expectations* as a Sunday teatime serial in the spring and *Bleak House* on Friday evenings in the autumn. It was apparent that a distinction was being made between those novels considered safe for the slot marked "Children's television," as it was actually called then, and those that are either unsuitable or incomprehensible for children. The separation persists to this day.

In Italy in 1958, *Le Avventure di Nicola Nickelby* appeared, the first of several television serials from Dickens, followed in the 1960s by *Il Grillo del Focolare (The Cricket on the Hearth), David Copperfield,* and *Il Circolo Pickwick*. Other European TV channels followed suit, mostly with the better-known stories.

Although ITV in Britain posed no challenge at all to the BBC with Dickens serials until 1960, it did present a lengthy series of *Tales from Dickens* begun in 1959 and widely shown and repeated over the next decade. These programs were made on film by the free-lance producer Harry Alan Towers, and sold extensively. In Britain, they were presented by the ABC Television company. They consisted of 25-minute episodes drawn chiefly from *The Pickwick Papers* and *David Copperfield*. Since only 15 of the originally announced 39 episodes were made, presumably it had been intended to use other books as well. The series ended with the irresistible *A Christmas Carol* and *Miss Havisham* (an excerpt from *Great Expectations*). The series began with an introductory episode called *Meet Mr. Dickens,* and was followed by the real surprise of the whole set *The Runaways,* a concoction of incidents and characters from three of Dickens's short stories.

Harry Alan Towers had assembled a strong company of actors, many of whose names now glitter with importance. The series was enhanced (no doubt in the interests of overseas sales) by the inclusion of Fredric March as host and narrator. March's wife, Florence Eldridge, was given the title role of Miss Havisham in the final episode, while Martita Hunt, who had been the intimidating

Miss Havisham in David Lean's 1946 film of *Great Expectations*, portrayed David Copperfield's aunt Betsy Trotwood instead. (Dramatists seem frequently to have discarded the letter E from Miss Trotwood's Christian name).

The fourth episode of the series included Donald Wolfit in his third appearance as Sergeant Buzfuz. He had earlier played the role in the 1952 Renown film of *Pickwick* and in the television *Bardell Versus Pickwick* in 1955. At the opposite end of the acting hierarchy from Wolfit at that time was the comparatively new actor Richard Briers, now a household name in Britain. "I was a very young and inexperienced actor at the time," he recalls, "and I remember being in the witness box and having to face Wolfit as Buzfuz. I was terrified. When he asked me my name I was so nervous I said Twinkle! Wolfit glared at me, and said 'Don't you mean Winkle, Mr. Winkle?' I was turned to stone."

Also noteworthy in the series were Robert Morley, Athene Seyler, Richard Pasco, Joan Hickson, Harry Fowler, and, in another appearance as Scrooge, the former portrayer of the implacable Mr. Murdstone and the unrepentant Marquis St. Evremonde—Basil Rathbone. It was Rathbone's only opportunity to play in a straight dramatization of *A Christmas Carol* (the others were musicals), and it receives no mention in either his memoirs or his biography.

At the same time as this series, there appeared an extract from *The Old Curiosity Shop* entitled *The Small Servant*, by American writers S. I. Abelow and Robert Cenedella. In the United States, it featured Laurence Harvey and Diane Cilento, and a separate British production was shown on New Years Day 1960.

ITV eventually entered the Dickens serial field in 1960 with an evening presentation of *The Mystery of Edwin Drood*, written by John Keir Cross, with an ending based on a solution provided by John Dickson Carr, a famous writer of locked-room mysteries. Before the serial was completed with Carr's solution, the sixth episode was embellished with a discussion as to Dickens's probable ending, between detective story writer Ngaio Marsh and Raymond Francis, then appearing on TV as Detective Chief Superintendent Lockhart in the immensely popular series *No Hiding Place*.

The first production of *Oliver Twist* on British television in 1962 was marked by questions in Parliament about violence being depicted in a Sunday teatime serial. Referring to the episode showing the murder of Nancy, the Postmaster General, who was then responsible for broadcasting, said, "I saw this particular scene and think it was brutal and quite inexcusable." The issue of violence and its possible influence on children—who would certainly be viewing at that time of day—caused the BBC to cut a shot showing the shadow of Bill Sikes's body hanging from a rope. The savagery of the murder of Nancy went unremarked when the story was redramatized as a Sunday serial in 1985. The death of Nancy—the first incident from Dickens ever to appear on the screen in 1897— had by 1985 lost its ability to make such a dramatic impact, so desensitized had audiences become to scenes of violent killing.

9

Reconstructing Dickens

> Dramatizing a Dickens novel fills me with joy and trepidation. Joy, because I know I am going to have a wealth of magnificent characters to work upon, and trepidation because of the breadth and scope of the work and the reconstruction and compression it will involve.
>
> Constance Cox, 1965

Constance Cox was responsible for writing a number of highly praised BBC Dickens serials during the 1960s, some of them from the less-well-used stories. She began in 1959 with *Bleak House* and followed that with the notorious *Oliver Twist* (1962), *The Old Curiosity Shop* (1962), *Martin Chuzzlewit* (1964), and *A Tale of Two Cities* (1965). Cox was one of the early writers who over some thirty years created memorable serials from the works of Dickens and many other famous authors. The group included Hugh Leonard, Arthur Hopcraft, Hugh Whitemore, and James Andrew Hall. These and other experienced playwrights fashioned a succession of television serials throughout the 1960s and 1970s, during which they perfected their methods of adaptation to a degree seldom surpassed. At the same time, they developed certain guidelines for their craft.

Constance Cox wrote:

> Rightly or wrongly, I begin by assuming that the majority of viewers are unfamiliar with the novel, and take particular care that the plot and sub-plots are clear and remain clear throughout a long serial often extending to thirteen episodes. This sometimes means writing scenes that are not in Dickens and transposing others....One must bear in mind that viewers do not always sit down uninterrupted to watch, and if one is too mysterious they may become weary of the effort to follow a tortuous plot from

week to week....There are various rules which apply to the writing of any serial. One is that, as far as possible, the leading characters must appear in every episode, and Dickens has a habit of leaving important characters out of the story for quite a time, while he follows the adventures of another set.

One of the outcomes of this professional approach that would have appealed to Dickens himself was the superb *Our Mutual Friend,* shown in 1976 by the BBC as a "Classic Serial" at peak evening viewing time. It ranks as one of television's finest adaptations of Dickens and was an opportunity to see a dramatization of one of the less-popular of his novels. The whole production was so finely mounted and so well cast that it raised the standard of quality in costume drama serials on TV.

Right from the somber, low-key opening with Gaffer Hexam and his daughter Lizzie scavenging on the Thames, it was clear that this serial had been adapted and produced with loving care and the firm intention to preserve the feeling of the book. Furthermore, the unfolding of the plot and the episode breaks were made with great skill, to intrigue and tantalize viewers unfamiliar with the story. Lesley Dunlop was excellent as the untamed Lizzie, and Lizzie's brother, the callow and selfish Charlie, was portrayed by Jack Wild, in a striking contrast to the winsome and sparky Artful Dodger he had played in the film *Oliver!*

The dramatization of *Hard Times* by Granada TV in 1977 claimed to be the most expensive television drama made in Britain, but the money was well spent. The 4-part serial marked ITV's maturity in the adaptation of Dickens for the small screen and, by raising the stakes in production values, it was a major challenge to the BBC's supremacy in that field. To reproduce the Coketown of Dickens's novel, the serial used surviving settings in a number of widespread locations that included a humpbacked canal bridge in Ashton-under-Lyme, an alley beneath a railway viaduct in Stockport, a flight of cobbled steps in Macclesfield, and a former ragged school in Manchester. Scenes shot with these genuine backgrounds were skillfully blended with those from sets built in a suitably grimy disused railway yard. The total effect recreated very convincingly the grim and forbidding Coketown of the 1840s that Charles Dickens intended his readers to visualize.

All this was splendidly complemented by the wonderful casting and performances of the actors involved who, with few exceptions, *looked* like mid-Victorians. Timothy West was a grand Bounderby, of appalling false humility, while Patrick Allen's slow and deliberate rendition of the morose Gradgrind was beautifully judged and delivered. Alan Dobie's features appear to have destined him for such tormented roles as the anguished Stephen Blackpool. The composition of some of the camera shots was intensely evocative of early Victorian photographs. The whole production was drenched in the atmosphere of the novel and did not shirk the exposures of social injustices and degradations on which Dickens had concentrated so vividly. It is a great pity that ITV faltered and did not hold to the original length of the serial, for when *Hard Times* was reshown in 1979, it was cut down to three episodes, which was a mistake and a disservice to a magnificent production. Happily, in 1983, the mistake must have been realized, and the further repeat was in 4 parts.

In the 1960s, in the wake of the storming stage successes of *Oklahoma!, Annie Get Your Gun, My Fair Lady, West Side Story,* and other overwhelming American shows, the British musical comedy was in a sorry state, and the astounding exuberance of Lionel Bart proved a life-saver. The most successful of his stage works was *Oliver!* (1960) a musical based on *Oliver Twist*. It became an international hit, holding the longest stage run in London, and is still being revived more than 30 years after its sensational opening. More than that, it achieved the rare distinction of a triumphant transfer to the cinema screen. The film version was heaped with praise and loaded with awards (six Oscars in 1968, including Best Picture). But for all its popularity and success, it was not a good Dickens film. The jollification of Dickens, long the cinema's way of moderating the difficult parts of the stories, swamped the subject, and fundamental changes were made to nearly all the principal characters. Soft-faced Mark Lester was clearly the opposite of a workhouse boy. Apple-cheeked Jack Wild as the Artful Dodger had obviously never roughed it for years. Fat, jovial Harry Secombe was the antithesis of the oily Bumble, and Shani Wallis as Nancy looked more like the girl next door than an ill-used whore. The despicable Fagin was turned into a picaresque old rogue who was allowed to escape to further villainy, scampering off down the road at the end in a Chaplinesque image of which director Carol Reed should have been ashamed.

Said Ron Moody:

> I'd done Fagin on the stage, and I'd always seen him as something of a tragic-comic kind of character. There's a great deal of humor there if you look for it. I spent one hour every morning being made up and when I looked in the mirror I was surprised by the image. It wasn't a really heavy make-up because I use my face and body and hands to convey the grotesque and comic aspects of the character and Carol Reed encouraged me to develop this image.

Reed should also have been ashamed of the unacknowledged borrowings from David Lean's *Oliver Twist* in story line and appearance. The similarities are too many to be coincidental. *Oliver!* is much closer to the David Lean film than to the Charles Dickens novel or Lionel Bart's stage musical. According to Lean's biographer Stephen Silverman, David Lean had seen the film *Oliver!* and could not bring himself to discuss it.

Pickwick, a musical by Wolf Mankowitz launched in 1963, followed the successful course laid down by *Oliver!* in the theater, but never made the step into a cinema film. However, it was restaged for BBC television in 1969, with Harry Secombe repeating his boisterous portrayal of Samuel Pickwick.

Scrooge (1970), on the other hand, did not originate on the stage but was directly prepared for the cinema, and seemed to benefit from being so planned. It was a Technicolor musical, which seems to be a questionable treatment of the story. But aside from the elaborate planning and lavish costuming, the film was directed by Ronald Neame, former collaborator of David Lean, and that ensured as close a presentation as could be expected with the present-day liberated style of musicals. As was customary by the 1970s, the characters were played by an awesome team of leading actors, including Alec Guinness as Marley's Ghost and Edith Evans as the Ghost of Christmas Past. Albert Finney's characterization of both the young and old Ebenezer Scrooge rightly consolidated the piece. Ronald Neame had the advantage of an excellent screenplay by Leslie Bricusse, whose skillful adaptation made certain drastic changes that worked satisfactorily. A good example is the scene of Christmas Yet To Come, in which Scrooge gleefully joins in the singing and dancing, ironically unaware that his own coffin is the cause of the general thanksgiving. With *Scrooge*, Neame and

Bricusse created a joyous musical version of fantasy, without sacrificing the moral and social lessons it contained.

"Why was I now and then inexplicably close to tears?" wrote film critic Dilys Powell.

> Not because of Edith Evans' voice; not because of Kenneth More's Ghost of Christmas Present, or David Collings' Bob Cratchit, or Richard Beaumont's Tiny Tim, or even Mr. Finney's funny and endearing and exhilarating Scrooge. There is another contributor to be thanked. Persistently the spirit of the original survives. It was Dickens who made me feel like crying. It always is.

David Copperfield was made in Britain for television in 1969, shown in the United States, but released in cinemas in the United Kingdom. It proved to be one of the most star-studded of all Dickens films. While that produced a number of interesting little cameo portrayals, it did not assist the picture, and the sole advantage it had over the Selznick version of 1935 was that it was in color. It was dreadfully dull, and a pitiful waste of the array of talent gathered together in it: Ralph Richardson as Micawber; Emlyn Williams as Mr. Dick, Edith Evans as Betsey Trotwood; Michael Redgrave as Daniel Peggotty, to mention only a few. With such a collection of characters and actors, it must have been hard work to make the film dull.

An ever-present problem with putting Dickens stories on the screen is their very popularity and familiarity. We know the plots beforehand, and directors' attempts at dramatic suspense have only a limited chance of real success. We are also familiar with a number of successful versions, and any new dramatization may have to stand comparison with a much-vaunted predecessor. Perhaps only with Dickens adaptations are there so many handicaps in the form of existing, and often resurrected, triumphs. Even so, it came as a rather irritating surprise when the company presenting the 1974 *Great Expectations* used such a comparison in their publicity. "It is the first film of the classic story since the memorable 1946 version became one of the all-time greats of the screen." This smacked of trying to ride on the tail of a famous film, implying that the new one might be just as good. In fact, it was inferior and had little to recommend it. Early reports heralded it as a musical to be called *Pip!* in obvious emulation of the one-word titles *Oliver!* and

Scrooge, but it ended up as an unexciting nonmusical TV film that was given a theatrical showing in Britain.

Michael York, the adult Pip in the film, wrote in his autobiography:

> [It] was conceived as a musical....I duly took singing lessons and even recorded such predictable ditties as "I had Great Expectations"...these songs went unfilmed. Instead of counterpointing, illuminating or advancing the action, it was found that they stopped it dead.

It was an expensively cast and elaborately mounted film, wasteful for so disappointing a result. Despite its impressive settings, the film lacked firm, imaginative direction and suffered a silly mistake in having Sarah Miles as both the young and the grown-up Estella. Margaret Leighton's Miss Havisham was not really frightening, and Joss Ackland's Joe Gargery, while admirably hesitant and nervously smiling, somehow did not attain an adequate contrast between his own awkwardness and gaucherie and the elevated status of a gentleman, hankered after by Pip. Michael York simply did not look Victorian. On the credit side, Rachel Roberts was a fearsome Mrs. Joe, and Anthony Quayle as Jaggers and Andrew Ray as Herbert Pocket were extremely well cast, Ray appearing to have modelled his performance on that of Alec Guinness in the earlier film.

The next major Dickens film, *Mister Quilp* (1975), really *was* a musical—and a tragedy. The tragedy was that it was ever made at all. The choice of *The Old Curiosity Shop* for filming may have been welcomed by Anthony Newley, judging by the gusto with which he played the loathsome Daniel Quilp, but it is hard to understand the idea of a musical built round such an unsympathetic character with no redeeming virtues at all. Even as played by Newley, Quilp was not funny, in spite of frenziedly vigorous efforts.

Turning any classic novel into a musical is always fraught with danger and seldom succeeds. In this particular case, the songs were quite unmemorable and were not helped by the frantic staging of the musical numbers. No doubt the excessive amount of close-ups and medium close camerawork was in the hope of television sales, but it certainly did not make for very agreeable watching in the cinema and was an unfortunate distraction from some of the very pleasant locations that had been chosen. The pictorial quality was there, backed by *Readers Digest* money. There was a perfectly charming Little Nell who has to die at the end of the film. That's all in accordance with the book, of course, but it's pretty unsuitable for a musical that is further burdened by Nell's helpless and selfish old grandfather. It is rather absurd to expect two youngsters to carry the audience, especially when one of them dies, leaving Kit Nubbles to close the film with a banal lament in a maudlin ending. Sarah Jane Varley was a perfectly sweet Nell who remained far too fresh and well-kept to make her ordeals believable.

Anthony Newley's Quilp was an extraordinary caricature of a character that Dickens meant to be menacing and detestable. True, Newley was never more detestable than when he was attempting to enliven the proceedings with a razzmatazz solo. His performance was overripe and grossly exaggerated, without conveying Quilp's essential malevolence. Michael Hordern was made for the role of pathetic Grandfather Trent, but the remaining principals—David Hemmings as Swiveller, David Warner as Sampson Brass, and Jill Bennett as Sally Brass—ought never to have been given such poorly written parts. There were some nice cameos among the lesser characters, but with so much of the film taken up with extended song-and-dance numbers, there was virtually no time or space for them to develop. As Dickens, it was a bit like a noisy Readers Digest Condensed Book.

As if that were not bad enough for 1975, the year also saw the emergence of the first—and probably only—pornographic Dickens film. *The Passions of Carol* featured Carol Scrooge, the tyrannical proprietor of a sex magazine. "Blah, humbug!" commented *Variety*.

10

Television Triumphs

> Sales were down to a fifth of the figure that *The Old Curiosity Shop* had attained weekly. To stir up the sluggish audience, Dickens decided that he would send young Martin Chuzzlewit off to the United States, and did so in the next installment. That sort of decision in a novelist sounds like an arbitrary one to us nowadays, although it is a familiar device in a television series (How Dickens would have relished writing for television!).
>
> Wolf Mankowitz

An unusual television drama series was *Dickens of London*, written by Wolf Mankowitz, whose earlier stage success with *Pickwick* had led him to study the author's life extensively. The result was 13 one-hour installments covering the first 32 years of Charles Dickens's life, beginning with an ailing Dickens on one of his last reading tours of America and turning in flashback to his childhood, youth, and early manhood. The versatile Roy Dotrice played the author's father, John Dickens (a model for Micawber), as well as the aging Charles Dickens and, in one episode, the character Quilp. The series was made by Yorkshire Television and was also shown by *Masterpiece Theatre* in America. To stop as it did when Dickens was in his thirties seemed strange, but Wolf Mankowitz explained. "I wrote 24 episodes, but the rest were never used. I don't know what the reason was. Perhaps the viewing figures were not good enough. It was rather absurd of them to think of doing 24 programs of a biography anyway."

The BBC continued their own straight serials with a very good *Nicholas Nickleby*, shown on Sunday afternoons in 1977. Nigel Havers was a first-rate Nicholas. Derek Francis, who had been

Ralph Nickleby in 1968, was this time Wackford Squeers. "So adept is the BBC at translating Dickens to the screen that it could do it in its corporate sleep," wrote Stanley Reynolds in *The Times*. "Indeed, it often seems to sleepwalk through a series like the new *Nicholas Nickleby*....The BBC seems timorous, if not plain tired when it comes to Dickens. The attitude appears to be: 'We've always done it so well this way in the past; why change a winning style?' " That seems a glib and rather unreasonable view of the BBC approach in general and the 1977 *Nickleby* in particular, for the BBC had, only one year earlier, raised the level of Dickens drama on television with its powerful *Our Mutual Friend*. In fact, the 1977 *Nickleby* was a remake in color of Hugh Leonard's adaptation first given in 1968, and the BBC repeated the 1977 one as a midweek evening serial in 1978, emphasizing their own confidence in its quality. It served to reaffirm one's opinion that only a television serial can present the sprawling *Nickleby* satisfactorily on the screen.

Sir Michael Hordern, one of the busiest of British acting knights, has had a number of Dickens roles in his career. He was Marley to Alastair Sim's Scrooge in the 1951 film and the voice of Marley in the Richard Williams animated version 20 years later. In between, he played Mr. Sowerberry on American TV in the CBS *Oliver Twist* of 1959. After playing Grandfather Trent in the film *Mr. Quilp*, he appeared on BBC television in the 1977 *A Christmas Carol*, this time as Scrooge. Hordern has developed an impressive line of diffident or befuddled characters over many years, but is rather too soft and harmless to convey the unpleasantness of the unreformed Scrooge. The contrast between the Ebenezers of the beginning and the end of the tale is thereby weakened. This production was an adequate realization of the well-worn tale, but added nothing to it.

The 1979 BBC serial was the second time *The Old Curiosity Shop* had been televised at length, and it put to shame the best-forgotten film *Mr. Quilp*. William Trevor, who wrote the serial, commented

> *The Old Curiosity Shop* is often said to be one of Dickens's less well constructed novels, to be in fact something of a rag-bag. This is so, but it is equally true that a novel which succeeds perfectly in its original form rarely succeeds as well in another. The film of *Great Expectations* is one of the very few instances of a superbly good novel remaining equally impressive in another medium....The huge popular audience that read *The Old Curiosity Shop* was very different from the popular audience that may watch it on television. Dickens knew his audience and wrote for

it, but because of passing time his point of view may easily become blurred or lost altogether. In this dramatization it was constantly a question of endeavouring to ensure that that didn't happen.

Hard on the heels of this fine production came a daring incursion by ITV into the Sunday afternoon serial space with *The Further Adventures of Oliver Twist*. This serial was not only a direct challenge for the BBC's traditional territory, it was a rare pastiche, using most of Dickens's original characters in a newly written extension of Oliver's escapades. Except for Sikes, the original villains reappear. Fagin escapes from prison and eludes the gallows. Bumble happens to obtain a job at the school into which Mr. Brownlow places Oliver. Noah Claypole and Monks turn up again, and Oliver suffers at the hands of each of them in turn in adventures at school, at sea, and up chimneys, his only comforter for much of the time being a nearly reformed Artful Dodger.

Seemingly undismayed by this intrusion into their customary time slot, in 1980, the BBC carried on with the second television serial of *A Tale of Two Cities*. It had Nigel Stock, Judy Parfitt, and Paul Shelley in an uneven version that was greatly reliant on the performances of the players, particularly Shelley, who undertook the unenviable task of doubling as Carton and Darnay, and managed a fairly good distinction between he two. The scenes where both characters appeared were technically brilliant, but it is questionable whether it is ever necessary for one actor to play both parts. It is hard to understand why the serial stretched to eight episodes when five would have done. The adaptation was worthy but wordy, and the complications and involvements of the plot did not emerge clearly enough.

In recent years the BBC has made a number of these serials in association with other companies, with consequent showings on American TV and elsewhere. But this 1980 *A Tale of Two Cities* clashed with a made-for-TV film of the same story shown in the United States by CBS two weeks after the BBC serial finished. The film was an elegant and very elaborately staged production made in France and England, with Billie Whitelaw as a ruthlessly vengeful Madame Defarge, Peter Cushing as Dr. Manette, and Christopher Sarandon in the dual roles of Carton and Darnay, alternately gloomy and dense. Kenneth More, in his last film part, was a suitably stodgy Jarvis Lorry. This well-made film was not shown on British TV until 1989, and then, ironically, by the BBC.

The BBC's *Two Cities* serial was followed in 1981 by a new and disappointing *Great Expectations* that had few saving features, among them a restrained but firm Miss Havisham by Joan Hickson (far better as Miss Marple), a pert Estella by Sarah Jane Varley (the Little Nell of *Mr. Quilp*), and a superior Jaggers by the versatile Derek Francis.

In 1980, the Royal Shakespeare Company embarked on one of its occasional bold experiments with a gigantic stage version of *Nicholas Nickleby* that took two evenings to perform. It was an incredible gamble but turned out to be such a tumultuous success that, despite original limitations, it was revived, revived again, taken to New York, and finally recorded for TV by two separate British television companies. One of the principal reasons for this well-deserved success was the exceptional collaboration among the writer, directors, and players, who jointly dissected the book, analyzed Dickens methods and motives, studied other dramatizations (including films), and together created and developed a piece of stage entertainment that was so unique that at first the theater critics were completely at odds as to how to respond to it. The regular reviewers were roundly lambasted by Bernard Levin in an article in *The Times*, which more than anything else ensured that the play became a sellout.

The adaptation finally confirmed the view that *Nicholas Nickleby* should not be condensed to a standard length for either stage or screen, but should be allowed ample time for its multiplicity of characters, its digressions, and its absurdities. These were presented with such verve and enthusiasm that the play was a dramatic landmark, both in English stage productions and in Dickens dramatizations.

The key to the whole production was indeed the tremendous enthusiasm of the entire RSC company, which communicated itself to the audiences, who stood and cheered at the end of each performance. The wonderful rapport between actors and audiences was understandably lacking in the television showings. The new British TV Channel Four proudly announced that its first important drama production would be an eight-hour screening of the new *Nickleby*, to be shown in installments in November 1982. It would be a virtually complete telerecording of the RSC version, but pre-

prepared, and performed especially for TV using the Old Vic theatre with the original cast, set, and costumes. The ink was barely dry on the announcement when London Weekend Television revealed that its videotapes of the RSC dress rehearsals would be shown in an abbreviated 2-hour selection in August 1981. While the keenness of this competition shows the importance of the RSC's epic presentation, it was still a *stage* version, adapted, prepared, and performed as such. In spite of that, it was enormously entertaining television, one of the greatest Dickens dramatizations on screen, because the skillful stage adaptation had been enhanced by the equally skillful lighting and camerawork of the TV team.

Although there was no attempt to disguise the staginess of the production, one was generally oblivious of it. When it *did* become apparent, the smooth moving of props and the swift scene transitions were admirable. The use of props was actually very meager, with players themselves becoming a variety of accessories. The acting was full-blooded; seldom over the top, but right up to the limit of the characters concerned. In the case of Dickens, that usually means fully ripe, anyway. Roger Rees and Emily Richard must rank as the best Nicholas and Kate Nickleby that have appeared on the screen. There was an added poignancy in the strain that showed on Nicholas's face and which in part must have been due to the strain on Rees at the end of his exhausting spell in the role. In an interview, he described the experience as having scarred him for life. If that is so, what must it have done to David Threlfall, whose agonized Smike was a tortured creation that remains long in the memory?

The telerecording of this production was shown in the United States on four consecutive nights, introduced by Peter Ustinov. The leading chronicler of United States television drama, Larry James Gianakos, in an overview of programs from 1982 to 1984, singled out this play as the sole dramatic production on American TV with any degree of social conscience.

> Perhaps even more remarkable than the production itself is the fact that it arrived in the United States at a time when this country, having ceded its leadership into the hands of the Newly Rich, had no longer a place for its Newly Poor. American television's current preoccupation with wealth and its acquisition gave this showing of *Nicholas Nickleby*, what with its throbbing concern for the poor, a certain revolutionary splendor. Odd that in the Age of

the Plutocrat, a foreign dramatization of a one-hundred-and-forty-five-year old novel should so lucidly drive the cry of the indigent home.

In *Dombey and Son*, the BBC serial that began in January 1983, Julian Glover, as the hard, unyielding Dombey senior, gave a performance described by one reviewer as "of unforgettable lethal gravity." In a well-paced production that allowed the story time to build up momentum, Lysette Anthony as Florence Dombey and Shirley Cain as Miss Tox gave first-class portrayals, and the liquid voice of James Cossins as Joe Bagstock was a priceless asset. Unfortunately, Barnaby Bulk as Paul Dombey did not look particularly ill and about to die, and the great flaw in the novel, which obliges a prolonged absence for two of the major characters, (Walter Gay and Solomon Gills), could not be concealed.

A few critics have taken to referring disparagingly to "BBC literature" when dealing with various TV dramatizations from the classics, especially with Dickens. Certainly the BBC has established a near monopoly in that particular field, but some of its more recent productions have been more than mere translations to the small screen, being triumphs of television drama in their own right. By some curious program planning, 1985 contained no fewer than three important Dickens serials on BBC. In the Sunday teatime slot came *The Pickwick Papers*, beginning in January 1985 and running for 12 episodes into March. Two weeks later came *Bleak House*, categorized as a major midweek evening serial with weekend repeats. In October a new adaptation of *Oliver Twist* in 12 episodes began.

The enjoyable *The Pickwick Papers* was almost certainly the best there has been on either large or small screen, with a delightful portrayal of Mr. Pickwick by the much underrated Nigel Stock, faithful to the character in spirit and appearance, in the manner of an excitable child. The level of casting was extremely high, with one or two outstanding impersonations, while the selection of settings and locations was of the usual excellent standard.

On the other hand, if there was any serious fault in *Bleak House*, it was an apparent obsession with the decor and trappings of period detail. The serial began as if it were likely to be overwhelmed with atmosphere at the expense of clarity of the story, but it soon developed so strongly that one readily forgave any slight excesses as one revelled in the visually arresting compositions and the magnificent performances by a matchless team of actors; Diana Rigg as Lady Dedlock; Denholm Elliott as John Jarndyce; and Peter Vaughan as Tulkinghorne. The adaptation was by Arthur Hopcraft, who had been responsible for the 1977 *Hard Times*.

Bleak House, Dickens's last completed novel, has never been made into a sound film, and it had not been on television for over 35 years. The 1985 production will probably last for another 35 years. Kevin Loader, a BBC producer, said of it in 1991, "There is a school of thought within the BBC that one of the reasons we haven't done any classic serials in recent years is because *Bleak House* elevated the level of production so high it is impossible to follow it."

After that, the third Dickens serial that year might have been expected to be an anticlimax, but *Oliver Twist* was by no means an unworthy conclusion to an unparalleled spate of Dickens on television. Settings were faultless, as always, and the cast was enriched by the repelling Fagin of Eric Porter, who was well matched by the grimly terrifying Bill Sikes of Michael Atwell. Bullseye, playing Sikes's dog, was a born scene stealer, too! It was good to see that at last boys of different ages were used to cover the growing-up of Oliver, almost certainly the first time it has been done. It worked well, especially as both boy actors were well chosen. This time, the violent murder of Nancy went unremarked.

11

Television Torments

> The idea of animation excited me....Never in a million years would I try to work on *A Christmas Carol* with real people...After people see it I don't want them to say "Look what they did to Dickens," but "Isn't Dickens fun!"
>
> Jule Styne, 1962

In addition to the wealth of Dickens material used for televised drama productions, there is one particular work by Charles Dickens that has been, and still is, a godsend for television comedy writers seeking an idea for a seasonal slant to a popular series. Because *A Christmas Carol* has become an institution, the regular characters in a successful situation comedy series can be fitted with very little difficulty into the various roles in the famous tale, and when that has been done, the parody has virtually written itself. The behavior of the characters is predictable, and the comedy is generated from the universally known situations in the story into which they are plunged.

No doubt many of these genial stealings from Dickens have disappeared from sight, but as early as 1953 there was an episode entitled *Christmas Carol* in the series *Topper*. Cosmo Topper the banker, whose haunted exploits had been enjoyed in Thorne Smith's stories and prewar films, was required, in this installment, to foreclose a mortgage on Christmas Eve. In 1956, English teacher Eve Arden of *Our Miss Brooks* put up with her school's rendition of *A Christmas Carol*. In 1960, *My Sister Eileen*'s Ruth (Elaine Stritch) and her sister Eileen (Shirley Bonne) managed to upset the Greek-American character Mr. Appopolous (Leon Belasco) when they forgot to invite him to their Christmas party, in an episode entitled

Ebenezer Scrooge Appopolous. In the same year in Britain, the enormously popular *Charlie Drake Show* presented "A Christmas Carol, with acknowledgements to Charles Dickens." The diminutive Drake (later to appear in a straight role in *Bleak House*), who was a regular loser in his television series, played Bob Cratchit, and confusion was added to the comedy by the inclusion of characters from five other Dickens books.

Dickens has not even been immune from space characters. In *My Favorite Martian,* Uncle Martin was a middle-aged Martian accidentally stranded on Earth, and in the episode *Humbug, Mrs. Brown* (1965) he tried to save the lady concerned from giving too much to charity by turning her into Scrooge. (More of an incidental borrowing from another Dickens story was the conjuring up of the Artful Dodger from *Oliver Twist* in an episode in the delightful and still popular series *Bewitched.*)

Animated versions of the story with well-known cartoon characters in the principal parts seem to have begun with *Mr. Magoo's Christmas Carol,* and who better to attempt a comic depiction of Scrooge than the ill-tempered Magoo, too short-sighted to be aware of the need around him. This was a musical version, with songs by composer Jule Styne. In 1967, the Smothers Brothers presented their revision of *A Christmas Carol,* with Tom Smothers as Scrooge and, in a notable piece of casting against type, Jack Benny as Cratchit. Peter Rogers's famous *Carry On* team demolished the story in *Carry On Christmas* (1969) with Sid James—he of the dirty laugh—as Scrooge and a chaotic cluster of characters that included Elizabeth Barrett, Robert Browning, Frankenstein, and Cinderella. In the series *The Ghost and Mrs. Muir,* a widow's house was still inhabited by the ghost of its former owner, so an episode entitled *The Ghost and Christmas Past* (1969) was no surprise. Also in 1969, an animated *Carol* made in Australia was the first of numerous straightforward animations of this and other Dickens stories.

Perhaps the most sophisticated animation of the *Carol* story was that made in Britain in 1971 by the acclaimed Richard Williams Studio (creators of the Pink Panther credit sequences) in the style of the original illustrations of Dickens's time. Made for the Foundation of Full Service Banks, in the United States, it was enhanced by the voices of Michael Redgrave as narrator, Alastair Sim as Scrooge, and Michael Hordern as Marley's ghost, and was first shown by ABC TV. It is the only animated Dickens film to have won an Oscar.

The stars of *The Honeymooners*, the celebrated comedy series of the 1950s and 1960s, were reunited briefly in 1977 in *The Honeymooners' Christmas Special*, a show that had Ralph Kramden (Jackie Gleason) directing a production of *A Christmas Carol* in which Ed Norton (Art Carney) ended up playing both Tiny Tim and Scrooge. Early in the life of the highly regarded series *The Odd Couple*, the peevish and pernickety Oscar Maddison turned down the role of Scrooge in a Christmas Play, only to dream his own version of the story in the episode *Scrooge Gets an Oscar* (1970).

Henry Winkler, the Fonz of *Happy Days*, portrayed the Scrooge character Benedict Slade in *An American Christmas Carol* in 1979. The story was transposed to New Hampshire in 1933, in the depths of the Depression, and Slade the furniture dealer was even repossessing furniture on Christmas Day. Although the revised setting of the tale was a clever idea, the production did not live up to the concept.

More recently, the team of *WKRP in Cincinnati* communicated their corruption of the celebrated story in 1981, when the outrageous disc jockey Johnny Fever offered his special brownies to the head of the station, Mr. Carlson, causing him a hallucinatory revision of Scrooge's experiences. Also in 1981, *Mel's Christmas Carol* was an installment in the comedy series *Alice*. The title character was a waitress in the diner when the owner Mel Sharples received a visit from the ghost of his former partner.

Rich Little, whose impressions of Scrooge as depicted by W. C. Fields, Cratchit by Paul Linde, and Marley by Richard Nixon, have been on the go for 30 years, has frequently presented them on stage and television as *Scrooge and the Stars* or as *Rich Little's Christmas Carol*.

In the immensely successful detective agency series *Moonlighting*, an episode of December 1986 cast Maddie Hayes as a Scrooge and the long-suffering Agnes Dipesto as Cratchit, while in Britain it was probably inevitable that the scheming and unscrupulous Blackadder, having wriggled and cheated his way through various epochs of English history, should surface again in the richly comic *Blackadder's Christmas Carol* (1988).

On the less hilarious side, borrowings from Dickens's books, and even the person of Charles Dickens himself, have turned up in a variety of renowned television series over the years. Musical versions, mostly of *A Christmas Carol,* have also been conspicuous, starting with the singing Scrooge of Fredric March in 1954, which was filmed and thus repeatable the following year. *The Merry Christmas,* another musical adaptation of the same story, was screened in Britain in 1955 and repeated with a new cast in 1958. Meanwhile Basil Rathbone, who previously was Marley's ghost to Fredric March's Scrooge, became Scrooge himself, still singing, in a different production called *The Stingiest Man in Town.* (More than 20 years later NBC presented an animated version of the same piece.) A straight operatic version of *A Tale of Two Cities* by Arthur Benjamin and Cedric Cliffe was first broadcast on radio, then performed on the stage, and finally televised in 1958 by the BBC. Four years later, the BBC commissioned an operatic version of *A Christmas Carol. Mr. Scrooge,* a musical created for the stage in Toronto in 1963, was performed on Canadian TV in 1964 with Cyril Ritchard as Scrooge and (unbelievably) "Two-Ton" Tessie O'Shea as Mrs. Cratchit.

A grimmer variation on the *Carol* story was *A Carol for Another Christmas,* televised in 1964. Rod Serling, responsible for the eerie cult series *The Twilight Zone,* wrote this antinuclear propaganda play, which was sponsored by the United Nations, directed by Joseph L. Mankiewicz with music by Henry Mancini, and included Sterling Hayden, Robert Shaw, Eva Marie Saint, Peter Sellers, and Britt Eklund. With such a pool of talent, it is surprising that the macabre piece has never been repeated, even as a now-dated curiosity.

Some television western series have taken advantage of the fact that the pioneering years in the west coincided with much of Dickens's output and Dickens's lifetime. The series *Wagon Train,* in an episode called *The Tom Tuckett Story,* used a western variation of *Great Expectations* themes, while *A Passion for Justice* in *Bonanza* had Charles Dickens visiting the Ponderosa.

Lighter-weight crime and adventure series have not been averse to poaching from Dickens, either. In *Mr. White's Christmas,* a 1965 episode in *The Rogues,* the dispassionate John McGiver portrayed a Scroogelike character who turns philanthropist, and in *Too Many Christmas Trees* (1965), Avengers John Steed and Emma Peel went as Sydney Carton and Oliver Twist to a house party given by a man so obsessed with Dickens that each room in his house was decorated as a tableau from one of the novels (standard *Avengers* stuff, really).

In a documentary vein, *Mr. Dickens of London* (1967) was a program designed "to show parts of London where the evidence of the author's impact is still preserved." The guide was Juliet Mills; Charles Dickens was impersonated by Michael Redgrave. Due to be shown on ABC during prime time, the show was delayed because of a speech by President Johnson. What would the bumptious Dickens have made of that? The centenary of his death was marked in 1970 by two 90-minute biographical programs made for British television: *The Hero of My Life* (also shown in the United States) and *The Great Inimitable Mr. Dickens*. In the latter, Dickens's father, John Dickens, was played by Arthur Lowe, who later was shrewdly cast as Mr. Micawber in a BBC serial of *David Copperfield*, Dickens having based much of the character on his own unreliable, profligate parent.

Other television trifles around this time were a pop musical "freely based on *Nicholas Nickleby*" called *Smike!* transmitted by the BBC in 1973 and a short animated educational film, *The Energy Carol* (1975) by the National Film Board of Canada, which depicted the reformation of an excessively energy-wasteful Scrooge.

Further operatic treatments of *Carol* were a specially commissioned version for the Welsh HTV channel, with Sir Geraint Evans as Scrooge in 1978, and the 1981 Granada Television presentation of Thea Musgrave's opera, as given at the Royal Opera House, Covent Garden.

There have been numerous American and Australian animated films of all the best-known Dickens stories, and these continue to be transmitted at all sorts of early morning and late-night hours.

12

The Great Inimitable

> I love bits of Dickens. I love the comic stuff—I get a bit bogged down with the melodrama.
>
> Alec Guinness, 1987

Clive Donner, who had edited the Alastair Sim film *Scrooge* in 1951, returned to the story in 1984 when he directed the film version of *A Christmas Carol* featuring George C. Scott as Ebenezer Scrooge. The film followed the now-familiar practice of being shown on television in America but theatrically in Britain, and it proved to be an exceptional presentation of the inexhaustible tale. Except for some weaknesses in the casting, it would rank among the foremost of Dickens films. Beautifully photographed, with elegant and impressive settings, the production conveyed a good feeling of the Dickensian milieu without resorting to period cliches or quaintness. This realistic approach was fully supported by the strongly acted Scrooge of George C. Scott. His performance was finely judged in its intensity, with no hint of caricature or grotesquerie. This was Scrooge—the ruthless hardheaded man of business yielding nothing in his dealings or his feelings until his conversion by the various spirits, and then only gradually, reluctantly, and quite believably.

The same story was used by the Walt Disney Studio, which decided to bring a long-absent Mickey Mouse back to the screen as Bob Cratchit in *Mickey's Christmas Carol* (1983), where he endured the temper of Donald Duck's crotchety uncle Scrooge McDuck. The universal understanding of the name "Scrooge" had been emphasized by the Disney Studio years earlier, when the tightfisted uncle made his first appearance in the aptly named cartoon *Scrooge McDuck and Money* (1967). Other favorite Disney cartoon characters were conscripted into the cast of this 35-minute film, dismissed by one commentator as Dickens in Disneyland.

Just when it seemed that television serials had established themselves as the latest and possibly best solution to the dramatization of Dickens, there came the mammoth cinema version of *Little Dorrit* (1987). At six hours, it is by far the longest Dickens feature film ever made and, happily, quantity was matched by quality, with exceptional performances by Alec Guinness and Derek Jacobi. The film was clearly a labor of love for writer and director Christine Edzard, who used the extended time to allow the story to develop gradually, in a manner reminiscent of Dickens's spaciousness. She made use of the practical necessity of dividing the film into two 3-hour parts by telling the story first from Arthur Clennam's point of view and then from that of Little Dorrit herself. Although that meant some of the same ground was covered twice, the subtle changes in camera set-up, dialogue, performance, and even visual design obviated any sense of repetition.

Alec Guinness gave a rich and delicately judged portrayal of the incorrigibly selfish and pretentious William Dorrit, vain and snobbish, full of skillful touches and sly business that make that splendid actor such a delight to watch. It is undoubtedly one of his finest film performances. Derek Jacobi was equally commendable as the perplexed and hapless Arthur Clennam. "The difficulty with the role is that it is very passive," said Jacobi. "The character often sets up scenes with other people and then takes a background place in it. I had to have help not to be the nice, kind, saintly gentleman who is around all the time—he had to be somebody you wanted to see again and enjoy his company." The docile Clennam, exasperated by the appalling Circumlocution Office, is shunned by his mother, the implacable Mrs. Clennam, formidably played by Joan Greenwood, who frankly described her part as "an awful person—a hypocrite, cruel, bible-thumping, religious mania. Awful." It was a memorable last role for that actress, who died soon after filming was completed.

The film was sprinkled with so many well-known actors playing small roles that it had the appearance of a prestige production that everyone wanted to join, and perhaps it was. Especially notable was Max Wall, born to play the baffling and eccentric

Flintwinch. Miriam Margoyles contributed a hilarious portrait of the sublimely foolish Flora Finching, delivered at breakneck speed and grandly entertaining. In the company of such a powerful team, Sarah Pickering gave little indication that she was a newcomer to the screen in her modest rendering of the self-effacing girl of the title. It was quite believable that she had been the child "born in the Marshalsea."

The settings, created in Edzard's own small Rotherhithe studio, captured amazingly the environments that Dickens intended to convey. The dank, cramped misery of the Marshalsea prison, with its dispiriting squalor, was presented in claustrophobic detail, as was the heavy, oppressive gloom of the Clennam family house. Outside, the London street scenes were a glorious bustle of noisy and confused activity. All these were depicted with a grimy realism of wear and neglect.

It is easy to forget that Verdi was contemporary of Dickens, and the choice of his music was an inspired embellishment to a film already rich in pleasures. Even with all the prodigious benefits of this massive production, there were still inevitable deletions of characters and occurrences from the original story, but they were very carefully and sensibly done.

Little Dorrit is a depressing novel, and perhaps Dickens's strongest social indictment, in the large combination of targets he attacks and condemns. It is no reckless flailing about at whatever happens to be in range, for by the time he wrote it he had learned to plan and prepare the structure of his novels, and much less of his writing was subject to market reactions.

Because of the unrelieved darkness of this, among Dickens's later works, the book has never been among his most popular. When it is realized that this epic film was made on a relatively tiny budget, the boldness of the venture becomes even more extraordinary. It was never likely to be a big box-office success—the subject matter and length ensured that—but it received widespread, almost universal critical acclaim and will surely remain the definitive dramatization of this very difficult story. With its exposure of crooked financiers, shifty politicians, inept and arrogant bureaucracy, and sheer greed, the film also presented a powerful fable for the selfish and materialistic 1980s, for those willing to see it.

The film *Hard Times* (1989) by Portuguese director João Botelho was regarded by some critics as a fairly important work by this rather vaunted filmmaker, but it was really an agonizingly slow adaptation, and badly cast. Presumably it was placed in a modern setting to lend more emphasis to the struggle between capital and labor, which is one of the principal strands of Dickens' book, but the treatment of the story made for boredom rather than tension. The film was crisply photographed in black and white (an interesting idea for this somber tale) and is the only talkie made of *Hard Times*, but the acting and direction were frequently so melodramatic as to appear absurd. For those not speaking Spanish, the version with English subtitles was rendered even more difficult by the use of some of Dickens' original dialogue and narration. For much of the time, none of the subtitles appeared to fit what was taking place on the screen or soundtrack. Even if merely regarded as a socialist parable, as is often the case with *Hard Times*, the film proved more laughable than laudable.

In the cinema film *Scrooged* (1988), the framework of Dickens's *Carol* story was used to depict a television network executive named Frank Cross, who lives only for his job and is completely unfeeling and ruthless toward his employees. Cross is preparing a prestige television production of *Scrooge* that promises to be correspondingly unfeeling and totally lacking in any spirit of Christmas goodwill. Cross by nature as well as by name, he manages to fall out with everyone round him and is duly visited by the decaying ghost of his former TV colleague. The customary trio of spirits take the form of a manic taxi-driver, an alternately sweet and sadistic fairy, and the more traditional cloaked and hooded figure of Death. Cross's eventual conversion is celebrated right in the middle of his live TV production, which he interrupts and changes into an impassioned homily on brotherly love. In an extraordinary way—and in spite of the syrupy sentimentality of the film's finale—the essence of the Dickens story exerts its wonderfully moving influence on its audience. The adaptation was stylishly produced and thoughtfully directed by Richard Donner. Above all, the film demonstrated the virtually indestructible nature of Charles Dickens' tale and confirmed the ability of *A Christmas Carol* to withstand transformation into almost any kind of narrative and entertainment.

Scrooged actually echoed rather closely an earlier idea from 1975, when Norman Stone, then a student at the Royal College of Art in London, wrote and directed a 20-minute pilot film entitled

Scrooge in which Ron Moody portrayed an equally detestable television chief actually named Scrooge, whose downtrodden minions—from floor-sweeper, chauffeur, and makeup man, to photographer, actor, secretary, and general dogsbody—are all Cratchits, played by Graham Stark. In a telling little scene, the charity solicitors, appealing for a donation from Scrooge to relieve the needy, are converted into representatives from a "Citizens Study Group of Mass Media and Social Responsibility," who come to express their shock and disappointment at the sensationalism and trivialization of television, "to gain the necessary ratings response, audience increases, greater profits, a larger slice of the market." "Is there not an OFF-SWITCH on every television in the land?" retorts Scrooge. "And is there not the freedom of the individual to use that switch?" Produced with an unbelievable budget of £423.00, this pilot film was shown on BBC television and made one wish that the clever concept had been completed by Stone.

Following the theatrical release of *Mickey's Christmas Carol*, the Walt Disney Studio produced a similar adaptation using cartoon animals as Dickens characters in *Oliver and Company* (1988), the orphan of the title being an orange kitten who is befriended by a larcenous dog named Dodger. This exposition of the story of Oliver Twist was reduced to escapades with Oliver and the gang who befriend him; another cute Disneyification.

Probably the only screen dramatization of Dickens to emanate from Australia was *Great Expectations—The Untold Story* (1987), a most unusual pastiche that added to the basis of the original story by relating what happened to the convict Magwitch when he was transported to the penal colony of New South Wales, and how he acquired the fortune he used to make Pip a gentleman. The serial showed these adventures in parallel with the familiar tale of Pip's upbringing in England, before merging into the customary ending of Magwitch's return to London. The concept was good, but seems not to have been too successfully accomplished, to judge from the reviews available. "This will irritate purists," declared *Variety*, "though one suspects that Dickens or any of the classic writers in the English language is so little read and respected in these days of encroaching sub-literacy that few will know enough to complain."

The year 1989 marked the bicentenary of the French Revolution. As part of the many events marking that anniversary, a lavish television production of *A Tale of Two Cities* was made as an Anglo-

French venture. For the first time, the respective English and French roles were played by actors of the appropriate nationality. The excellent adaptation was by Arthur Hopcraft, previously responsible for the magnificent serials *Hard Times* (1977) and *Bleak House* (1985), but this time the story was delivered in two lengthy installments on separate evenings. It was a superior production, worthy of the bicentenary commemoration, and Hopcraft's sensitive adaptation was performed with grace and conviction by a splendid team of players. In spite of the relative blankness of the character, Serena Gordon managed to inject firmness and feeling into the role of Lucie Manette. Her wide-eyed beauty made it quite conceivable that the dissolute Sydney Carton (in an admirably restrained performance by James Wilby) would willingly die for her.

Among the French actors, Jean-Pierre Aumont was a highly persuasive Dr. Manette, and the hot-eyed, vindictive Madame Defarge of Kathie Kriegel practically spat venom with every utterance. The all-round strong cast had the benefit of superb sets, locations, and costumes. A subtle color scheme dressed the English in browns and sepias and the French in grays and slatey blues. Two versions of the teleplay were made. For the French language version, the English actors' voices were dubbed, suggesting that the English education system has not advanced all that much since Dickens's time.

If there had been any doubt that the Dickens television serial had passed its peak, it must have been dispelled when the latest *Great Expectations* appeared in 1989. Most of the lessons learned from its recent predecessors in the way of authenticity of sets, locations, and costumes seemed to have been overlooked or ignored (*Variety* commented that even the dirt looked clean), and the casting of the characters was a serious disappointment. Perhaps it is significant that the idea for this unnecessary remake came from the Disney Channel, which provided 50 percent of the financing. Certainly the garish piece was given some big names—Anthony Hopkins as Magwitch, and Jean Simmons returning to the story as Miss Havisham, 45 years after playing the young Estella in David Lean's film—but that did not help a lackluster production. With a story familiar from previous screen versions, slackness in screenplay and direction just will not do. Moments of real dramatic tension were seldom experienced.

The superior screen versions of Dickens stories are not only evocative of the period in which they are set but also generally reflective of the times in which they were made. There is charm and innocence in the films made before the Second World War that disappears thereafter. Postwar social changes are similarly noticeable, while the reckless abandon of the 1960s and 1970s was marked by a distinct leaning toward escapism. The money-grubbing 1980s brought forth due acknowledgment of ruthless men of business and their crooked counterparts. Dickens, it seems, is adaptable to all eras. His messages of morality, integrity, and social responsibility indicate that little has changed since his lifetime.

Supposedly there is always room for another solution to *The Mystery of Edwin Drood*. Unfortunately the 1993 version, one of the few wholly British films of the 1990s, did not provide it, but followed much on the lines of the Universal version of 1935. With an excess denied to films of the 1930s, Robert Powell's John Jasper becomes wildly deranged and attempts further murders before being apprehended. The film enhanced one's respect for Claude Rains, as well as for the tight discipline of the old Hollywood studio system.

Most of Dickens's novels have been adapted for the screen in one or more forms, first with short extracts and then longer versions on silent film, succeeded by remakes on sound film and in color, some with music. Overlapping the later stages came live and recorded television versions, inevitably remade in color. The advent of home video players meant that many of the film and TV versions could be purchased and viewed at will on video cassettes. Many animated films of the stories have appeared during the last decade.

In the earlier films, the general treatment of the stories varied enormously. A common fault was setting the action in a vaguely mid-Victorian environment, taking little or no account of the changes in English social life that the novels reflect. In *Pickwick*, Dickens was writing about the 1830s, which was the era of stagecoaches and post chaises. By the time he died in 1870, leaving *Edwin Drood* unfinished, railway travel was long established and public road transport had changed to broughams, hansom cabs, and horse-drawn buses. Thus the term *Dickensian* can be extremely misleading when used to indicate an historical period. In recent years, due recognition of these changes has been made by adapters and producers.

Except for the two Selznick M-G-M films, many of the sound films demonstrated that the Hollywood star system was largely defeated by Dickens's huge casts of characters, for there are really very few starring roles—or too many starring roles. While recognizing the importance of dramatizations that will be enjoyed by those who have not read the books, it should be realized that the musical films effectively blunt the thrust and soften the impact of Dickens's novels, leaving them rather simple morality tales, shorn of many of their deeper issues and darker aspects and largely reduced to brilliantly staged costume pieces with music.

There seems to be a combination of familiarity and popularity that encourages ever more versions of certain of the stories, while others are neglected. In the cinema, *Oliver Twist* and *A Christmas Carol* have been about equally popular with filmmakers, followed at some distance by *Pickwick, Curiosity Shop, Copperfield,* and *Two Cities*. On television, *A Christmas Carol* far outstrips all the others, although the high number of productions is partly explained by the great number of parodies of *Carol* perpetrated in comedy series. Yet there has been no great *Martin Chuzzlewit* or *Barnaby Rudge*, perhaps because they are difficult to dramatize satisfactorily and costly to stage, although surely no more costly than *A Tale of Two Cities*. However, production costs have now become a dominating factor in all costume dramas for the screen.

During the 1970s and 1980s, American television screened much British-made period drama, some as straight imports and some made as coproductions. Even the formerly exclusive BBC found it necessary to spread the ever-rising costs of such costume dramas by associating with overseas TV channels, and the commercial TV companies in Britain have never had any qualms about the practice.

With a proliferation of channels over which the spread of quality has become thinner and thinner, it has long been easier and cheaper for American TV to use quality drama from Britain, where there has usually been a fairly steady supply. Unfortunately, with the restructuring of British independent TV in 1992 and the simultaneous cost-cutting rationalization of the BBC, combined with the rocketing costs of production, it now seems unlikely that many more large-scale costume dramas will be mounted in the foreseeable future. It is ironic that, as a consequence of the deep and long-lasting world recession, more people have been staying at home and watching TV or videos, and there is a distinct need for more quality television.

In 1991, Michael Wearing, the BBC's head of serials, admitted the dangerously high cost of making period films.

> Something like three-quarters of your budget goes on design-related expenditure...When ITV joined in the game people started copying each other. ITV made *Hard Times*, which was shot very beautifully and very expensively, and the BBC responded with *Bleak House*. We were both bankrupting ourselves.

It is likely that several of the more recent adaptations of Dickens will remain the standard and lasting versions, augmented by periodic repeats of some of the older films. For example, fairly recently a "colorized" edition of the 1951 Alastair Sim monochrome film *Scrooge* has been issued, thereby extending its screen life for many more years. There seems to be little chance of there being any end of Charles Dickens on the screen, and there is always hope for some great new versions. Dickens often referred to himself as The Great Inimitable. The catalogue of adaptations that follows shows that he is also The Great Inextinguishable.*

---

* As this book went to print, there came news of a big new BBC TV serial of *Martin Chuzzlewit*, and a new Disney film of *The Old Curiosity Shop*. Inextinguishable indeed!

Catalog of Film, Television, and Video Productions

The catalog of Dickens screen dramatizations lists motion picture films and then television productions, each in chronological order. Parodies, pastiches, and spoofs have been included, indicating a presumed familiarity with the original stories by the general public. Videos are included with television.

Reading through the catalog not only reveals the development of the dramatization of the stories in the different media but also the progress and versatility of particular actors in their careers, the relative popularity of the various tales from a dramatic viewpoint, and the international appeal of Charles Dickens on the screen.

In the later large productions, shortened cast lists are given, with references to where full details may be found. An exception is the RSC production of *Nicholas Nickleby*. The full cast cannot easily be found elsewhere and a full listing shows the many roles performed by each member of the cast.

Although this is the most comprehensive catalog of such dramatizations ever published, there are bound to be some omissions and errors. Information on additions and corrections will be welcomed by the author, care of the publisher.

Abbreviations

ABC	American Broadcasting Company
or	Associated British Picture Corporation
or	Australian Broadcasting Corporation
AFI	American Film Institute
AM&B	American Mutoscope and Biograph Co.
ATV	Associated Television
BBC	British Broadcasting Corporation
BFI	British Film Institute
C	Camera
CBC	Canadian Broadcasting Corporation
CBN	Christian Broadcasting Network
CBS	Columbia Broadcasting System
D	Director
HTV	Harlech Television, Wales
LOC	Library of Congress
M	Music
MD	Music Director
MFB	*Monthly Film Bulletin* of the British Film Institute
N	Narrator
NBC	National Broadcasting Company
NFB	National Film Board of Canada
OU	The Open University
P	Producer
PBS	Public Broadcasting Service
R	Repeated
RCA	Royal College of Art, London
Reg	Registered
Rel	Released
S&S	*Sight & Sound*, Journal of the British Film Institute
T	Transmitted
UK	United Kingdom
US or USA	United States of America
W	Writer

Cinema Films

Silent Films

DEATH OF NANCY SYKES
American Mutoscope Co., USA, Apr 1897, 37 ft?
Bill Sykes: Charles Ross. Nancy: Mabel Fenton. From *Oliver Twist*.

MR. BUMBLE THE BEADLE
R. W. Paul, UK, Aug 1898, 60 ft
From *Oliver Twist*.

MR. PICKWICK'S CHRISTMAS AT WARDLE'S
R. W. Paul, UK, Nov 1901, 140 ft
D: W. R. Booth?

SCROOGE: OR MARLEY'S GHOST
R. W. Paul, UK, Nov 1901, 620 ft
D: W. R. Booth. From *A Christmas Carol*.

DOTHEBOYS HALL; OR NICHOLAS NICKLEBY
Gaumont, UK, Nov 1903, 225 ft.
D: Alf Collins. Reg LOC 17 Nov 1903. Dist US AM&B. Pupil: William Carrington.

GABRIEL GRUB THE SURLY SEXTON
Williamson, UK, 1904, 445 ft
D: James Williamson. Rel UK Nov 1904, US 8 Feb 1908. From *The Pickwick Papers*.

OLIVER TWIST
Gaumont, France, 1906, 750 ft
Rel UK 10 Mar 1906.

THE MODERN OLIVER TWIST: OR THE LIFE OF A PICKPOCKET
Vitagraph, USA, 1906, 800 ft
Reg LOC 12 Feb 1906. Rel UK 17 Mar 1906.

DOLLY VARDEN
Gaumont, UK, 1906, 740 ft
D: Alf Collins. Rel UK July 1906. From *Barnaby Rudge*.

LITTLE NELL
Gaumont, UK, 1906, Length?
D: Arthur Gilbert. Rel UK Aug 1906. With: Thomas Nye. From *The Old Curiosity Shop*.

A TALE OF TWO CITIES
Selig, USA, 1908, 1,000 ft
Rel US 16 Jul 1908.

A CHRISTMAS CAROL
Essanay, USA, 1908, 1,000 ft
Rel US 9 Dec 1908. 10 scenes.
Scrooge: Thomas Ricketts.

THE OLD CURIOSITY SHOP
Essanay, USA, 1909, 1,000 ft
Rel US 20 Jan 1909.
With: Marcia Moore.

THE MYSTERY OF EDWIN DROOD
Gaumont, UK, 1909, 1,030 ft
D: Arthur Gilbert. Rel UK Feb 1909. 13 scenes.
Edwin Drood: Cooper Willis. Rosa Budd: Nancy Bevington. Neville Landless: James Annard.
In July 1909, *Der Kinematograph* (Dusseldorf) carried advertisements for "*Edwin Droud* [sic], Englisches Kriminal-Drama, 260 metres." Same film?

OLIVER TWIST
Vitagraph, USA, 1909, 995 ft
D: J. Stuart Blackton. W: Eugene Mullin. Rel US 1 Jun 1909. Nancy: Elita Otis. Also: William Humphrey.

THE CRICKET ON THE HEARTH
Biograph, USA, 1909, 985 ft
D: D. W. Griffith. W: Frank Woods. C: Billy Bitzer, Arthur Marvin. Rel US 27 May 1909, UK Jul 1909.
Dot: Linda Arvidson. May Plummer: Violet Mersereau. John Peerybingle: Herbert Pryor. Edward Plummer: Owen Moore. Also: Harry Salter, Clara T. Bracey, Mary Pickford, Mack Sennett, Charles Inslee, Dorothy Bernard.

THE BOY AND THE CONVICT
Williamson, UK, 1909, 750 ft.
D: Dave Aylott? Rel UK Jun 1909.
From *Great Expectations*.

A KNIGHT FOR A NIGHT
Edison, USA, 1909, 370 ft
Rel US 24 Sep 1909.
From *The Pickwick Papers*.

OLIVER TWIST
Film d'Art, France, 1910, 316 metres
D: Camille de Morlhon. Rel Germany May 1910, US 13 Aug 1910. 15 scenes (Berlin censor's report 21 May 1910).
With: Jean Perier, Renee Pré.

JO THE CROSSING SWEEPER
Walturdaw, UK, 1910, 450 ft
Rel UK Sep 1910. From *Bleak House*.

A YORKSHIRE SCHOOL
Edison, USA, 1910, 800 ft
D & C: James H. White. Rel US 29 Apr 1910, UK 22 June 1910.
With: Verner Clarges. From *Nicholas Nickleby*.

LOVE AND THE LAW
Edison, USA, 1910, 1,000 ft
D: Charles Kent? Rel US 23 Aug 1910, UK 22 Oct 1910.
With: Edwin August, Charles J. Brabin. From *David Copperfield*.

IL SOGNO DEL VECCHIO USURAIO
(English title DREAM OF OLD SCROOGE or OLD SCROOGE)
Cines, Italy, 1910, 206 metres
Rel UK 21 Dec 1910.
From *A Christmas Carol*.

A CHRISTMAS CAROL
Edison, USA, 1910, 1,000 ft
D: J. Searle Dawley? Rel US 23 Dec 1910, UK 9 Dec 1911.
With: Charles Ogle, William Bechtell, Carey Lee, Marc McDermott, Viola Dana.

OLIVER TWIST
Cines, Italy, 1911, 1,424 ft
Rel UK 6 May 1911.

THE OLD CURIOSITY SHOP
Thanhouser, USA, 1911, 1,000 ft
D: Barry O'Neil. Rel US 20 Jan 1911.
Grandfather Trent: Frank Crane. Little Nell: Marie Eline. Also: Marguerite Snow, Alphonse Ethier, William Bowman, Harry Benham.

A TALE OF TWO CITIES
Vitagraph, USA, 1911, c3,034 ft
D: William J. Humphrey. P: J. Stuart Blackton. W: Eugene Mullin. Rel US 21, 24 & 25 Feb 1911. Rel UK 1911; reissued UK 24 May 1913.
Lucie Manette: Florence Turner. Sydney Carton: Maurice Costello. Seamstress: Norma Talmadge. Charles Darnay: Leo Delaney. Darnay as child: Kenneth Casey. Marquis St. Evremonde: William J. Humphrey. Miss Pross: Julia Swayne Gordon. Dr. Manette: Charles Kent. Ernest Defarge: Tefft Johnson. Madame Defarge: Helen Gardner. Jarvis Lorry: William Shea. Jailer: John Bunny. Peasant: James Morrison. Peasant girl: Lillian Walker. Also: Ralph Ince, Edith Storey, Lydia Yeamans Titus, Anita Stewart, Eleanor Radinoff, E. R. Phillips, Dorothy Kelly. The *American Film Index* gives lengths of 3 parts as 1,014, 1,013, and 994 ft respectively.

HOW BELLA WAS WON
Edison, USA, 1911, 1,000 ft
Reg LOC 10 Mar 1911. Rel UK 28 Jun 1911.
From *Our Mutual Friend*.

EUGENE WRAYBURN
Edison, USA, 1911, 1,000 ft
Reg LOC 3 Oct 1911. Rel UK 23 Dec 1911.
Eugene Wrayburn: Darwin Karr. Mortimer Lightwood: Richard Ridgeley. Lizzie Hexam: Bliss Milford. Charley Hexam: Edwin Clarke. Bradley Headstone: Charles M. Seay. Lockkeeper: William West.
From *Our Mutual Friend*.

THE EARLY LIFE OF DAVID COPPERFIELD
Thanhouser, USA, 1911, 950 ft
D: George O. Nichols. Rel US 17 Oct 1911, UK 10 Feb 1912.
David Copperfield: Flora Foster. David's mother: Anna Seer. Aunt Betsey: Viola Alberti. Ham: Justus D. Barnes. Little Em'ly as child: Marie Eline. Also: Frank Crane, Alphonse Ethier, Maude Fealy, Mignon Anderson, William Garwood, Harry Benham.

Oliver asks for more. Unknown players in Vitagraph's *Oliver Twist,* 1909 *(Courtesy of Museum of Modern Art).*

Oliver (Jackie Coogan) asks for more. Mr. Bumble (James Marcus) is astounded. *Oliver Twist,* 1922 *(Courtesy of Museum of Modern Art).*

On the tumbril, the seamstress (Norma Talmadge) is comforted by Sydney Carton (Maurice Costello). *A Tale of Two Cities,* 1911 *(Courtesy of Museum of Modern Art).*

Lucie Manette (Jewel Carmen), Miss Pross (Olive White), Jarvis Lorry (Marc Robbins), and either Charles Darnay or Sydney Carton (William Farnum played both). *A Tale of Two Cities,* 1917 *(Courtesy of Museum of Modern Art).*

Bob Cratchit (John Cook) with wife (Clare McDowell) and family. *The Right to be Happy,* 1916 *(Courtesy of Museum of Modern Art).*

The Cratchit family home, M-G-M style, with Kathleen and Gene Lockhart. *A Christmas Carol,* 1938 *(Courtesy of British Film Institute).*

This rare still shows a splendid-looking Micawber impersonated by Charles Laughton before he left the film, with Jean Cadell as Mrs. Micawber, Freddie Bartholomew as David, and Elsa Lanchester as Clickett. *David Copperfield,* 1935 *(Courtesy of the Academy of Motion Picture Arts and Sciences).*

W. C. Fields replaced Charles Laughton as Micawber, seen here with David (Frank Lawton) and Uriah Heep (Roland Young). *David Copperfield,* 1935 *(Courtesy of British Film Institute).*

Quilp (Hay Petrie) threatens Grandfather Trent (Ben Webster). *The Old Curiosity Shop,* 1934 *(Courtesy of British Film Institute).*

Grandfather Trent (Michael Hordern) cannot stand up to Quilp (Anthony Newley). *Mister Quilp,* 1975.

Fagin (Alec Guinness), Sikes (Robert Newton), and Nancy (Kay Walsh). *Oliver Twist,* 1948 *(Courtesy of British Film Institute).*

Nicholas (Derek Bond) restrains Squeers (Alfred Drayton) from caning Smike (Aubrey Woods), as Mrs. Squeers (Sybil Thorndike) and Wackford Jr. (Ray Hermitage) look on. *Nicholas Nickleby,* 1947 *(Courtesy of British Film Institute).*

Smike (David Threlfall) and Nicholas (Roger Rees) in the epic RSC production of *Nicholas Nickleby*, 1982.

Carol Reed directing Nancy (Shani Wallis), Fagin (Ron Moody), and Sikes (Oliver Reed, Carol's nephew). *Oliver!,* 1968.

Scrooge (Albert Finney) in the musical film *Scrooge,* 1970.

Another singing Scrooge (Sir Geraint Evans) in the television opera *A Christmas Carol,* 1978.

Neville Landless (Douglass Montgomery), Rosa Bud (Heather Angel), and Helena Landless (Valerie Hobson). *Mystery of Edwin Drood,* 1935 *(Courtesy of British Film Institute).*

Marley's ghost (Leo G. Carroll) and Scrooge (Reginald Owen). *A Christmas Carol,* 1938 *(Courtesy of British Film Institute).*

Pickwick (James Hayter), Jingle (Nigel Patrick), Winkle (James Donald), Rachel Wardle (Kathleen Harrison), Miss Tomkins (Hermione Gingold), Buzfuz (Donald Wolfit), Mrs. Leo Hunter (Joyce Grenfell), Mrs. Bardell (Hermione Baddeley), Sam Weller (Harry Fowler), Tupman (Alexander Gauge), Snodgrass (Lionel Murton), Tony Weller (George Robey). *The Pickwick Papers,* 1951 *(Courtesy of British Film Institute).*

Sydney Carton (Ronald Colman) and Stryver (Reginald Owen). *A Tale of Two Cities*, 1935.

Oliver (Mark Lester) about to ask for more in the musical *Oliver!,* 1968.

LITTLE EM'LY AND DAVID COPPERFIELD
Thanhouser, USA, 1911, 950 ft
D: George O. Nichols. Rel US 24 Oct 1911, UK 24 Feb 1912.
David Copperfield: Ed Genung. Ham: William Russell. Little Em'ly: Florence LaBadie.

THE LOVES OF DAVID COPPERFIELD
Thanhouser, USA, 1911, 1,000 ft
D: George O. Nichols. Rel US 31 Oct 1911, UK 2 Mar 1912.
David Copperfield: Ed Genung. Dora: Mignon Anderson. All 3 reels rel Germany 23 Mar 1912 by Pathé.

LITTLE EMILY
Britannia, UK, 1912, 1,254 ft
D: Frank Powell. Rel UK 6 Jan 1912.
Little Emily: Florence Barker. From *David Copperfield*.

LEAVES FROM THE BOOKS OF CHARLES DICKENS
Britannia UK 1912 740 ft
D: Frank Powell. W: Thomas Bentley. Rel UK Jan 1912.
All roles: Thomas Bentley. "Character studies performed on the sites of the novels" (Gifford).

THE OLD CURIOSITY SHOP
Britannia, UK, 1912, 990 ft
D: Frank Powell. Rel UK 28 Feb 1912.

MARTIN CHUZZLEWIT
Edison, USA, 1912, 3 reels
D: Oscar Apfel, J. Searle Dawley. Rel US 10 Jun 1912, UK 9 Mar 1912.
Tom Pinch: Harold Shaw. Jonas: Guy Hedlund. Also: Marion Brooks, Miriam Nesbitt, Mary Fuller, Charles Ogle, William West.

NICHOLAS NICKLEBY
Thanhouser, USA, 1912, 2 reels
D: George O. Nichols. Rel US 19 Mar 1912, UK 1 Jan 1913.
Nicholas Nickleby: Harry Benham. Madeleine Bray: Mignon Anderson. Kate Nickleby: Frances Gibson. Mrs. Nickleby: Inda Palmer. Ralph Nickleby: Justus D. Barnes. Smike: N. S. Wood. Wackford Squeers: David Thompson. Mrs. Squeers: Isabel Madigan. Wackford, Jr.: Marie Eline. Fanny Squeers: Grace Eline. Gryde: Etienne Giradot. Crummles: Harry A. Marks. Mrs. Crummles: Louise Trinder. Crummles youngsters: Grace Eline, Will Morgan. Mr. Bray: George Moss. Lord Frederick Verisopht: John Ashley. Sir Mulberry Hawk: Reginald Carrington. Newman Noggs: Oren

Hooper. Cheeryble brothers: Harry Blakemore, John Maher. Miss LaCreevy: Victory Bateman. Mr. Pluck: Walter Thomas. Mr. Pyke: Carl Grimmer. Lenville: Mikail Mitsoraz. Nicholas' support in play—Benvolio: John Harkness. Juliet: Ethyle Cook. Lady Capulet: Eleanor Rose. The Tragedian: Carl LeViness.

OLIVER TWIST
General Film Publicity and Sales Co., USA, 1912, 5 reels
P: H. A. Spanuth. Rel US 20 May 1912.
Fagin: Nat C. Goodwin. Oliver Twist: Vinnie Burns. Artful Dodger: Charles Rogers. Bill Sykes: Mortimer Martine. Nancy: Beatrice Moreland. Monks: Edwin McKim. Bates: Daniel Read. Mr. Brownlow: Hudson Liston. Mr. Grimwig: Frank Kendrick. Bumble the Beadle: Stuart Holmes. Rose: Lillian DeLesque. Mrs. Maylie: Mrs. Liston. Giles: Will Scherer. Brittles: Frank Stafford. Agnes Fleming: Louise White. Charles Leeford: Jack Hopkins. Nurse: Agnes Stone. (From the stage play by J. Comyns Carr.)

THE MYSTERY OF EDWIN DROOD
Film d'Art France, 1912, 1,970 ft
Rel UK 29 May 1912.

MR. PICKWICK'S PREDICAMENT
Edison, USA, 1912, 1,000 ft
D: J. Searle Dawley. Rel US 21 Aug 1912, UK 12 Oct 1912.
Mr. Pickwick: William Wadsworth. Sam Weller: Barry O'Moore. Winkle: Bigelow Cooper. Tupman: William Bechtel. Snodgrass: Henry Tomlinson. Mrs. Bardell: Mrs. Wallace Erskine. Mrs. Cluppins: Elizabeth Miller. Master Bardell: Yale Boss. Dodson: Marc MacDermott. Fogg: Julian Reed. Buzfuz: Charles Ogle. Snubbin: William West. Judge: Harry Eytinge.

MRS. LIRRIPER'S LODGERS
Vitagraph, USA, 1912, 1,000 ft
D: Van Dyke Brooke. W: W. A. Tremayne. Rel US 15 Oct 1912, UK 25 Jan 1913.
Mrs. Lirriper: Mary Maurice. Major Jackman: Van Dyke Brooke. Mr. Edson: Courteney Foote. Mrs. Edson: Clara Kimball Young.

OLIVER TWIST
Hepworth, UK, 1912, 3,700 ft
D & W: Thomas Bentley. Rel UK 24 Oct 1912.
Oliver Twist: Ivy Millais. Fagin: John McMahon. Bill Sikes: Harry Royston. Nancy: Alma Taylor. Rose Maylie: Flora Morris. Mr. Brownlow: E. Rivary. Artful Dodger: Willie West. (First British 4-reel feature film.)

MRS. LIRRIPER'S LEGACY
Vitagraph, USA, 1912, 1,000 ft
D: Van Dyke Brooke. Rel US 5 Dec 1912, UK 20 Mar 1913.

MR. HORATIO SPARKINS
Vitagraph, USA, 1913, 1,000 ft
D: Van Dyke Brooke. Rel US 13 May 1913, UK 25 Aug 1913.
Horatio Sparkins: Courteney Foote. Miss Malderton: Flora Finch. From *Sketches by Boz*.

THE PICKWICK PAPERS
Vitagraph, UK/USA, 1913, 3 reels
D & W: Larry Trimble. Rel: First 2 reels US 28 Feb 1913, UK 9 Jun 1913. 3rd reel US 5 Sep 1913, UK 18 Dec 1913.
Samuel Pickwick: John Bunny. Tupman: James Pryor. Snodgrass: Sidney Hunt. Winkle: Fred Hornby. Jingle: Arthur Ricketts. Sam Weller: H. P. Owen. Fat boy: George Temple. Mrs. Budger: Minnie Rayner. Dr. Slammer: Arthur White. Beadle: David Upton. Captain Boldwig: Arthur Jackson.
Individual reels were entitled *The Honourable Event, The Westgate Seminary, The Shooting Party*.

LITTLE DORRIT
Thanhouser, USA, 1913, 2,000 ft
D: James Kirkwood. W: Lloyd F. Lonergan. Rel US 29 Jul 1913, UK 15 Dec 1913.
Little Dorrit: Maude Fealy. Little Dorrit as child: Helen Badgley. Arthur Clennam: William Russell. William Dorrit: James Cruze. Also: Harry Benham, Gerda Holmes, Mrs. Lawrence Marston, Sidney Bracey.

DAVID COPPERFIELD
Hepworth, UK, 1913, 7,500 ft
D & W: Thomas Bentley. Rel UK Aug 1913, US Oct 1913.
David Copperfield: Kenneth Ware. David as child: Eric Desmond. David as youth: Len Bethel. Dora Spenlow: Alma Taylor. Micawber: H. Collins. Uriah Heep: Jack Hulcup. Daniel Peggotty: Jamie Darling. Little Emily: Amy Verity. Emily as child: Edna May. Steerforth: Cecil Mannering. Agnes Wickfield: Miss Harcourt. Murdstone: Johnny Butt. Mrs. Micawber: Miss West. Mr. Wickfield: Shiel Porter. Ham: Tom Arnold. Mr. Creakle: Harry Royston. Mrs. Gummidge: Marie de Solla. (First British 8-reel film.)

DOLLY VARDEN
Edison, USA, 1913, 1,000 ft
D & W: Charles Brabin. Rel US 5 Aug 1913, UK 20 Oct 1913.

Dolly Varden: Mabel Trunnelle. Joe Willets: Willis Secord. Gabriel Varden: Robert Brower. Simon: Barry O'Moore. From *Barnaby Rudge*.

SCROOGE
Zenith Film Co., UK, 1913, 2,600 ft
D: Leedham Bantock. W: Seymour Hicks. Rel UK 16 Sep 1913, US Nov 1913.
Scrooge: Seymour Hicks. Also: Ellaline Terriss, William Lugg, Leedham Bantock, J. C. Buckstone, Dorothy Buckstone, Leonard Calvert, Osborne Adair, Adela Measor. From *A Christmas Carol*.

PICKWICK VERSUS BARDELL
Clarendon, UK, 1913, 1,000 ft
D: Wilfred Noy. Rel UK Nov 1913.
No. 1 of a series of Clarendon Speaking Pictures—dramatizations of stories to accompany stage reciters.

MR. PICKWICK IN A DOUBLE BEDDED ROOM
Clarendon, UK, 1913, 1,000 ft
D: Wilfred Noy. Rel UK Nov 1913.
Clarendon Speaking Pictures No. 8

MRS. CORNEY MAKES TEA
Clarendon, UK, 1913, 1,000 ft
D: Wilfred Noy. Rel UK Nov 1913.
Clarendon Speaking Pictures No. 9. From *Oliver Twist*.

THE OLD CURIOSITY SHOP
Hepworth, UK, 1914, 5,300 ft
D & W: Thomas Bentley. Rel UK Jan 1914, US Apr 1914.
Little Nell: Mai Deacon. Grandfather Trent: Warwick Buckland. Quilp: E. Felton. Mrs. Quilp: Alma Taylor. The Single Gentleman: Jamie Darling. Dick Swiveller: Willie West. Tom Codlin: Billy Rex. Sampson Brass: S. May. Short: Bert Stowe. Jerry: Sydney Locklynne. The Marchioness: Moya Nugent. Mrs. Jarley: R. Phillips.

A CHRISTMAS CAROL
London Film Co., UK, 1914, 1,340 ft
D & W: Harold Shaw. Rel UK Jan 1914, US Oct 1914.
Scrooge: Charles Rock. Belle: Edna Flugrath. Bob Cratchit: George Bellamy. Mrs. Cratchit: Mary Brough. Fred: Franklyn Bellamy. Jacob Marley: Edward O'Neill. Christmas Past: Arthur Cullin. Christmas Present: Windham Guise. Christmas Yet To Come: Assheton Tonge.

THE CRICKET ON THE HEARTH
American Film Co. (Flying A), USA, 1914, 2,000 ft
D & W: Lorimer Johnston. Rel US 16 Feb 1914, UK 7 May 1914.
With: Sidney Ayres, Jack Richardson, Harry von Meter, Caroline Cooke, Louise Lester, Charlotte Burton, Vivian Rich, Harris L. Forbes.

THE CHIMES
Hepworth, UK, 1914, 2,500 ft
D & W: Thomas Bentley. Rel UK Aug 1914, US 29 Aug 1914.
Richard: Stewart Rome. Meg Veck: Violet Hopson. Trotty Veck: Warwick Buckland. Sir Richard Bowley: Harry Gilbey. Alderman Cute: Johnny Butt. Will Fern: John MacAndrews. Lillian: Muriel Smith.

THE CHIMES
US Amusement Corporation, USA, 1914, 5 reels
D: Herbert Blaché, Tom Terriss. Rel US 7 Sep 1914.
Trotty Veck: Tom Terriss. Meg; Faye Cusick. Alderman Cute: Alfred Hemming. William Fern: Clarence Harvey. Richard: Harry Hitchcock. Sir Joseph Bowley: Robert Vivian. Fern's daughter: Milly Terriss. Lillian: Vinnie Burns. Mr. Fish: William Terriss. Tugby: Eliza Mason.

THE CRICKET ON THE HEARTH
Biograph, USA, 1914, 2 reels
D: L. Marston. Rel US 8 Sep 1914.
With: Jack Drumier, Alan Hale, Marie Newton, Betty Gray, Gretchen Hartman, Robert Drouet, William Russell, A. C. Marston.

THE MYSTERY OF EDWIN DROOD
World Film Corporation, USA, 1914, 5 reels
D: Herbert Blaché, Tom Terriss. W: Tom Terriss. Rel US 19 Oct 1914, UK Sep 1915.
John Jasper: Tom Terriss. Edwin Drood: Rodney Hickok. Rosa Budd: Vinnie Burns. Neville Landless: Paul Sterling. Helena Landless: Margaret Prussing. Princess Puffer: Faye Cusick.

MARTIN CHUZZLEWIT
Biograph, USA, 1914, 2,114 ft
D: Travers Vale. Rel US Oct 1914, UK 21 Dec 1914.
Young Martin: Alan Hale. Old Martin: Jack Drumier. Anthony Chuzzlewit: Thornton Cole. Jonas Chuzzlewit: Edward Cecil. Mark Tapley: Hector V. Sarno. Seth Pecksniff: Selden Powell. Tom Pinch: Arthur Rankin. Mary Graham: Isabel Rea. Mercy Pecksniff: Helen Hart. Charity Pecksniff: Kate Toncray.

OLIVER TWIST SADLY TWISTED
Crystal Film Co., USA, 1915, Length?
Rel US 17 Jan 1915. Burlesque.

BARNABY RUDGE
Hepworth, UK, 1915, 5,325 ft
D & W: Thomas Bentley. P: Cecil Hepworth. Rel UK Jan 1915, US Feb 1915.
Barnaby Rudge: Tom Powers. Emma Haredale: Violet Hopson. Maypole Hugh: Stewart Rome. Dolly Varden: Chrissie White. Edward Chester: Lionelle Howard. Geoffrey Haredale: John MacAndrews. Sir John Chester: Henry Vibart. Lord George Gordon: Barry Gilbey. Dennis: Harry Royston. Simon Tappertit: Harry Buss. Mr. Rudge: William Felton. Gabriel Varden: William Langley.

SVERCHOK NA PECHI (The Cricket on the Hearth)
Golden Series, Russia, 1915, 2,330 ft
D & W: Boris Suskevich, A. Uralsky. Rel Russia 20 May 1915.
With: Grigori Khmara, Yevgeni Vakhtangov, Mikhail Chekhov, M. Durasova, Vera Soloviova.

HARD TIMES
Trans-Atlantic, UK, 1915, 4,000 ft
D & W: Thomas Bentley. Rel UK Sep 1915.
Gradgrind: Bransby Williams. Tom Gradgrind: Leon M. Lion. Louisa: Dorothy Bellew. Rachael: Madge Tree. Stephen Blackpool: Mr. Forrest. Josiah Bounderby: F. Lymons. Sleary: Will Corrie. Cissie Jupe: Clara Cooper. James Harthouse: J. Wynn Slater.

OLIVER TWIST
Jesse L. Lasky Feature Play Co., USA, 1916, 5 reels
D: James Young. W: Winthrop Ames, James Young. Rel US 10 Dec 1916.
Oliver Twist: Marie Doro. Bill Sikes: Hobart Bosworth. Fagin: Tully Marshall. Artful Dodger: Raymond Hatton. George Brownlow: James Neill. Nancy Sikes: Elsie Jane Wilson. Mr. Bumble: Harry Rattenbury. Monks: Carl Stockdale. Charles Dickens: W. S. Van Dyke.

THE RIGHT TO BE HAPPY
Bluebird Photoplays Inc, USA, 1916, 5 reels
D: Rupert Julian. W: E. J. Clawson. Rel US 25 Dec 1916.
Scrooge: Rupert Julian. Bob Cratchit: John Cook. Mrs. Cratchit: Clare McDowell. Tiny Tim: Francis Lee. Jacob Marley: Harry Carter. Fred: Emory Johnson. Caroline: Roberta Wilson. Scrooge's sweetheart. Francelia Billington. Miss Fezziwig: Lydia Yeamans Titus. Christmas Past:

Wadsworth Harris. Christmas Present: Dick LeStrange. Christmas Future: Tom Figee. From *A Christmas Carol*.

GREAT EXPECTATIONS
Famous Players Film Co., USA, 1917, 5 reels
D: Robert G. Vignola. W: Paul West, Doty Hobart. (Joseph Kaufman completed direction when Vignola was taken ill.) Rel US 8 Jan 1917, UK 23 Jul 1917.
Estella: Louise Huff. Pip: Jack Pickford. Magwitch: Frank Losee. Joe Gargery: W. W. Black. Mrs. Gargery: Marcia Harris. Miss Havisham: Grace Barton. Mr. Jaggers: Herbert Prior.

A TALE OF TWO CITIES
Fox Film Corporation, USA, 1917, 7 reels
D & W: Frank Lloyd. Rel US 12 Mar 1917, UK May 1917. Reissued US 4 Feb 1920.
Sydney Carton/Charles Darnay: William Farnum. Lucie Manette: Jewel Carmen. Marquis St. Evremonde: Charles Clary. Roger Cly: Ralph Lewis. Jacques Defarge: Herschel Mayall. Madame Defarge: Rosita Marstini. Dr. Manette: Joseph Swickard. Gabelle: William Clifford. Jarvis Lorry: Marc Robbins. Sergeant Stryver: Willard Louis. Miss Pross: Olive White. Gaspard: Harry de Vere.

OLIVER TWISTED
Piccadilly, UK, 1917, 2,360 ft
D & W: Fred and Joe Evans. Rel UK Apr 1917. Burlesque.

KLEIN DOORTJE (Little Dorrit)
Berliner Film Manufaktur, Germany, 1917, 4 reels
D: Friedrich Zelnik. W: Eddy Beuth, Richard Wilde. Rel Germany 17 Sep 1917; reissued Sep 1921.
Little Dorrit: Lisa Weisse. Also: Grete Weixler, Carl Beckersachs, Hermann Picha, Anderly Lebius

DOMBEY AND SON
Ideal, UK, 1917, 6,800 ft
D: Maurice Elvey. W: Eliot Stannard. Rel UK Oct 1917, US Jul 1919.
Paul Dombey: Norman McKinnel. Edith Dombey: Lillian Braithwaite. Walter Gay: Hayford Hobbs. Florence Dombey: Odette Grimbault. Sol Gills: Douglas Munro. Carker: Jerrold Robertshaw. Bagstock: Fewlass Llewellyn. Captain Cuttle: Will Corrie. Mrs. Skewton: Evelyn Walsh Hall.

MY LITTLE BOY
Bluebird Photoplays, USA, 1917, 5 reels

D: Elsie Jane Wilson. W: Elliot J. Clawson, Rupert Julian. Rel US 17 Dec 1917.
Clara: Ella Hall. Paul: Zoe Rae. Fred: Emory Johnson. Uncle Oliver: Winter Hall. Joe: Harry Holden. Clara's mother: Gretchen Lederer.
From portions of *A Christmas Carol* and the nursery rhyme "Little Boy Blue."

JO THE CROSSING SWEEPER
Barker, UK, 1918, 5,000 ft
D: Alexander Butler. W: Irene Miller. Rel UK Jun 1918.
Lady Dedlock: Dora de Winton. Bucket: Rolf Leslie. From *Bleak House*.

TWIST OLIVER
?, Hungary, 1919, Length ?
D: Marton Garas. W: Laszlo Vajda.
Oliver: Tibor Lubinszky. Also: Jeno Torzs, Laszlo Molnar, Gyula Szoreghy, Sari Almasi.

STORE FORVENTNINGER (Great Expectations)
Nordisk, Denmark, 1920, 2,517, metres
D: A. W. Sandberg. W: Laurids Skands. Premiere Denmark 1920. Rel Denmark 28 Aug 1922, US 6 Mar 1923.
Estella: Olga d'Org. Pip: Harry Komdrup. Pip as boy: Martin Herzberg. Miss Havisham: Marie Dinesen. Joe Gargery: Gerhard Jessen. Mrs. Gargery: Ellen Rovsing. Magwitch: Emil Helsengreen. Orlick: Peter Nielsen. Jaggers: Egill Rostrup. Biddy: Ellen Lillien. Herbert Pocket: Hjalmar Bendtsen. Pumblechook: A. Meyer. Also: Gorm Schmidt.

OLIVER TWIST
Rex Film, Germany, 1920, Length?
D: Lupu Pick.
Reported in *Der Kinematograph* 11 Feb 1920, but in view of the Richard Oswald film (see below), same subject, same year, this was possibly not completed.

THE BIRTH OF A SOUL
Vitagraph, USA, 1920, 4,986 ft
D: Edwin L. Hollywood. W: Arthur Edwin Krows. Rel US Jan 1920. Philip Gray/Charles Drayton: Harry T. Morey. Dorothy Barlow: Jean Paige. Lem Barlow: Charles Eldridge. Joe Barlow: George Cooper. Hap Barlow: Charles Kent. George Drayton: Walter Lewis. Parson: Robert Guillard. Sheriff: Bernard Siegel. Based on parts of *A Tale of Two Cities*.

Cinema Films 129

BLEAK HOUSE
Ideal, UK, 1920, 6,400 ft
D: Maurice Elvey. W: William J. Elliott. Rel UK Mar 1920.
Lady Dedlock: Constance Collier. Esther Summerson: Bertha Gellardi. Tulkinghorne: E. Vivian Reynolds. Guppy: Norman Page. Bucket: Clifford Heatherley. Capt. Hawdon: Ion Swinley. Sir Leicester Dedlock: A. Harding Steerman. Jo: Anthony St. John. Miss Barbay: Helen Haye. George: Teddy Arundel. Rachel: Beatrix Templeton.

LITTLE DORRIT
Progress, UK, 1920, 6,858 ft
D & W: Sidney Morgan. P: Frank Spring. Rel UK Aug 1920.
Mrs. Clennam: Lady Tree. Arthur Clennam: Langhorne Burton. Amy Dorrit: Joan Morgan. Pancks: Compton Coutts. William Dorrit: Arthur Lennard. John Chivery: J. Denton-Thompson. Merdle: George Foley. Flintwinch: Arthur Walcot. Old Bob: Judd Green. Fanny Dorrit: Betty Doyle. Mrs. Merdle: Mary Lyle. Daniel Doyce: Fred Gladman. Mr. Meagles: Clive Pembroke. Sparkler: Derick Zoya. Mrs. General: Louie Dare Smith. Frederick Dorrit: George Bellamy. Rigaud: J. Warris Lindon. Tip: Pett Francis. Chivery: Charles Levy. Maggie: Lena Brothy.

DIE GEHEIMNISSE VON LONDON (Secrets of London)
Richard Oswald Film, Germany, 1920, 2,137 metres
D: Richard Oswald. Rel Germany 22 Dec 1920.
Percy (Oliver): M. Lubinsky. Brown: Max Devrient. Smith, sein Freund: Julius Strobl. Dr. White: Hans Homma. Mary, seine Tochter: Maria West. Ein Fremder: Curt von Lessen. Bumble, Aufsieher: Ferdinand Bonn. Frau Winkle, Aufsieherin: Alice Hetsey. Fagin: Adolf Weise. Jim: Louis Ralph. Dick: Joseph Konig. Bill: Arthur Guttman. Bob: Fritz Strassny. Tom: Rudolf Merstallinger.
From *Oliver Twist*.

OLIVER TWIST JR.
Fox Film Corporation, USA, 1921, 5 reels
D: Millard Webb. W: F. McGrew Willis. Rel US 13 Mar 1921.
Oliver Twist, Jr.: Harold Goodwin. Ruth Norris: Lillian Hall. Schoolmaster: George Nichols. Dick: Harold Esboldt. Artful Dodger: Scott McKee. Fagin: Wilson Hummell. Bill Sykes: G. Raymond Nye. Monks: Hayward Mack. Mrs. Norris: Pearl Lowe. James Harrison: George Clair. Judson: Fred Kirby. Nancy: Irene Hunt.

VOR FAELLES VEN (Our Mutual Friend)
Nordisk, Denmark, 1921, 4,664 metres

D: A. W. Sandberg. W: Laurids Skands. Rel Denmark 27 Sep 1921, UK May 1921, US Nov 1921.
John Harmon/Handford/Rokesmith: Aage Fonss. Bella Wilfer: Kate Riise. Lizzie Hexam: Karen Caspersen. Gaffer Hexam: Peter Fjelstrup. Rogue Riderhood: Svend Kornbeck. Mortimer Lightwood: Egill Rostrup. Eugene Wrayburn: Peter Malberg. Mr. Boffin: Jonna Neiiendam. Bradley Headstone: Peter Nielsen. Silas Wegg: Bertel Krause. Mr. Venus: Charles Wilken. Reginald Wilfer: Carl Madsen.
Produced in 1919; not released until 1921. Presumably the Danish premiere took place before the UK release.

THE OLD CURIOSITY SHOP
Welsh-Pearson, UK, 1921, 6,587 ft
D: Thomas Bentley. W: G. A. Atkinson. P: George Pearson. Rel UK May 1921, US Aug 1921.
Little Nell: Mabel Poulton. Grandfather Trent: William Lugg. Tom Codlin: Hugh E. Wright. Daniel Quilp: Pino Conti. Single gentleman: Bryan Powley. Tom Scott: Barry Livesey. Sampson Brass: Cecil Bevan. Sally Brass: Beatie Olna Travers. Mrs. Jarley: Minnie Rayner. Short: Dennis Harvey. Mrs. Quilp: Dezma du May. Dick Swiveller: Colin Craig. Marchioness: Fairy Emlyn. Mr. Marton: A. Harding Steerman.

THE ADVENTURES OF MR. PICKWICK
Ideal, UK, 1921, 6,000 ft
D: Thomas Bentley. W: Eliot Stannard, E. A. Baughan. Rel UK Nov 1921.
Mr. Pickwick: Frederick Volpe. Tupman: Frank J. Arlton. Snodgrass: John Kelt. Winkle: Arthur Cleave. Jingle: Ernest Thesiger. Wardle: Thomas Weguelin. Mrs. Wardle: Lizzie Primmer. Rachael Wardle: Athene Seyler. Emily Wardle: Joyce Dearsley. Isabella Wardle: Anna Dearsley. Arabella Allen: Kathleen Vaughan. Sam Weller: Hubert Woodward. Mary: Amy Gilbert. Sergeant Buzfuz: Bransby Williams. Mr. Justice Stareleigh: Norman Page. Mrs. Bardell: Mary Brough. Fat Boy: John E. Zecchini. Dodson: Townsend Whitling. Fogg: Harry Gilbey. Jackson: Joynson Powell. Perker: Douglas Fox. Magnus: Hugh Higson. Miss Witherfield: Jose Brooks. Mrs. Cluppins: Eileen Moore. Mrs. Sanders: Nannie Goldman. Mr. Skimpin: Rice Cassidy. Sergeant Snubbin: Charles Clifford. Mr. Phunky: Keith Williams.

NANCY
Master Films, UK, 1922, 1,578 ft
D & P: H. B. Parkinson. W: W. C. Rowden. Rel UK Jan 1922.
Nancy: Sybil Thorndike. Fagin: Ivan Berlyn.
No. 4 in series of Tense Moments With Great Authors. From *Oliver Twist*.

FAGIN
Master Films, UK, 1922, 1,260 ft
D & P: H. B. Parkinson. Rel UK Jan 1922.
Fagin: Ivan Berlyn.
No. 5 in series of Tense Moments With Great Authors. From *Oliver Twist*.

SCROOGE
Master Films, UK, 1922, 1,280 ft
D: George Wynn. P. H. B. Parkinson. W: W. C. Rowden. Rel UK Jan 1922.
Scrooge: H. V. Esmond.
No. 7 in series of Tense Moments With Great Authors. From *A Christmas Carol*.

A TALE OF TWO CITIES
Master Films, UK, 1922, 1,174 ft
D: W. C. Rowden. P: H. B. Parkinson. Rel UK Jan 1922.
Dr. Manette: J. Fisher White. Sydney Carton: Clive Brook. Lucie Manette: Ann Trevor.
No. 10 in series of Tense Moments With Great Authors.

LA BOTTEGA DELL'ANTIQUARIO (The Old Curiosity Shop)
Tespi-Film, Italy, 1922, 1,987 metres
D & W: Mario Corsi. P: Gustavo Salvini. Rel Italy 23 Jan 1922.
Grandfather: Gustavo Salvini. Nell: Egle Valery. Kit: Renato Visca. Quilp: Roberto Pla (Robert Sortsch-Pla).

LE GRILLON DU FOYER (The Cricket on the Hearth)
Film Eclipse, France, 1922, 1,800 metres
D & W: Jean Manoussi. Rel France May 1922, UK Jul 1922.
Dot Peerybingle: Sabine Landray. May Fielding: Suzanne Dantes. Nurse: Marcelle Monthil. Bertha: Henriette Moret. John Peerybingle: Marcel Vibert. Caleb: Paul Jorge. Edouard: Charles Boyer. Tackleton: Gouget.

BLEAK HOUSE
Master Films, UK, 1922, 3,100 ft
D & P: H. B. Parkinson. W; Frank Miller. Rel UK Jun 1922.
Lady Dedlock: Sybil Thorndike. Esther: Betty Doyle. Sir Leicester Dedlock: Stacey Gaunt. Bucket: Harry J. Worth. Jo: Alec Alexander.
No. 2 in series of Tense Moments From Great Plays.

OLIVER TWIST
Jackie Coogan Prodns/Sol L. Lesser, USA, 1922, 7,761 ft
D: Frank Lloyd. W: Frank Lloyd, Harry Weil. Rel US 5 Nov 1922, UK 26 Dec 1922.

Oliver Twist: Jackie Coogan. Fagin: Lon Chaney. Nancy: Gladys Brockwell. Bill Sikes: George Siegmann. Artful Dodger: Edouard Trebaol. Mr. Brownlow: Lionel Belmore. Monks: Carl Stockdale. Toby Crackit: Eddie Boland. Charlie Bates: Taylor Graves. Noah Claypole: Lewis Sargent. Bumble: James Marcus. Mrs. Corney: Aggie Herring. Charlotte: Joan Standing. Rose Maylie: Esther Ralston. Mrs. Bedwin: Florence Hale. Sowerberry: Nelson McDowell. Mr. Grimwig: Joseph Hazleton. Mrs. Maylie: Gertrude Claire.

DAVID COPPERFIELD
Nordisk, Denmark, 1922, 3,180 metres
D: A. W. Sandberg: W: Laurids Skands. Rel Denmark 5 Dec 1922, US Sep 1923, UK Jul 1924.
Dora: Karina Bell. Micawber: Frederick Jensen. David as boy: Martin Herzberg. Betsey Trotwood: Marie Dinesen. Mrs. Copperfield: Margarete Schlegel. Chillip: Charles Wilken. Emily: Karen Caspersen. Uriah Heep: Rasmus Christiansen. David: Gorm Schmidt. Agnes Wickfield: Karin Winther. Murdstone: Robert Schmidt. Mrs. Murdstone: Ellen Rovsing. Mr. Wickfield: Poul Reumert. Mrs. Micawber: Anne Marie Wiehe. Mr. Dick: Peter Malberg. Agnes as child: Else Nielsen. Peggotty: Bodil Ipsen.

SCROOGE
B & C, UK, 1923, 1,600 ft
D: Edwin Greenwood. P: Edward Godal. W: Eliot Stannard. Rel UK Apr 1923.
Scrooge: Russell Thorndike. Alice: Ninna Vanna. Bob Cratchit: Jack Denton. Marley: Forbes Dawson.
No. 5 in series Gems of Literature. From *A Christmas Carol*.

DICKENS UP-TO-DATE
Bertram Phillips, UK, 1923, 1,900 ft
D: Bertram Phillips. Rel UK Apr 1923.
No. 4 in series Syncopated Picture Plays (comedy burlesques).

THE CRICKET ON THE HEARTH
Paul Gerson Pictures, USA, 1923, 7 reels
D: Lorimer Johnston. W: Caroline Cooke. Rel US 11 Aug 1923.
Caleb Plummer: Joseph Swickard. Bertha Plummer: Fritzi Ridgeway. John Peerybingle: Paul Gerson. Dot Marley: Virginia Brown Faire. Edward Plummer: Paul Moore. Josiah Tackleton: Lorimer Johnston. May Fielding: Margaret Landis. Tillie Slowboy: Joan Standing

LILLE DORRIT (Little Dorrit)
Nordisk, Denmark, 1924, 3,245 metres

D: A. W. Sandberg. W: Sam Ask. Rel Denmark 26 Dec 1924.
Amy Dorrit: Karina Bell. William Dorrit: Frederick Jensen. Fanny Dorrit: Karin Winther. Arthur Clennam: Gunnar Tolnaes. Tip: Knud Schroder. Frederick Dorrit: Georg Bush. Also: Ingeborg Pehrsson.

DICKENS' LONDON
Graham-Wilcox Prodns, UK, 1924, 807 ft
D: Frank Miller, H. B. Parkinson, In series *Wonderful London*.
A travelog featuring places and characters from the novels, and clips from earlier feature films.

THE ONLY WAY
Herbert Wilcox Prodns, UK, 1925, 10,075 ft
D, P & W: Herbert Wilcox. Rel UK Sep 1925, US Apr 1926.
Sydney Carton: John Martin Harvey. Mimi: Madge Stuart. Lucie Manette: Betty Faire. Marquis St. Evremonde: Ben Webster. Dr. Manette: J. Fisher White. Charles Darnay: Frederick Cooper. Miss Pross: Mary Brough. Jarvis Lorry: Frank Stanmore. Barsad: Gibb MacLaughlin. Ernest Defarge: Gordon McLeod. Jeanne Defarge: Jean Jay. Jacques Defarge: C. Burton. Stryver: Harold Carton. Judge: H. Ibberson. Citizen Prosecutor: Martin Conway. The Vengeance: Margaret Yarde. Prosecutor: Judd Green. President: Fred Rains. Jacques 1: Jack Raymond. No. 46: Michael Martin Harvey.
Adapted from the stage play by Freeman Wills and Frederick Longbridge. From *A Tale of Two Cities*.

Sound Films

GRANDFATHER SMALLWEED
British Sound Film Prodns, UK, 1928, 9 mins
D: Hugh Croise. Rel UK Oct 1928.
Smallweed: Bransby Williams.
From *Bleak House*.

SCROOGE
British Sound Film Prodns, UK, 1928, 9 mins
D: Hugh Croise. Rel UK Dec 1928.
Scrooge: Bransby Williams. From *A Christmas Carol*.

RICH MAN'S FOLLY
Paramount Publix Corp, USA, 1931, 80 mins
D: John Cromwell. W: Edward Paramore, Grover Jones.
Rel US 14 Nov 1931, UK 4 Jul 1932.
Brock Trumbull: George Bancroft. Anne Trumbull: Frances Dee. Joe Warren: Robert Ames. Paula Norcross: Juliette Compton. Brock junior: David

Durand. Katherine Trumbull: Dorothy Peterson. McWylie: Harry Allen. Kincaid: Gilbert Emery. Dayton: Guy Oliver. Anne as child: Dawn O'Day. Marton: George McFarlane. Jackson: William Arnold.
From *Dombey and Son*.

OLIVER TWIST
Monogram Pictures Corp, USA, 1933, 8 reels
D: William J. Cowen. P: Herbert Brenon, I. E. Chadwick. W: Elizabeth Meehan. Rel US Mar 1933, UK Sep 1933.
Oliver Twist: Dickie Moore. Fagin: Irving Pichel. Nancy: Doris Lloyd. Bumble: Lionel Belmore. Bill Sikes: William Stage Boyd. Mr. Brownlow: Alec B. Francis. Artful Dodger: Sonny Ray. Rose Maylie: Barbara Kent. Toby Crackit: George K. Arthur. Thomas Chitling: Clyde Cook. Charley Bates: George Nash. Mrs. Corney: Tempe Piggott. Sowerberry: Nelson McDowell. Mrs. Sowerberry: Virginia Sale. Noah Claypole: Bobby Nelson. Grimwig: Harry Holman. Reissued UK 1947.

A DICKENSIAN FANTASY
Gee Films, UK, 1933, 10 mins
D: Aveling Ginever. Rel UK Nov 1933.
All characters: Lawrence Hanray.
"Man reads *A Christmas Carol* and dreams characters come to life" (Gifford).

LE GRILLON DU FOYER (The Cricket on the Hearth)
Acropole Cine Co-op, France, 1933, Length?
D & W: Robert Boudrioz.
John Peerybingle: Jim Gerald. Dot: Nane Germon. Caleb: Gustave Hamilton. Bertha: Jeanne Boitel. Edward: Maurice Cloche. May: Mona Cartier. Tackleton: Guy Favieres. Mrs. Fielding: Henriette Moret. Tilly: Rose May. La mere de Dot: Martha Sarbel. Le Pere de Dot: Pierre Finaly. Also: Paul Bascol.

KLEIN DORRIT (Little Dorrit)
Ondra-Lamac Film GmbH, Germany, 1934, 99 mins
D: Karel Lamac. P: Karel Lamac, Anny Ondra. W: Kurt J. Braun. Rel Germany 21 Aug 1934, US 23 Oct 1935, UK Oct 1935.
Amy Dorrit: Anny Ondra. William Dorrit: Gustav Waldau. Lilli: Hilde Hildebrand. Pit: Kurt Meisel. Arthur Clennam: Matthias Wieman. Also: Antonie Jaeckel, Otto Streckel, Fritz Rasp, Joseph Eichheim.

THE OLD CURIOSITY SHOP
British International Pictures, UK, 1934, 95 mins

D: Thomas Bentley. P: Walter C. Mycroft. W: Margaret Kennedy, Ralph Neale. Rel UK Dec 1934, US Jan 1935.
Grandfather Trent: Ben Webster. Nell: Elaine Benson. Quilp: Hay Petrie. Mrs. Quilp: Beatrix Thompson. Sampson Brass: Gibb McLaughlin. Dick Swiveller: Reginald Purdell. Marchioness: Polly Ward. Single gentleman: James Harcourt. Schoolmaster: J. Fisher White. Sally Brass: Lily Long. Tommy Codlin: Dick Tubb. Short: Roddy Hughes. Mrs. Jarley: Amy Veness. Kit Nubbles: Peter Penrose. George: Wally Patch. Showman: Fred Groves.

GREAT EXPECTATIONS
Universal Pictures, USA, 1934, 100 mins
D: Stuart Walker. W: Gladys Unger. Rel US Dec 1934, UK Jan 1935.
Pip as boy: Georgie Breakston. Estella: Jane Wyatt. Pip: Phillips Holmes. Miss Havisham: Florence Reed. Magwitch: Henry Hull. Jaggers: Francis L. Sullivan. Joe Gargery: Alan Hale. Mrs. Gargery: Rafaela Ottiano. Herbert Pocket: Walter Armitage. Herbert as boy: Jackie Searle. Sarah Pocket: Eily Malyon. Molly: Virginia Hammond. Estella as girl: Anne Howard. Uncle Pumblechook: Forrester Harvey. Orlick: Harry Cording. Compeyson: George Barraud. Drumble: Philip Dakin. Wopsle: Douglas Wood.

DAVID COPPERFIELD
M-G-M, USA, 1935, 133 mins
D: George Cukor. P: David O. Selznick. W: Howard Estabrook, Hugh Walpole. Rel US 18 Jan 1935, UK 7 Mar 1935.
David as boy: Freddie Bartholomew. David as man: Frank Lawton. Micawber: W. C. Fields. Peggotty: Lionel Barrymore. Dora: Maureen O'Sullivan. Agnes Wickfield: Madge Evans. Mr. Wickfield: Lewis Stone. Mrs. Copperfield: Elizabeth Allan. Betsey Trotwood: Edna May Oliver. Mr. Murdstone: Basil Rathbone. Uriah Heep: Roland Young. Clickett: Elsa Lanchester. Mrs. Micawber: Jean Cadell. Nurse Peggotty: Jessie Ralph. Mr. Dick: Lennox Pawle. Miss Murdstone: Violet Kemble-Cooper. Mrs. Gummidge: Una O'Connor. Ham: John Buckler. Steerforth: Hugh Williams. Littimer: Ivan Simpson. Barkis: Herbert Mundin. Little Emily as child: Fay Chaldecott. Agnes as child: Marilyn Knowlden. Little Emily: Florence McKinney. Dr. Chillip: Harry Beresford. Mary Ann: Mabel Colcord. Vicar: Hugh Walpole. Janet: Renee Gad.

MYSTERY OF EDWIN DROOD
Universal Pictures, USA, 1935, 87 mins
D: Stuart Walker. W: John L. Balderston, Gladys Unger. Rel US Mar 1935, UK Jun 1935.
John Jasper: Claude Rains. Neville Landless: Douglass Montgomery. Rosa Bud: Heather Angel. Helena Landless: Valerie Hobson. Edwin Drood:

David Manners. Mr. Crisparkle: Francis L. Sullivan. Hiram Grewgious: Walter Kingsford. Thomas Sapsea: E. E. Clive. Mrs. Tope: Vera Buckland. Durdles: Forrester Harvey. Mrs. Crisparkle: Louise Carter. Miss Twinkleton: Ethel Griffies. Deputy: George Ernest. Princess Puffer: Zeffie Tilbury. Tope: Joseph M. Kerrigan. Mrs. Tisher: Elsa Buchanan.

A TALE OF TWO CITIES
M-G-M, USA, 1935, 121 mins
D: Jack Conway. P: David O. Selznick. W: W. P. Lipscomb, S. N. Behrman. Rel US 25 Dec 1935, UK 10 Apr 1936.
Sydney Carton: Ronald Colman. Lucie Manette: Elizabeth Allan. Madame Defarge: Blanche Yurka. Marquis St. Evremonde: Basil Rathbone. Miss Pross: Edna May Oliver. Stryver: Reginald Owen. Dr. Manette: Henry B. Walthall. Charles Darnay: Donald Woods. Barsad: Walter Catlett. Gaspard: Fritz Lieber. Gabelle: H. B. Warner. Ernest Defarge: Mitchell Lewis. Jarvis Lorry: Claude Gillingwater. Jerry Cruncher: Billy Bevan. Seamstress: Isabel Jewell. La Vengeance: Lucille Laverne. Woodcutter: Tully Marshall. Prosecutor: Ralf Harolde. Lucie's child: Fay Chaldecott. Morveau: John Davidson. Mrs. Cruncher: Eily Malyon. Tellson, Jr.: Tom Ticketts. Old Bailey Judge: E. E. Clive. Jerry Cruncher, Jr.: Donald Haines. Prosecutor: Lawrence Grant. Tribunal Judge: Robert Warwick. Jacques 116: Barlow Borland.

SCROOGE
Twickenham Films, UK, 1935, 78 mins
D: Henry Edwards. P: Julius Hagen, Hans Brahm. W: Seymour Hicks, H. Fowler Mear. Rel UK Aug 1935, US Dec 1935.
Scrooge: Seymour Hicks. Bob Cratchit: Donald Calthrop. Fred: Robert Cochran. Belle: Mary Glynne. Christmas Present: Oscar Asche. Charwoman: Athene Seyler. Poor Man's wife: Mary Lawson. Poor Man: Maurice Evans. Belle's husband: Garry Marsh. Mrs. Cratchit: Barbara Everest. Fred's wife: Eve Gray. Christmas Future: C. V. France. Poulterer: Morris Harvey. Tiny Tim: Philip Frost. Undertaker: D. J. Williams. Laundress: Margaret Yarde. Joe: Hugh E. Wright. Middlemark: Charles Carson. Christmas Past: Marie Ney. Worthington: Hubert Harben. From *A Christmas Carol.*

A CHRISTMAS CAROL
M-G-M, USA, 1938, 69 mins
D: Edwin L. Marin. P: Joseph L. Mankiewicz. W: Hugo Butler. Rel US 16 Dec 1938, UK Dec 1938.
Scrooge: Reginald Owen. Tiny Tim: Terry Kilburn. Bob Cratchit: Gene Lockhart. Mrs. Cratchit: Kathleen Lockhart. Fred: Barry Mackay. Bess: Lynne Carver. Marley's Ghost: Leo G. Carroll. Christmas Past: Ann Ruth-

erford. Christmas Present: Lionel Braham. Christmas Future: D'Arcy Corrigan. Young Scrooge: Ronald Sinclair.

GREAT EXPECTATIONS
Cineguild, UK, 1946, 118 mins
D: David Lean. P: Anthony Havelock-Allan, Ronald Neame. W: Lean, Neame, Havelock-Allan, Kay Walsh, Cecil McGivern. Rel UK Dec 1946.
Pip: John Mills. Estella: Valerie Hobson. Joe Gargery: Bernard Miles. Jaggers: Francis L. Sullivan. Miss Havisham: Martita Hunt. Magwitch: Finlay Currie. Pip as boy: Anthony Wager. Estella as child: Jean Simmons. Herbert Pocket: Alec Guinness. Wemmick: Ivor Barnard. Mrs. Gargery: Freda Jackson. Bentley Drummle: Torin Thatcher. Biddy: Eileen Erskine. Uncle Pumblechook: Hay Petrie. Compeyson: George Jayes. Aged Parent: O. B. Clarence. Sergeant: Richard George. Sarah Pocket: Everly Gregg. Mr. Wopsle: John Burch. Mrs. Wopsle: Grace Denbigh-Russell. Pale Young Gentleman: John Forrest.

NICHOLAS NICKLEBY
Ealing Studios, UK, 1947, 105 mins
D: Alberto Cavalcanti. P: Michael Balcon. W: John Dighton. Rel UK Mar 1947. Reissued UK 1953.
Ralph Nickleby: Cedric Hardwicke. Vincent Crummles: Stanley Holloway. Wackford Squeers: Alfred Drayton. Alfred Mantalini: Cyril Fletcher. Newman Noggs: Bernard Miles. Nicholas Nickleby: Derek Bond. Kate Nickleby: Sally Ann Howes. Mrs. Nickleby: Mary Merrall. Mrs. Squeers: Sybil Thorndike. Mrs. Crummles: Vera Pearce. Miss Knag: Cathleen Nesbitt. Miss la Creevy: Athene Seyler. Sir Mulberry Hawke: Cecil Ramage. Mr. Bray: George Relph. Frank Cheeryble: Emrys Jones. Madame Mantalini: Fay Compton. Madeline Bray: Jill Balcon. Smike: Aubrey Woods. Ned/Charles: James Hayter. Fanny Squeers: Vida Hope. Tim Linkinwater: Roddy Hughes. Lord Verisopht: Timothy Bateson. Mercury: Frederick Burtwell. Wackford Squeers, Jr.: Ray Hermitage. Phoebe: Patricia Hayes. Infant Phenomenon: Una Bart. Miss Snevellici: June Elvin. Mrs. Grudden: Drusilla Wills. Mr. Gregsbury, MP: Michael Shepley. Mr. Gride: Laurence Hanray. Mr. Lillyvick: John Salew. Mr. Snawly: Arthur Brander. Postman: Eliot Makeham.

LEYENDA DE NAVIDAD (A Christmas Carol)
Panorama Films, Spain, 1947, 88 mins
D: Manuel Tamayo.
Scrooge: Jesus Tordesillas. Mary: Lina Yegros. Jack: Angel Picazo. Marley: Ramon Martori. Christmas Past: Fernando Aguirre. Christmas Present: Manuel Requena. Christmas Future: Joaquin Soler Serrano. Elizabeth: Charito Montemar. Bob: Emilio Santiago.

OLIVER TWIST
Cineguild, UK, 1948, 116 mins
D: David Lean. P: Anthony Havelock-Allan. W: David Lean, Stanley Haynes. Rel UK Jul 1948, US Jul 1951.
Bill Sikes: Robert Newton. Fagin: ALec Guinness. Nancy: Kay Walsh. Bumble: Francis L. Sullivan. Oliver Twist: John Howard Davies. Mr. Brownlow: Henry Stephenson. Mrs. Corney: Mary Clare. Artful Dodger: Anthony Newley. Oliver's mother: Josephine Stuart. Monks: Ralph Truman. Mrs. Sowerberry: Kathleen Harrison. Mr. Sowerberry: Gibb McLaughlin. Mrs. Bedwin: Amy Veness. Charlotte: Diana Dors. Mr. Grimwig: Frederick Lloyd. Chief of Police: Maurice Denham. Bookseller: W. G. Fay. Official: Henry Edwards. Singer: Hattie Jacques.

GREAT EXPECTATIONS
BFI, UK, 1949, 6 mins
No. 1 in series *Critic and Film.* Jympson Harman, then film critic for the London *Evening News,* analyzes the editing of the graveyard scene from the opening of David Lean's 1946 film.

SCROOGE
Renown, UK, 1951, 86 mins
D: Brian Desmond Hurst. P: George Minter. W: Noel Langley. Rel UK Oct 1951, US Nov 1951. Reissued UK 1955.
Scrooge: Alastair Sim. Mrs. Dilber: Kathleen Harrison. Mr. Jorkins: Jack Warner. Bob Cratchit: Mervyn Johns. Mrs. Cratchit: Hermione Baddeley. Mr. Wilkins: Clifford Mollison. Jacob Marley: Michael Horden. Scrooge as youth: George Cole. Marley as youth: Patrick McNee. Alice: Rona Anderson. Peter Cratchit: John Charlesworth. Tiny Tim: Glyn Dearman. Christmas Present: Francis de Wolff. Fan: Carol Marsh. Fred: Brian Worth. Old Joe: Miles Malleson. Undertaker: Ernest Thesiger. Christmas Past: Michael Dolan. Fezziwig: Roddy Hughes. Christmas Future: C. Konarski. Laundress: Louise Hampton. Collectors: Noel Howlett, Fred Johnson. Business men: Peter Bull, Douglas Muir. (Entitled *A Christmas Carol* in US.)

THE PICKWICK PAPERS
Renown, UK, 1952, 115 mins
D & W: Noel Langley. P: George Minter, Noel Langley. Rel UK Nov 1952.
Samuel Pickwick: James Hayter. Jingle: Nigel Patrick. Winkle: James Donald. Rachel Wardle: Kathleen Harrison. Mrs. Leo Hunter: Joyce Grenfell. Miss Tomkins: Hermione Gingold. Serjeant Buzfuz: Donald Wolfit. Mrs. Bardell: Hermione Baddeley. Sam Weller: Harry Fowler. Emily Wardle: Diane Hart. Tony Weller: George Robey. Cabman: William Hartnell. Isabella Wardle: Joan Heal. Mr. Wardle: Walter Fitzgerald. Job Trotter: Sam Costa. Tupman: Alexander Gauge. Snodgrass: Lionel Murton. Miss

Witherfield: Athene Seyler. Dodson: D. A. Clarke-Smith. Fogg: Alan Wheatley. Arabella: June Thorburn. Fat boy: Gerald Campion. Grandma Wardle: Mary Merrall. Surgeon: Raymond Lovell. Mr. Justice Stareleigh: Cecil Trouncer. Dr. Slammer: Felix Felton. Aide: Max Adrian. Sergeant Snubbin: Barry Mackay. Mrs. Nupkins: Hattie Jacques. Roker: Noel Purcell. Foreman: Gibb McLaughlin. Dr. Slammer's dancing partner: Dandy Nichols. Mrs. Budger: Helen Goss. Mr. Nupkins: Jack McNaughton. Mr. Perker: Noel Willman. Mrs. Cluppins: Helen Burls. Mrs. Saunders: May Hallett. Jackson: Raf de la Torre. Master Bardell: David Hannaford.

A CHARLES DICKENS CHRISTMAS
Encyclopaedia Britannica, UK/USA, 1956, 22 mins
P: John Barnes.
Mr. Pickwick: Roddy Hughes. Mr. Wardle: Felix Felton. From the chapter "A Good Humoured Christmas" in *The Pickwick Papers*. Made at Merton Park Studios, London. The first Dickens color film.

A TALE OF TWO CITIES
Rank, UK, 1958, 117 mins.
D: Ralph Thomas. P: Betty Box. W: T. E. B. Clarke. Rel UK Feb 1958.
Sydney Carton: Dirk Bogarde. Lucie Manette: Dorothy Tutin. Jarvis Lorry: Cecil Parker. Dr. Manette: Stephen Murray. Miss Pross: Athene Seyler. Charles Darnay: Paul Guers. Marie Gabelle: Marie Versini. Gabelle: Ian Bannen. Jerry Cruncher: Alfie Bass. Stryver: Ernest Clark. Madame Defarge: Rosalie Crutchley. The Vengeance: Freda Jackson. Ernest Defarge: Duncan Lamont. Marquis St. Evremonde: Christopher Lee. Attorney General: Leo McKern. Barsad: Donald Pleasance.

A CHRISTMAS CAROL
Alpha, UK, 1960, 28 mins
D & P: Robert Hartford-Davis. Rel UK Nov 1960.
With: James Hayter, Stewart Brown, Gordon Mulholland.

OLIVER!
Warwick-Romulus, UK, 1968, 146 mins
D: Carol Reed. P: John Woolf. W: Vernon Harris. Rel UK Apr 1968, US Sep 1968.
Fagin: Ron Moody. Nancy: Shani Wallis. Bill Sikes: Oliver Reed. Bumble: Harry Secombe. Magistrate: Hugh Griffith. Artful Dodger: Jack Wild. Charlie Bates: Clive Moss. Oliver Twist: Mark Lester. Mrs. Corney: Peggy Mount. Mr. Sowerberry: Leonard Rossiter. Mr. Brownlow: Joseph O'Connor. Mrs. Sowerberry: Hylda Baker. Bet: Sheila White. Noah Claypole: Kenneth Cranham. Mrs. Bedwin: Megs Jenkins. Jessop: James Hayter. Chairman: Fred Emney.

DAVID COPPERFIELD
Omnibus, UK, 1969, 118 mins
D: Delbert Mann. P: Frederick H. Brogger. W: Jack Pulman. Rel UK Nov 1969. T: NBC TV 15 Mar 1970.
David Copperfield: Robin Phillips. Mr. Micawber: Ralph Richardson. Mr. Dick: Emlyn Williams. Betsey Trotwood: Edith Evans. Mr. Peggotty: Michael Redgrave. Mr. Tungay: Richard Attenborough. Barkis: Cyril Cusack. Dora: Pamela Franklin. Agnes Wickfield: Susan Hampshire. Mrs. Micawber: Wendy Hiller. Uriah Heep: Ron Moody. Mr. Creakle: Laurence Olivier. Clara Copperfield: Isobel Black. Emily: Sinead Cusack. Mr. Murdstone: James Donald. Porter: James Hayter. Clara Peggotty: Megs Jenkins. Jane Murdstone: Anna Massey. Traddles: Nicholas Pennell. Steerforth: Corin Redgrave. Quinion: Liam Redmond.

UNEASY DREAMS; THE LIFE OF MR. PICKWICK
?, UK, 1970, 26 mins
D: Jeremy Marre.
A film biography that uses cartoons, reconstructed scenes, and clips from Dickens films.

SCROOGE
Waterbury Films, UK, 1970, 118 mins
D: Ronald Neame. P: Leslie Bricusse, Robert Solo. W: Leslie Bricusse. Rel UK Nov 1970.
Scrooge: Albert Finney. Ghost of Jacob Marley: Alec Guinness. Christmas Past: Edith Evans. Christmas Present: Kenneth More. Fred: Michael Medwin. Fezziwig: Laurence Naismith. Bob Cratchit: David Collings. Tom Jenkins: Anton Rodgers. Isabel: Suzanne Neve. Mrs. Cratchit: Frances Cuka. Charity gentlemen: Derek Francis, Roy Kinnear. Fred's wife: Mary Peach. Christmas Yet To Come: Paddy Stone. Mrs. Fezziwig: Kay Walsh. Friend: Gordon Jackson. Tiny Tim: Richard Beaumont.

GREAT EXPECTATIONS
?, Switzerland, 1971, 35 mins
D: Leopold H. Ginner.
With: Petra von der Linde, Volker Vogeler, Gerard Vandenberg.

GREAT EXPECTATIONS
Transcontinental, UK, 1974, 124 mins
D: Joseph Hardy. P: Robert Fryer. W: Sherman Yellen. T: NBC TV 22 Nov 1974. Rel UK Jan 1976.
Pip: Michael York. Estella: Sarah Miles. Miss Havisham: Margaret Leighton. Magwitch: James Mason. Uncle Pumblechook: Robert Morley. Jaggers: Anthony Quayle. Biddy: Heather Sears. Joe Gargery: Joss Ackland. Her-

bert Pocket: Andrew Ray. Bentley Drummle: James Faulkner. Mrs. Gargery: Rachel Roberts. Pip as boy: Simon Gipps-Kent. Sarah Pocket: Maria Charles. Sergeant: Noel Trevarthen. Molly: Celia Hewitt. Mr. Wopsle: John Clive. Compeyson: Sam Kydd. Wemmick: Peter Bull. Herbert Pocket as boy: Richard Beaumont. (For full cast and credits see MFB Dec 1975.)

THE PASSIONS OF CAROL
Ambar Films, USA, 1975, 76 mins
D & W: Amanda Barton. Rel US 14 Mar 1975.
Carol Screwge: Mary Stuart. Marley: Marc Stevens. Mr. Hatchet: Jamie Gillis. Mrs. Hatchet: Kim Pope. Spirits: Arturo Millhouse, Kevin Andre, Helmut Richler.

MISTER QUILP
Readers Digest, UK, 1975, 119 mins
D: Michael Tuchner. P: Helen M. Strauss. W: Louis and Irene Camp. Rel US 15 Oct 1975, UK Nov 1975.
Daniel Quilp: Anthony Newley. Richard Swiveller: David Hemmings. Sampson Brass: David Warner. Grandfather: Michael Hordern. Henry Trent: Paul Rogers. Sally Brass: Jill Bennett. Nell Trent: Sarah Jane Varley. Duchess: Sarah Webb. Mrs. Jarley: Mona Washbourne. Mrs. Quilp: Yvonne Antrobus. Kit: Peter Duncan. (For full cast and credits, see MFB Oct 1975.) Retitled *The Old Curiosity Shop.*

OLIVER TWIST
Claridge Group/Grafton, UK, 1982, 102 mins
D: Clive Donner. P: Ted Child, Norton Romsey. W: James Goldman. T: CBS TV 23 Mar 1982. Rel UK Nov 1983.
Fagin: George C. Scott. Bill Sikes: Tim Curry. Mr. Brownlow: Michael Hordern. Mr. Bumble: Timothy West. Mrs. Mann: Eileen Atkins. Nancy: Cherie Lunghi. Monks: Oliver Cotton. Oliver Twist: Richard Charles. Artful Dodger: Martin Tempest. Charlie Bates: Matthew Duke. Rose Maylie: Eleanor David. Mr. Sowerberry: Philip Locke. Mrs. Corney: Ann Tirard. Mrs. Sowerberry: Ann Beach. Mrs. Bedwin: Brenda Cowling. Oliver's mother: Lysette Anthony. Noah Claypole: Philip Davis. Chairman: Michael Logan. Mr. Fang: John Savident. Charlotte: Debbie Arnold. (For full cast and credits, see MFB Nov 1983.)

MICKEY'S CHRISTMAS CAROL
Walt Disney Prodns, USA, 1983, 30 mins
D & P: Burny Mattinson. Rel UK Dec 1983.
Scrooge: Uncle Scrooge McDuck. Bob Cratchit: Mickey Mouse. Mrs. Cratchit: Minnie Mouse. Scrooge's nephew: Donald Duck. Marley's Ghost:

Goofy. Christmas Past: Jiminy Cricket. Voice of Scrooge McDuck: Alan Young.

A CHRISTMAS CAROL
Entertainment Partners, UK, 1984, 101 mins
D: Clive Donner. P: William F. Storke, Alfred R. Kelman. W: Roger O. Hirson. Rel UK Dec 1984. T: CBS TV 17 Dec 1984.
Scrooge: George C. Scott. Ghost of Jacob Marley: Frank Finlay. Christmas Past: Angela Pleasance. Christmas Present: Edward Woodward. Christmas Yet To Come: Michael Carter. Bob Cratchit: David Warner. Mrs. Cratchit: Susannah York. Tiny Tim: Anthony Walters. Fred Holywell: Roger Reese. Janet Holywell: Caroline Langrishe. Belle: Lucy Gutteridge. Silas Scrooge: Nigel Davenport. Young Scrooge: Mark Strickson. Fan: Joanne Whalley. Fezziwig: Timothy Bateson. (For full cast and credits, see MFB Dec 1984.)

LITTLE DORRIT
Sands Films/Canon, UK, 1987, Part 1 176 mins, Part 2 181 mins
D & W: Christine Edzard. P: John Brabourne, Richard Goodwin. Rel UK Dec 1987.
Arthur Clennam: Derek Jacobi. Mrs. Clennam: Joan Greenwood. Flintwinch: Max Wall. Affery: Patricia Hayes. Flora Finching: Miriam Margolyes. Mr. Casby: Bill Fraser. Mr. Pancks: Roshan Seth. Tite Barnacle: John Savident. Clarence Barnacle: Brian Pettifer. Ferdinand Barnacle: John Harding. Daniel Doyce: Edward Burnham. Mr. Rugg: Harold Innocent. Mr. Plornish: Christopher Whittingham. Mrs. Plornish: Ruth Mitchell. William Dorrit: Alec Guinness. Frederick Dorrit: Cyril Cusack. Little Dorrit (Amy): Ruth Pickering. Fanny Dorrit: Amelda Brown. Tip Dorrit: Daniel Chatto. Bob: Howard Goorney. Milliner: Celia Bannerman. Dancing master: Murray Melvin. John Chivery: Richard Stirling. Mrs. Merdle: Eleanor Bron. Mr. Merdle: Michael Elphick. Lord Decimus Barnacle: Robert Morley. Bishop: Alan Bennett. Duchess: Brenda Bruce. Mrs. Chivery: Jo Warne. Maggy: Pauline Quirke.
(For full cast, numbering 215, and credits, see MFB Dec 1987.)

TEMPOS DIFICEIS, ESTE TEMPO (Hard Times)
Botelho/Artificial Eye, Portugal/UK, 1988, 96 mins
D, P & W: João Botelho. Rel UK 2 June 1989.
Tomazinho Cremalheira (Tom Gradgrind, Jr.): Luis Estrela. Luisa Cremalheira (Louisa Gradgrind): Julia Britton (voice Rita Blanco). D. Tereza Cremalheira (Mrs. Gradgrind): Isabel de Castro. Tomaz Cremalheira (Tom Gradgrind): Ruy Furtado. Cecilia (Cissy Jupe): Ines Madeiros. Jose Grandela (Mr. Bounderby): Henrique Viana. Raquel (Rachel): Lia Gama. Sebastião (Stephen Blackpool): Joaquim Mendes. Sebastião's wife: Isabel Ruth. Dr. Julio Vaz Simoes (Capt. Harthouse): Pedro Cabrita Reis. D.

Josefina Vilaverde (Mrs. Sparsit): Eunice Munoz. Bastos (Bitzer): Pedro Hestnes.
(For full cast and credits, see MFB Jul 1989.)

SCROOGED
Paramount/Mirage Prodns, USA, 1988, 101 mins
D: Richard Donner. P: Donner, Art Linson. W: Mitch Glazer, Michael O'Donoghue. Rel US & UK Nov 1988.
Frances Xavier Cross: Bill Murray. Lew Hayward: John Forsythe. Ghost of Christmas Past: David Johansen. Ghost of Christmas Present: Carol Kane.
From *A Christmas Carol*.
(For full cast and credits, see MFB Dec 1988.)

OLIVER AND COMPANY
Walt Disney Studios, USA, 1988, 74 mins
D: George Scribner. Rel US Nov 1988, UK Jan 1989.
From *Oliver Twist*.
(For full production credits, see MFB Jan 1990.)

THE MUPPET CHRISTMAS CAROL
Walt Disney/Jim Henson, USA, 1992, 86 mins
D: Brian Henson. P: Henson, Martin G. Baker. W: Jerry Juhl. Rel UK Dec 1992.
Scrooge: Michael Caine. Bob Cratchit: Kermit the Frog. Emily Cratchit: Miss Piggy. Charles Dickens: The Great Gonzo. Rizzo the rat: Himself. Fozziwig: Fozzie Bear. Fred: Stephen Mackintosh. Belle: Meredith Braun. Clara: Robin Weaver. Ghost of Christmas Present: Donald Austen. Scrooge, 7: Edward Sanders. Scrooge, 9: Theo Sanders. Scrooge, 11: Kristopher Milnes. Scrooge, 14: Russell Martin. Scrooge, 18: Raymond Coulthard.
(For full credits, see S&S Feb 1993.)

THE MYSTERY OF EDWIN DROOD
Bevanfield Films, UK, 1993, 100 mins
D & W: Timothy Forder. P: Keith Hayley. Rel UK 28 Apr 1993.
John Jasper: Robert Powell. Helena Landless: Michelle Evans. Edwin Drood: Jonathan Phillips. Neville Landless: Rupert Rainsford. Rosa Bud: Finty Williams. Tope: Ken Wynne. Opium woman: Kate Williams. Reverend Crisparkle: Peter Pacey. Mrs. Crisparkle: Nanette Newman. Dean: Ronald Fraser. Miss Twinkleton: Gemma Craven. Bazzard: Barry Evans. Crisparkle's maid: Emma Healey. Minor canon: David Homewood. Mr. Grewgious: Glyn Houston. Mr. Sapsea: Freddie Jones. Sapsea's maid: Nabila Khashoggi. Durdles: Andrew Sachs. Deputy: Leonard Kirby. Mrs. Tope: Rosemary Leach. Reverend Honeythunder: Marc Sinden. Choir boy:

Gareth Arnold. Nun's maid: Delia Lindsay. Wagon driver: Geoff Loynes. Head ruffian: Rocky Taylor.

Television and Video Productions

MR. PICKWICK
BBC, UK, 1936, 25 mins
Extracts from Albert Coates's opera, transmitted by the London Television Service of the BBC from Alexandra Palace, 13 Nov 1936.

BARDELL AGAINST PICKWICK
BBC, UK, 1938, 25 mins
P & W: Stephen Harrison. T: 6 & 11 Jul 1938.
Sam Weller: Alan Wheatley. Sergeant Buzfuz: A. R. Whatmore. Winkle: Ernest Jay. Sergeant Snubbin: Wilfred Fletcher. Foreman of Jury: Christopher Steele. Mr. Skimpin: Mark Dignam. Mr. Justice Stareleigh: Ray Byford. Mr. Pickwick: Cameron Hall. Mrs. Cluppins: Edie Martin. Mrs. Bardell: Jean Webster Brough. Mr. Perker: Roddy Hughes. Tupman: Kaye Seely. Fogg: Patrick Glover. Dodson: Andre Morell. Mr. Phunky: Stuart Latham. Clerk of Court: Harding Steerman. Master Bardell: Arthur Payne.
From *The Pickwick Papers*.

A CHRISTMAS CAROL
WBKB, USA, 1945, 30 mins
D, P & W: Beulah Zachary. T: 20 Dec 1945.
Presented by Admiral Radio on the WBKB Chicago channel. An amateur production.

THE STRANGE CHRISTMAS DINNER
?, USA, 1945, Length?
From *A Christmas Carol*.

BARDELL AGAINST PICKWICK
BBC, UK, 1946, 45 mins
P & W: Stephen Harrison. T: 25 & 27 Sep 1946.
Mr. Pickwick: John Salew. Sam Weller: Alan Wheatley. Mr. Justice Stareleigh: Aubrey Mallalieu. Sergeant Buzfuz: James Gale. Mrs. Bardell: Jean Webster Brough. Mr. Skimpin: Richard Hurndall. Sergeant Snubbin: Cecil Bevan. Mr. Phunky: Stuart Latham. Winkle: Charles Heslop. Tupman: Fred Essex. Mrs. Cluppins: Edie Martin. Dodson: Alban Blakelock.

Fogg: Peter Bennett. Foreman of Jury: Wilfrid Caithness. Clerk of Court: Nicholas Hill. Master Bardell: Brian Parker. From *The Pickwick Papers*.

CHRISTMAS NIGHT
BBC, UK, 1946, 60 mins
P & W: Philip Bate. T: 25 Dec 1946.
A family fireside story told by Hubert Foss, with a ballet, and with music by Vaughan Williams. From *A Christmas Carol*.

A CHRISTMAS CAROL
WABD, DuMont, USA, 1947, 60 mins
D & P: James L. Caddigan. T: 25 Dec 1947.
Scrooge: John Carradine. Also: Bernard Hughes, Eve Marie Saint, Somer Alder, Sam Fertig, Helen Stenborg, Jonathan Marlowe.

THE ONLY WAY
BBC, UK, 1948, 90 mins
P: Fred O'Donovan. T: 1 & 3 Feb 1948.
Sydney Carton: Andrew Osborn. Dr. Manette: Harold Scott. Jarvis Lorry: Graveley Edwards. Charles Darnay: Hattan Duprez. Lucie Manette: Jeanette Tregarthen. Jean Defarge: Roger Snowdon. Marquis St. Evremonde: Alan Judd. Vicomte St. Evremonde: Philip Ashley. Peasant: MacGregor Urquhart. Ernest Defarge: Thomas Gallagher. Sergeant Stryver: Alastair Hunter. President: Michael O'Halloran. Public Prosecutor: Sydney Tafler. Comte de Fauchet: Geoffrey Steele. M. de Maury: Richard Fulford. Marquis de Boulanvilliers: John Arnatt. Gabelle: Stanley Lemin. Barsad: Roland Caswell. Citizen: George Selway. The Vengeance: Rose Power. Citizeness: Anne Blake. Mimi: Viola Merrett. From the stage play by Freeman Wills and Frederick Longbridge; based on *A Tale of Two Cities*.

A CHRISTMAS CAROL
NBC, USA, 1948, 60 mins
D & P: Fred Coe. W: Samuel Taylor. T: 19 Dec 1948. In series *Philco Television Playhouse*.
Scrooge: Dennis King. Also: Bing Crosby and the Mitchell Boys Choir.

DICKENS'S CHRISTMAS CAROL
ABC, USA, 1948, 60 mins
P: Leonard Steinman. T: 24 Dec 1948.
A performance by the Rufus Rose Marionettes.

THE CRICKET ON THE HEARTH
NBC, USA, 1949, 30 mins
D: Sobey Martin. P: Eugene Laurie. W: Louis Lantz.

Television and Video Productions   147

T: 8 Jul 1949.
With: Heather Wilde, Thomas P. Dillon.
TV film made by Marshal Grant/Realm TV Productions.

A CHRISTMAS CAROL
BBC, UK, 1950, 90 mins
P: Eric Fawcett. W: Dominic Roche, Eric Fawcett.
T: 25 and 27 Dec 1950.
Scrooge: Bransby Williams. Bob Cratchit: John Ruddock. Marley's Ghost: W. E. Holloway. Mrs. Dilber: Dorothy Summers. Mrs. Cratchit: Kathleen Saintsbury. Fred: Robert Cawdron. Portly gentleman: Julian d'Albie. Crossing sweeper: Leonard Sharp. Night watchman: John Bentley. Christmas Past: Arthur Hambling. Boy Scrooge: Sean Lynch. Fanny: Patricia Fryer. Fiancee: Barbara Murray. Young Scrooge: John Bentley. Christmas Present: Julian d'Albie. Boy Cratchit: Adrian Evans. Girl Cratchit: Shirley Hose. Martha Cratchit: Pamela Cameron. Tiny Tim: Thomas Moore. Peter Cratchit: John Young. Waifs: Michael Edwards, Patricia Fryer. Christmas Yet To Come: W. E. Holloway. Gentlemen of Stock Exchange: Arthur Hambling, Howard Douglas, Stanley Vines. Joe: Leonard Sharp. Boy with goose: Tony Lyons. Mrs. Fred: Ann Wriggs.

MARLEY'S GHOST
CBS, USA, 1951, 30 mins
T: 26 June 1951. In series *Danger*.
With: Joseph Anthony, Rita Gam.

EMLYN WILLIAMS AS CHARLES DICKENS
BBC, UK, 1951, 35 mins
T: 10 Dec 1951. Introduced by Dilys Powell.
Excerpts from Emlyn Williams's one-man show of readings in the manner of the author.

A CHRISTMAS CAROL
NBC, USA, 1951, 30 mins
D: Gordon Duff. P: Fred Coe. W: David Swift.
T: 25 Dec 1951. In series *Fireside Theatre*.
Scrooge: Ralph Richardson. Marley's Ghost: Malcolm Keen. Bob Cratchit: Norman Barr. Tiny Tim: Robert Hay Smith. Christmas Present: Arthur Treacher. Christmas Past: Melville Cooper. Mrs. Cratchit: Margaret Phillips. Mrs. Fezziwig: Gypsy Raine. Carol singer: Bobby White. Ghost of Christmas Present: Alan Napier.

THE MYSTERY OF EDWIN DROOD
CBS, USA, 1952, Serial 2x60 mins

D & P: Robert Stevens: W: Halstead Welles. T: 18 & 25 Mar 1952. In series *Suspense*.
John Jasper John Baragrey. Rosa Bud: Susan Douglas. Also: William Smithers, Betty Sinclair, Elizabeth Johnson.

HUNTED DOWN
CBS, USA, 1952, 60 mins
T: 20 May 1952. In series *Suspense*.
With: John Baragrey.

THE CRICKET ON THE HEARTH
NBC, USA, 1952, 60 mins
T: 11 Jun 1952. In series *Kraft Television Theatre*.
With: Grace Kelly, Russell Hardie.

A TALE OF TWO CITIES
BBC, UK, 1952, 15 mins
P: Pamela Brown. Devised & introduced: Robert MacDermot. T: 31 Jul 1952. In series *How Does It End?* based on famous books.
Sydney Carton/Charles Darnay: Desmond Llewellyn. Lucie Manette: Sheila Shand Gibbs. Dr. Manette: Leslie Firth. Madame Defarge: Margot van der Burgh. Mons. Defarge: Francis de Wolff.

THE HUMOUR OF DICKENS
BBC, UK, 1952, 35 mins
T: 14 Sep 1952.
Emlyn Williams and a group of distinguished British cartoonists reviewed a selection of Dickens illustrations old and new. With: Low, Searle, Vicky, Lancaster, Illingworth, Ardizzone.

THE PICKWICK PAPERS
BBC, UK, 1952, Serial, 7x30 mins
P: Douglas Allen. W: Robert Christie. Settings: Richard Greenhough, based on Phiz illustrations. T: 6 Dec 1952 to 17 Jan 1953. *The first Dickens television serial*. Mr. Pickwick: George Howe. Snodgrass: Robert Beaumont. Winkle: Geoffrey Sumner. Tupman: Campbell Gray. Dr. Slammer: Aubrey Mather. Lt. Payne: Percy Herbert. Mr. Wardle: David Horne. Joe: Rodney Bewes. Emily Wardle: Margaret Lane. Isabella Wardle: Claire Pollock. Rachel Wardle: Betty Marsden. Old Mrs. Wardle: Nancy Roberts. Jingle: Peter Copley. Mr. Perker: Wyndham Goldie. Sam Weller: Sam Kydd. Mrs. Bardell: Edna Morris. Master Bardell: John Pitt. Mistress of Seminary: Elizabeth Maude. Cook at Seminary: Madge Brindley. Jackson: John Vere. Dodson: Frank Bird. Fogg: Richard Caldicott. Tony Weller: Peter Bull. Mrs. Cluppins: Violet Gould. Mrs. Weller: Janet Voye. Mr. Stiggins: Kynaston

Television and Video Productions 149

Reeves. Arabella Allen: Petra Davies. Mary: Fanny Carby. Benjamin Allen: Gordon Bell. Bob Sawyer: Robert Brown. Sergeant Snubbin: Erik Chitty. Sergeant Buzfuz: Arthur Young. Mr. Justice Stareleigh: Aubrey Mather.

THE TRIAL OF MR. PICKWICK
CBS, USA, 1952, 27 mins
D: Ralph Nelson. P: William Spier. W: Alistair Cooke. T: 21 Dec 1952. In series *Omnibus*.
Mr. Pickwick: Mercer McCleod. Buzfuz: Francis L. Sullivan. Snubbin: Richard Purdy. Judge: Sir Cedric Hardwicke.

A CHRISTMAS CAROL
NBC, USA, 1952, 60 mins
D: Fielder Cook. W: Robert Howard Lindsay. T: 24 Dec 1952. In series *Kraft Television Theatre*.
Scrooge: Malcolm Keen. Marley's Ghost: Richard Purdy. Bob Cratchit: Harry Townes. Mrs. Cratchit: Valerie Cossart. Christmas Present: Melville Cooper. Christmas Past: Noel Leslie.

A CHRISTMAS CAROL
?, USA, 1952 ,30 mins
P: Jerry Fairbanks. A Stokey & Ebert production on kinescope. T: 1952; repeated 23 Dec 1983 on CBN.
Scrooge: Taylor Holmes. Tiny Tim: Bobby Hyatt. Narrator: Vincent Price.

THE FANCY BALL
CBS, USA, 1953, c30 mins
T: 26 Apr 1953. Program segment in series *Omnibus*. Emlyn Williams, as Charles Dickens, reading from *A Tale of Two Cities*.

A TALE OF TWO CITIES
ABC, USA, 1953, 2x30 mins
D: Dik Darley. P: Robert Banker. W: John Blahos. M: Dimitri Tiomkin. T: 3 & 10 May 1953. In series *ABC Album*.
Sydney Carton: Wendell Corey. Charles Darnay: Carleton Young. Lucie Manette: Wandra Hendrix. Dr. Manette: Murray Matheson. Mme. Defarge: Judith Evelyn.

THE SIGNALMAN
CBS, USA, 1953, 30 mins
W: Ben Radin. T: 23 Jun 1953. In series *Suspense*.
With: Boris Karloff, Alan Webb.

BRANSBY WILLIAMS
BBC, UK, 1953, 25 mins
P: Kenneth Milne Buckley. T: 21 Dec 1953. R: 21 Dec 1955.
A telerecording of Williams as Scrooge in his own version of *A Christmas Carol*.

A CHRISTMAS CAROL
ABC, USA, 1953, 60 mins
T: 24 Dec 1953. In series *Kraft Television Theatre*.
Scrooge: Melville Cooper. Also: Noel Leslie, Dennis Greene, Harry Townes, Geoffrey Lumb, Valerie Cossart.

CHRISTMAS CAROL
CBS, USA, 1953, 30 mins
In series *Topper*. Cosmo Topper: Leo G. Carroll.

GREAT EXPECTATIONS
NBC, USA, 1954, 2x60 mins
D: Norman Felton. W: Dora Folliott. T: 14 & 21 June 1954.
In series *Robert Montgomery Presents*.
Pip as boy: Rex Thompson. Pip as man: Roddy McDowall. Miss Havisham: Estelle Winwood. Also: Jacques Aubuchon, Scott Forbes, Malcolm Lee Beggs.
Part I The Promise. Part II The Reality.

DAVID COPPERFIELD
NBC, USA, 1954, 2x60 mins
D: Norman Felton. W: Dora Folliott. T: 20 & 27 Dec 1954. In series *Robert Montgomery Presents*.
David as boy: Rex Thompson. David as man: David Cole. Uriah Heep: Earl Montgomery. Micawber: J. Pat O'Malley. Jane Murdstone: Cavada Humphrey. Also: Ralph Bunker, Frederick Worlock, Sarah Marshall, Ethel Owen, Isobel Elsom, Frederic Tozere, Betty Sinclair, Lynn Bailey.

A CHRISTMAS CAROL
CBS, USA, 1954, 60 mins
D & P: Ralph Levy. W: Maxwell Anderson. M: Bernard Herrman. T: 23 Dec 1954. R: 15 Dec 1955. In series *Shower of Stars*.
Scrooge: Frederic March. Marley's Ghost: Basil Rathbone. Scrooge's nephew/Christmas Present: Ray Middleton. Bob Cratchit: Bob Sweeney. Tiny Tim: Christopher Cook. Mrs. Cratchit: Queenie Leonard. Young Scrooge: Craig Hill. Belle/Spirit of Christmas Past: Sally Fraser. Belinda: Janine Perrau. Peter: Peter Miles. Scrooge's housekeeper: Juney Ellis. Lamplighter: John Murphy. Man in bookshop: Billy Griffiths. Boy in candy

shop: Jimmy Baird. Portly gentlemen: Rex Evans, Tony Pennington. Children: Ronnie and Judy Franklin. Fezziwig: Dick Elliott. Goose boy: John Meek. Town crier: John Murphy. Woman: Ezelle Poule. Also the Roger Wagner Chorale. Host: William Lundigan.

THE SIGNALMAN
CBS, USA, 1954, 15 mins
In *Christmas Story Hour*. T: 25 Dec 1954. With: Monty Woolley.

BRANSBY WILLIAMS
BBC, UK, 1954 to 1956, ?x15 mins
Between Dec 1954 and Dec 1956, Williams appeared in at least eighteen 15-minute programs, reminiscing about his long career. Some of the programs may have been repeats, and some certainly included examples of his Dickens studies.

THE MAN FROM THE MOORS
BBC, UK, 1955, 40 mins
P & W: Shaun Sutton. A play for Easter, first shown in Children's Television on Easter Sunday, 10 Apr 1955. R: 30 Mar 1956 & 28 May 1961.
Mr. Dickens: Barry Letts. Polly: Dorothy Gordon. Tom: Jonathan Swift. Stubbs: Dawson France. Mrs. Grimshaw: Gladys Spencer. Mr. Grimshaw: Raymond Rollett. Mr. Milling: Leonard Sachs. Charley: James Doran. Sam: Barrie Martin. Ned: Kenneth Woodage.

BARDELL V. PICKWICK
ABC, UK, 1955, 30 mins
D: Desmond Davis. W: George Kerr, Desmond Davis. T: 25 Sep 1955, in series *Theatre Royal*. US 14 Nov 1956, in series *Lilli Palmer Theatre*.
Mr. Pickwick: Roddy Hughes. Sergeant Buzfuz: Donald Wolfit. Mrs. Bardell: Edna Morris. Snodgrass: Robert Lankasheer. Winkle: Desmond Walter-Ellis. Tupman: Campbell Gray. Master Bardell: Graham Harper. Dodson: Raymond Rollett. Fogg: Tony Sympson. Mr. Perker: George Benson. Clerk: Alec Finter. Judge: Frank Birch. Sergeant Snubbin: John Boddington. Sam Weller: Sam Kydd. Groffin: Stuart Latham. From *The Pickwick Papers*.

THE SMALL SERVANT
NBC, USA, 1955, 60 mins
W: S. I. Abelow, Robert Cenedela. T: 30 Oct 1955. In series *Alcoa Hour*.
Dick Swiveller: Laurence Harvey. Small servant: Diane Cilento. From *The Old Curiosity Shop*.

THE MERRY CHRISTMAS
Associated Rediffusion, UK, 1955, 45 mins
P: Douglas Hurn. W: Donald Cotton. M: Brian Burke. MD: Steve Race. T: 21 Dec 1955.
Scrooge: Hugh Griffith. Night watchman: John Gower. Mr. Topper: Michael O'Halloran. Bob Cratchit: Norman Tyrrell. Fred: Peter Reeves. Marley's Ghost: Edmund Willard. Christmas Past: Martin Lawrence. Mr. Fezziwig: George Murcell. Young Scrooge: Peter Reeves. Belle: Eira Heath. Mrs. Cratchit: Irene Byatt. Tiny Tim: Barry Huband. Mrs. Fred: Madi Head.
From *A Christmas Carol*.

THE STORY OF THE CHRISTMAS CAROL
NBC, USA, 1955, 30 mins
D: David Barnhizer. T: 22 Dec 1955 on Chicago stations WNBQ and WMAQ.
Narrator: Ken Nordine. Scrooge: Norman Gottschalk. Bob Cratchit: Eugene Troobnick. Mrs. Cratchit: Gertrude Breen. Tiny Tim: Morton Freedman. Fezziwig: Kurt Kupfer. Young Scrooge: George Greer. From *A Christmas Carol*.

CHRISTMAS EVE WITH CHARLES LAUGHTON
NBC, USA, 1955, 60 mins
D: Boris Segal. T: 24 Dec 1955.
A program of readings that included passages from *The Pickwick Papers*.

THE MATING OF WATKINS TOTTLE
NBC, USA, 1956, 60 mins
T: 6 Mar 1956. In series *Matinee Theatre*.
Based on "A Passage in the Life of Mr. Watkins Tottle" from *Sketches By Boz*.

DAVID COPPERFIELD
BBC, UK, 1956, Serial 13x30 mins
D: Stuart Burge. P: Douglas Allen. W: Vincent Tilsley. T: 28 Sep to 21 Dec 1956. R: 4 Jan to 29 Mar 1957.
David as boy: Leonard Cracknell. David's mother: Diane Fairfax. Clara Peggotty: Edna Morris. Mr. Murdstone: William Devlin. Barkis: Meadows White. Daniel Peggotty: George Woodbridge. Ham: Andrew Downie. Mrs. Gummidge: Mabel Constanduros. Emily as child: Patricia Roots. Jane Murdstone: Dorothy Black. Waiter: Sam Kydd. Mr. Tungay: Wensley Pithey. Mr. Creakle: Elwyn Brook-Jones. Young Traddles: Keith Davis. Topsawyer: David Tilley. Kemble: Terry Cooke. Peel: Brian Franklin. Steerforth: Anthony Tancred. Mealy Potatoes: Ian Thompson. Mick Walker: James Doran. Mr. Quinion: John Kidd. Micawber: Hilton Edwards.

Mrs. Micawber: Olga Lindo. Betsey Trotwood: Sonia Dresdel. Mr. Dick: Richard Goolden. Janet: Ann Cherry. Mr. Wickfield: George Skillan. Uriah Heep: Maxwell Shaw. Young Agnes: Valerie Smith. Littimer: John Vere. Young Rosa: Jill Balcon. Mrs. Steerforth: Mary Hinton. David Copperfield: Robert Hardy. Mr. Spenlowe: Andre van Gyseghem. Jorkins: Geoffrey Tyrrell. Mrs. Crupp: Vi Stevens. Traddles: Bernard Cribbins. Mr. Guppidge: Graham Crowden. Agnes Wickfield: Mary Watson. Lavinia Spenlowe: Joan Hickson. Clarissa Spenlowe: Nora Nicholson. Dora Spenlowe: Sheila Shand Gibbs. Rosa Dartle: Gwen Watford. Little Emily: Dorothy Gordon. Mrs. Heep: Gretchen Franklin. Mr. Bellstruther: Peter Copley. Sophy Traddles: Barbara Bolton.
(Episode 12, repeated on 23 Mar 1957, was followed by a 10-minute program of *Songs That Dickens Knew*, sung by Marian Studholme.)

THE STINGIEST MAN IN TOWN
NBC, USA, 1956, 90 mins
D: Daniel Petrie. P: Joel Spector. W: Janice Torr. M: Fred Spielman. T: 23 Dec 1956. In series *Alcoa Hour*. Scrooge: Basil Rathbone. Marley's Ghost: Robert Weede. Bob Cratchit: Martyn Green. Tiny Tim: Dennis Kohler. Also: Vic Damone, Johnny Desmond, Patrice Munsel, John McGiver, Betty Madigan, Robert Wright, Alice Frost, Olive Dunbar, Bryan Herbert, Philippa Bevans, Ian Martin, Keith Harrington, Richard Morse, Karol Ann Trautman, Karson Woods, Karin Wolfe, John Heawood, The Four Lads. From *A Christmas Carol*.

LE GRILLON DU FOYER (The Cricket on the Hearth)
CBC, Canada, 1956, 60 mins
D: Paul Leduc. W: Francois Valere. T: 30 Dec 1956.
In series Théâtre Populaire, by Societé Radio-Canada. May Fielding: Monique Champagne. Caleb Plummer: Camille Ducharme. Dot Peerybingle: Marjolaine Hebert. Bertha Plummer: Helene Loiselle. Tackleton: Henri Norbet. John Peerybingle: Gilles Pelletier. Mme. Fielding: Rose Rey-Duzil. Edouard Plummer: Pierre Valcour.

MUSIC REVIEW
CBS, USA, 1956, 30 mins
Connie Brooks: Eve Arden. In series *Our Miss Brooks*. From *A Christmas Carol*.

THE BOOTS AT THE HOLLY TREE INN
BBC, UK, 1957, 15 mins
T: 23 Feb 1957. R: 21 Apr 1958. In series *Moira Lister Tells a Story*. From *The Holly Tree*.

A TALE OF TWO CITIES
BBC, UK, 1957, Serial 8x30 mins
P: Kevin Sheldon. W: John Keir Cross. T: 28 Jul to 15 Sep 1957. R: 21 Apr to 16 Jun 1959.
Jarvis Lorry: Mervyn Johns. Lucie Manette: Wendy Hutchinson. Dr. Manette: Fred Fairclough. Miss Pross: Joan Ingram. Mme. Defarge: Margaretta Scott. Ernest Defarge: Kenneth Thornett. Jerry Cruncher: Ronald Radd. Jacques 1, 2, and 3: Julian Orchard, Kenneth Warren, Anthony Bate. Charles Darnay: Edward de Souza. Sydney Carton: Peter Wyngarde. Sergeant Stryver: Gareth Jones. Barsad: Gordon Gostelow. Marquis St. Evremonde: Heron Carvic. Gabelle: Harry Moore. Jerry Cruncher, Jr.: Malcolm Knight. Mrs. Cruncher: Joan Duan. Seamstress: Carol Marsh.

NICHOLAS NICKLEBY
BBC, UK, 1957, Serial 10x30 mins
D: Eric Taylor. W: Vincent Tilsley. T: 18 Oct to 20 Dec 1957. R: 4 Apr to 6 June 1958.
Nicholas Nickleby: William Russell. Newman Noggs: Richard Wordsworth. Ralph Nickleby: Malcolm Keen. Miss LaCreevy: Rosamund Greenwood. Mrs. Nickleby: Gillian Lind. Kate Nickleby: Jennifer Wilson. Wackford Squeers: Esmond Knight. Master Wackford: David Lord/Keith Davis. Mr. Snawley: Roy Hepworth. Mr. Mantalini: Carl Bernard. Mme. Mantalini: Fabia Drake. Smike: Brian Peck. Mrs. Squeers: Fay Compton. Fanny Squeers: Rosalind Knight. Matilda Price: Sheila Ballantine. John Browdie: Brian Rawlinson. Miss Knag: Daphne Newton. Mrs. Witterly: Veronica Turleigh. Mr. Witterly: William Mervyn. Sir Mulberry Hawk: Douglas Wilmer. Lord Frederick Verisopht: Jack May. Pluck: Victor Platt. Pyke: Graham Crowden. Vincent Crummles: Wensley Pithey. Mrs. Crummles: Madeline Christie. Crummles children: Alan Coleshill, David Franks, Maria Charles. Mr. Folair: Aubrey Woods. Mrs. Grudden: Vi Stevens. Thomas Lenville: David Lander. Mrs. Lenville: Edna Petrie. Cheeryble brothers: George Howe, Roddy Hughes. Tim Linkinwater: Bartlett Mullins. Madeline Bray: Marilyn James. Walter Bray: Maurice Colbourne. Frank Cheeryble: Barry Foster. Arthur Gride: Anthony Jacobs. Peg Sliderskew: Ada Reeve. Gentleman in small clothes: Leslie Henson. Mr. Westwood: Roger Winton. Captain Adams: John Hussey. Mrs. Grimshaw: Betty Hare.

TRAIL TO CHRISTMAS
CBS, USA, 1957, 30 mins
D: James Stewart. P: William Frye. W: Frank Burt, Valentine Davies. T: 14 Dec 1957. In series *General Electric Theatre*.
Host: Ronald Reagan. Scrooge: John McIntire. Runaway: Richard Eyer. Also: James Stewart, Sam Edwards, Will Wright, Kevin Hagen, Sally

Frazier, Mary Lawrence, Dennis Holmes, Russell Simpson, Tom Pittman, Tony Hilder, Ted Mapes, Gregg Barton, Hope Summers. From *A Christmas Carol*.

THE STINGIEST MAN IN TOWN
CBS, USA, 1957, 60 mins
In *CBS Television Workshop*. Based on the 1956 production. R: 14 Dec 1985. Scrooge: Gerald Floyd. From *A Christmas Carol*.

FACT IN FICTION
BBC, UK, 1958, 4x25 mins
P: Ronald Eyre. W: Rosemary Hill. In series *For the Schools*. Introduced by Hugh Ross Williamson, with excerpts from BBC telerecordings of drama productions.
7 Mar 1958 Some bad schools of the last century—Dotheboys Hall; excerpt from *Nicholas Nickleby*, with Esmond Knight as Squeers.
14 Mar 1958 Children at work in the last century. In a factory; excerpt from *David Copperfield*, dramatized by Jo Manton, with Richard O'Sullivan as David. In domestic service; excerpt from *The Old Curiosity Shop*.
21 Mar 1958 Children working on their own account in the last century. The Dolls Dressmaker; excerpt from *Our Mutual Friend*, dramatized by Jo Manton.
28 Mar 1958 Children at leisure in the last century. The Crummles Theatre; excerpt from *Nicholas Nickleby*.

A TALE OF TWO CITIES
CBS, USA, 1958, 90 mins
D: Robert Mulligan. P: David Susskind. W: Michael Dyne. T: 27 Mar 1958. In series *DuPont Show of the Month*. Sydney Carton: James Donald. Mme. Defarge: Agnes Moorehead. Lucie Manette: Rosemary Harris. Dr. Manette: Eric Portman. Charles Darnay: Denholm Elliott. Miss Pross: Gracie Fields. Jacques: George C. Scott. Barsad: Fritz Weaver. Ernest Defarge: Bruce Gordon. Marquis St. Evremonde: Max Adrian. Jarvis Lorry: Walter Fitzgerald. Gabelle: Francis Compton. Stryver: David Hurst. Jerry Cruncher: Bill Duell. Gaspard: Alfred Ryder. Seamstress: Margaret Linn.

THE MAGIC FISHBONE
NBC, USA, 1958, 60 mins
D: Oscar Rudolph. P: Alvin Cooperman. W: Margaret Fitts. T: 19 Aug 1958. In series *Shirley Temple's Storybook*. King Watkins I: Barry Jones. Princess Alicia: Lisa Daniels. Fairy Grandmarina: Estelle Winwood. Prince Certainpersonio: Richard Lupino. Also: Leo G. Carroll, Gary von Euer, Philip Walters, Jimmy Carter, Keva Zajic, Christine Anderson, Terry Burnham, J. M. Kerrigan, Rex Evans.

From *A Holiday Romance*.

A TALE OF TWO CITIES
BBC, UK, 1958, 120 mins
P: Rudolph Cartier. M: Arthur Benjamin. W: Cedric Cliffe. T: 2 Oct 1958. Opera, first broadcast BBC Third Program, 1953; first performed on the stage, 1957.
Marquis St. Evremonde: Michael Langdon. Gabelle: John Camburn. Mme. Defarge: Amy Shuard. Defarge: James Atkins. Jacques 1, 2, and 3: Frederick Sharp, Eric Shilling, Alfred Hallett. Lucie Manette: Heather Harper. Jarvis Lorry: Ronald Lewis. Dr. Manette: Heddle Nash. Sydney Carton: John Cameron. Miss Pross: Janet Howe. Charles Darnay: Alexander Young. Narrator: William Devlin. New Opera Chorus, Royal Philharmonic Orchestra, conductor Leon Lovett.

OUR MUTUAL FRIEND
BBC, UK, 1958, Serial 12x30 mins
D: Eric Taylor. P: Douglas Allen. W: Freda Lingstrom. T: 7 Nov 1958 to 23 Jan 1959.
John Harman: Paul Daneman. Radfoot: Brian Worth. Mrs. Wilfer: Daphne Newton. Bella Wilfer: Zena Walker. Reginald Wilfer: George Howe. Lavinia Wilfer: Jill Dixon. George Sampson: Bruce Gordon. Rogue Riderhood: Richard Leech. Pleasant Riderhood: Dorothy Gordon. Gaffer Hexam: Julian Somers. Lizzie Hexam: Rachel Roberts. Charley Hexam: Melvyn Hayes. Mortimer Lightwood: Basil Henson. Eugene Wrayburn: David McCallum. Mrs. Veneering: Barbara Lott. Mr. Veneering: Keith Banks. Mr. Podsnap: Raymond Rollett. Mrs. Podsnap: Miriam Raymond. Georgiana Podsnap: Olive McFarland. Julius Handford: Paul Daneman. Inspector: William Mervyn. Miss Potterson: Peggy Thorpe-Bates. Bob Gliddery: Henry Soskin. Nicodemus Boffin: Richard Pearson. Young Blight: John Stirling. John Rokesmith: Paul Daneman. Silas Wegg: Esmond Knight. Mr. Venus: Gerald Cross. Mrs. Boffin: Marda Vanne. Alfred Lammle: Carl Bernard. Mrs. Lammle: Rachel Gurney. Mr. Twemlow: Patrick Boxill. Mrs. Higden: Fay Compton. Sloppy: Robert Scroggins. Bradley Headstone: Alex Scott. Jenny Wren: Helena Hughes. Mr. Dolls: Wilfred Brambell. Mr. Riah: Malcolm Keen. Mr. Fledgeby: Charles Hodgson. Reverend Frank Milvey: Roger Ostime. Mrs. Milvey: Edna Petrie. Job Potterson: Richard Aylen. Jacob Kible: Ronald Elms.

THE MERRY CHRISTMAS
Associated Rediffusion, UK, 1958, 45 mins
D: Ronald Marriott. W: Donald Cotton. M: Brian Burke. MD: Steve Race. T: 24 Dec 1958.

Scrooge: Stephen Murray. Night watchman: Forbes Robinson. Topper: Hugh Latimer. Bob Cratchit: John Glyn Jones. Fred: Peter Gilmore. Marley's Ghost: Percy Cartwright. Christmas Past: Julian Orchard. Fezziwig: Cameron Hall. Young Scrooge: Peter Gilmore. Belle: Frances Youles. Christmas Present: Colin Cunningham. Mrs. Cratchit: Beryl Ede. Tiny Tim: Dennis Mallard. Christmas Future: Howard Williams. Peter Cratchit: Peter Soule. Martha Cratchit: Judy Robinson. Boy: Anthony Wilson. Mrs. Fred: Paddy Turner. Cousin Arabella: Joan Brown. From *A Christmas Carol*.

LE AVVENTURE DI NICOLA NICKLEBY
RAI, Italy, 1958, Serial 8x60 mins
D: Daniele d'Anza. W: Alessandro de Stefani. T: 24 May to 12 Jul 1958.
Nicholas Nickleby: Antonio Ciffariello. Ralph Nickleby: Arnoldo Foa. Squeers: Aroldo Tieri. Also: Leonora Ruffo, Elisa Cegani, Maria Grazia Spina, Franco Volpi.

GREAT EXPECTATIONS
BBC, UK, 1959, Serial 13x30 mins
P: Dorothea Brooking. W: P. D. Cummings. T: 5 Apr to 28 Jun 1959. R: 30 Mar to 22 Jun 1960.
Pip as boy: Colin Spaull. Magwitch: Jerrold Wells. Joe Gargery: Michael Gwynn. Mrs. Joe: Margot van der Burgh. Orlick: Richard Warner. Compeyson: Robert Mooney. Mr. Wopsle: William Lyon Brown. Uncle Pumblechook: Raymond Rollett. Estella as girl: Sandra Michaels. Miss Havisham: Marjory Hawtrey. Herbert Pocket as boy: Nicholas Chagrin. Pip: Dinsdale Landen. Biddy: Gabrielle Hamilton. Sarah Pocket: Elsie Wagstaff. Jaggers: Kenneth Thornett. Mr. Trabb: Geoffrey Taylor. Trabb's boy: Frazer Hines. Wemmick: Ronald Ibbs. Herbert Pocket: Colin Jeavons. Bentley Drummle: Nigel Davenport. Startop: Roger Kemp. Molly: Rozanne Clare. Aged Parent: Frederick Victor. Estella: Helen Lindsay.

BLEAK HOUSE
BBC, UK, 1959, Serial 11x30 mins
P: Eric Taylor. W: Constance Cox. T: 16 Oct to 25 Dec 1959. Mr. Kenge: William Mervyn. Esther Summerson: Diana Fairfax. Mrs. Rachael: Anne Blake. William Guppy: Timothy Bateson. Richard Carstone: Colin Jeavons. Ada Clare: Elizabeth Shepherd. Lord Chancellor: Frederick Leister. Miss Flite: Nora Nicholson. Krook: Wilfred Brambell. John Jarndyce: Andrew Cruickshank. Sir Leicester Dedlock: David Horne. Lady Dedlock: Iris Russell. Mrs. Rouncewell: Eileen Draycott. Mr. Snagsby: Leslie French. Alan Woodcourt: Jerome Willis. Jo: Malcolm Knight. Mrs. Bayham Badger: Fabia Drake. Mr. Bayham Badger: Laurence Hardy. Hortense: Annette Carell. Mrs. Woodcourt: Noel Hood. Mrs. Snagsby: Molly Lumley. Mrs.

Chadband: Ann Blake. Reverend Chadband: Willoughby Goddard. Inspector Bucket: Richard Pearson. Tony Jobling: Aubrey Woods. Mr. George: Michael Aldridge. Mr. Smallweed: Terence Soall. Judy Smallweed: Ann Way. Phil Squod: Tex Fuller. Mrs. Blinder: Vi Stevens. Charley: Angela Crow. Mr. Vholes: Gerald Cross. Matthew Bagnett: Geoffrey Tyrell. Mrs. Bagnett: Megan Latimer. Mrs. Guppy: Gretchen Franklin.

OLIVER TWIST
CBS, USA, 1959, 90 mins
D: Daniel Petrie. P: David Susskind. W: Michael Dyne. T: 4 Dec 1959. In series *DuPont Show of the Month*. Fagin: Eric Portman. Mr. Brownlow: Robert Morley. Bumble: John McGiver. Artful Dodger: William Hickey. Monks: John Collicos. Oliver: Frederick Clark. Dick: Richard Thomas. Rose: Inga Swenson. Bill Sikes: Tom Clancy. Nancy: Nancy Wickwire. Mr. Sowerberry: Michael Hordern. Fang: George Rose. Noah Claypole: James Valentine. Grimwig: Ronald Lang. Bookseller: George Turner. Mrs. Sowerberry: Lucy Landau. Policeman: Richard O'Neill. Also: Rex O'Malley, Beulah Garrick.

MEET MR. DICKENS
ABC, UK, 1959, 25 mins
First in series *Tales From Dickens*, all produced by Harry Alan Towers. The series was made on film in both 35mm and 16mm format, and was available for hire as well as being shown and repeated in ITV regions in UK. Exact transmission dates have proved difficult to trace.

THE RUNAWAYS
ABC, UK, 1959, 25 mins
D: Robert Lynn. T: 27 Dec 1959. R: 6 May 1962, 30 Dec 1969. In series *Tales From Dickens*.
Boots: Bobby Howes. Harry: Martin Stephens. Flora: Caroline Sheldon. Mrs. Piff: Athene Seyler. Lettie: Susan Westerby. Second maid: Ann Lancaster. Stout lady: Tottie Truman Taylor. Old gentleman: Campbell Cotts. Mrs. Lirriper: Beatrice Kane. Mr. Lirriper: Peter Stephens. Guardian: Ralph Truman. From *The Holly Tree, Mugby Junction*, and *Mrs. Lirriper's Lodgings*.

CHRISTMAS AT DINGLEY DELL
ABC, UK, 1959, 25 mins
D: Robert Lynn. T:(?R) 25 Dec 1960. R: 13 May 1962, 26 Dec 1968, 23 Dec 1969. In series *Tales From Dickens*.
Mr. Pickwick: John Salew. Jingle: James Donald. Winkle: Richard Briers. Snodgrass: Jack Watling. Tupman: John Hewer. Mr. Wardle: Gerald William Mervyn. Rachel Wardle: Ambrosine Phillpotts. Emily Wardle: Karal Gardner. Isabella Wardle: Pamela Binns. Old Mrs. Wardle: Nancy Roberts.

Television and Video Productions 159

Fat boy: Kenneth Parry. Sam Weller: John Sherlock. Innkeeper's wife: Nan Marriott Watson. Innkeeper: Humphrey Heathcote. Servants: Pat Goddferey, Ronald Howe. From *The Pickwick Papers*.

BARDELL VERSUS PICKWICK
ABC, UK, 1959, 25 mins
D: Ross MacKenzie. T: ? R: 27 May 1962, 7 Nov 1969. In series *Tales From Dickens*.
Mr. Pickwick: John Salew. Mrs. Bardell: Edna Morris. Sergeant Buzfuz: Donald Wolfit. Tupman: John Hewer. Snodgrass: Jack Watling. Winkle: Richard Briers. Sam Weller: Harry Fowler. Master Bardell: Malcolm Knight. Jackson: Robert Raikes. Dodson: Felix Felton. Fogg: Tony Sympson. Mrs. Crubbins: Vi Stevens. Perker: Victor Wolf. Judge: Charles Heslop. Sergeant Snubbin: John Geedan. Usher: Nicholas Tanner. Foreman: Henry Longhurst. From *The Pickwick Papers*.

MR. PICKWICK'S DILEMMA
ABC, UK, 1959, 25 mins
D: Ross MacKenzie. T: ? R: 20 May 1962. In series *Tales From Dickens*.
Mr. Pickwick: John Salew. Sam Weller: Harry Fowler. Jingle: James Donald. Job Trotter: Roger Snowden. Cook: Diana Beaumont. Peter Magnus: Alexander Dore. Miss Witherfield: Joan Sterndale Bennett. Grummer: Harold Scott. Dubbly: Michael Moore. Nutkins: Mark Dignam. Jinks: Michael Anthony. Muzzle: Philip Holles. Mary: Gillian Watt. From *The Pickwick Papers*.

SAM WELLER AND HIS FATHER
ABC, UK, 1959, 25 mins
D: Robert Lynn. T: ? R: 3 Jun 1962. In series *Tales From Dickens*.
Sam Weller: Harry Fowler. Tony Weller: Wilfred Lawson. Mrs. Bardell: Edna Morris. Mrs. Weller: Janet Joye. Stiggins: George Benson. Mr. Pickwick: John Salew. Anthony Humm: Gerald Cross. Jonas Mudge: Robert Lankisheer. Brother Tradger: Alex Sinter. Namby: Jack Melford. Perker: Victor Wolf. From *The Pickwick Papers*.

DAVID AND HIS MOTHER
ABC, UK, 1959, 25 mins
D: Robert Lynn. T: ? R: 10 Jun 1962. In series *Tales From Dickens*.
David Copperfield as boy: Martin Stephens. Mr. Murdtone: Alan Wheatley. Mrs. Copperfield: Anne Gudrun. Miss Murdstone: Patricia Jessel. Mr. Quinion: Fred Kitchen. Peggotty: Barbara Ogilvie. Akers: Keith Banks. Mr. Mell: Anton Rodgers. Mr. Creakle: Peter Bull. Mrs. Creakle: Marjorie Fleeson. From *David Copperfield*.

DAVID AND MR. MICAWBER
ABC, UK, 1959, 25 mins
D: ? T: ? R: 24 Jun 1962. In series *Tales From Dickens*.
David Copperfield as boy: Martin Stephens. Mr. Micawber: Robert Morley. Mrs. Micawber: Irene Handl. Miss Micawber: Regina Clow. Master Micawber: Robert Howe. Walker: Ross Yeo. Mealy: Michael Scoble. Mr. Quinion: Fred Kitchen. Captain Hopkins: Keith Smith. Creditors: Robert Raglan, Frank Pemberton. From *David Copperfield*.

DAVID AND BETSEY TROTWOOD
ABC, UK, 1959, 25 mins
D: ? T: ? R: 17 Jun 1962, 10 Oct 1969.
David Copperfield as boy: Martin Stephens. Betsey Trotwood: Martita Hunt. Mr. Murdstone: Alan Wheatley. Miss Murdstone: Patricia Jessel. Mr. Dick: Russell Thorndike. Mrs. Copperfield: Ann Gudrun. Peggotty: Barbara Ogilvie. Dr. Chillip: Robert Sansom. Landlord: John Sharpe. Landlord's wife: Kathleen Canty. Mr. Dolloby: Sidney Arnold. Old clothes man: Lionel Jeffries. Janet: Shirley Patterson. Young man: Brian Peck. Tramp: Harold Siddons. Mealy: Michael Scoble. From *David Copperfield*.

DAVID AND DORA
ABC, UK, 1959, 25 mins
D: ? T: ? R: 1 Jul 1962. In series *Tales From Dickens*.
David Copperfield: William Russell. Dora Spenlow: June Laverick. Miss Murdstone: Patricia Jessel. Mrs. Crupp: Violet Gould. Lavinia Spenlow: Phillida Sewell. Clarissa Spenlow: Gladys Boot. Mr. Spenlow: Noel Howlett. Miss Mills: Kate Cameron. Tiffey: Erik Chitty. Clerks: Anthony Sheppard, Alan Barry. Mr. Masters: Stewart Hillier. Blonde girl: Dawn Berrington. From *David Copperfield*.

DAVID AND DORA MARRIED
ABC, UK, 1959, 25 mins
D: ? T: ? R: 8 Jul 1962. In series *Tales From Dickens*.
David Copperfield: William Russell. Dora: June Laverick. Betsey Trotwood: Martita Hunt. Traddles: Kendrick Owen. Officer of the Lifeguard: Brian Wilde. Paragon: Marjorie Wilde. Treasure: Marjorie Gresley. Dr. Chillip: Robert Sansom. Sophie: Marjorie Lawrence. Page: Peter Mander. From *David Copperfield*.

THE OLD SOLDIER
ABC, UK, 1959, 25 mins
D: Ross MacKenzie. W: Peter Holiday. T: ? R: 25 Dec 1966. In series *Tales From Dickens*.

Television and Video Productions 161

David Copperfield: William Russell. Mrs. Markleham: Nora Nicholson. Annie Strong: Sally Home. Uriah Heep: Richard Pasco. Mr. Wickfield: Henry Oscar. Maldon: Gerald Harper. Dr. Strong: Clive Morton. From *David Copperfield*.

URIAH HEEP
ABC, UK, 1959, 25 mins
D: Ross MacKenzie. T: (?R) 24 Dec 1960.
In series *Tales From Dickens*.
David Copperfield: William Russell. Mr. Micawber: Robert Morley. Betsey Trotwood: Martita Hunt. Uriah Heep: Richard Pasco. Mrs. Heep: Beatrice Varley. Mr. Wickfield: Henry Oscar. Agnes Wickfield: Jacqueline Ellis. Mrs. Crupp: Violet Gould. From *David Copperfield*.

A CHRISTMAS CAROL
ABC, UK, 1959, 25 mins
D: Robert Lynn? W: Desmond Davis. T: 27 Dec 1959. R: 10 Dec 1969. In series *Tales From Dickens*.
Scrooge: Basil Rathbone. Scrooge as boy: Kaplam Kaye. Scrooge as young man: Howard Williams. Bob Cratchit: Toke Townley. Mrs. Cratchit: Mary Jones. Peter Cratchit: Michael Lewis. Martha Cratchit: Monica Marlow. Tiny Tim: Mark Milcham. Fan: Laura Henderson. Fred: Brian McDermott. Mrs. Fred: Patricia Cree. Sisters: Roberta Wooley, Stella Riley. Jacob Marley: Wilfred Fletcher. Christmas Past: Walter Hudd. Christmas Present: Alexander Gauge. Christmas Future: Michael McCarthy. Belle: Mary Webster. Fezziwig: Gabriel Toyne. Charwoman: Rita Webb. Old Joe: Sydney Arnold. Urchin boy: Joey White. Thin and fat businessmen: Keith Smith, Michael Logan.

MISS HAVISHAM
ABC, UK, 1959, 25 mins
D: Robert Lynn. W: Peter Holiday. T: ? R: 25 Dec 1966, 3 Oct 1969. In series *Tales From Dickens*.
Miss Havisham: Florence Eldridge. Joe Gargery: Michael Aldridge. Mrs. Gargery: Joan Hickson. Estella: Jill Haworth. Biddy: Fiona Duncan. Sarah Pocket: Phyllis Morris. Cousin Camilla: Betty Turner. Pip: Jon Skinner. Herbert Pocket: Karl Lanchbury. From *Great Expectations*.

THE SMALL SERVANT
Granada, UK, 1960, 60 mins
D: Desmond Davis. W: S. I. Abelow, Robert Cenedella. T: 1 Jan 1960.
Sally Brass: Anita Sharp Bolster. Sampson Brass: Michael Aldridge. Small servant: Dudy Nimmo. Dick Swiveller: Ian Bannen. Sophie: Pat Coombs.

Wrasp: Michael Logan. Mr. Garland: Ralph Tovey. Padgett: Cardew Robinson. From *The Old Curiosity Shop*.

THE TOM TUCKETT STORY
NBC, USA, 1960, 60 mins
W: Jean Holloway. T: 2 Mar 1960. Episode in series *Wagon Train*.
Tom Tuckett (Pip): Ben Cooper. Also: Robert Middleton, Josephine Hutchinson.
A western variation of the theme of *Great Expectations*.

THE MYSTERY OF EDWIN DROOD
Associated Rediffusion, UK, 1960, Serial 8x30 mins
D: Mark Lawton. W: John Keir Cross; completed from an idea by John Dickson Carr. T: 28 Sep to 16 Nov 1960.
John Jasper: Donald Sinden. Princess Puffer: Sonia Dresdel. Reverend Crisparkle: Richard Pearson. Edwin Drood: Tim Seely. Mrs. Tope: Beatrice Varley. Miss Twinkleton: Rosamund Greenwood. Rosa Bud: Barbara Brown. Durdles: Frederick Piper. Mr. Sapsea: George Woodbridge. Neville Landless: Clifford Elkin. Mrs. Crisparkle: Elsie Wagstaff. Helena Landless: Catherine Woodville. Miss Twinkleton's young ladies: Wendy Terry, Marian Collins, Carole Lorimer. Mr. Grewgious: Laidman Brown. Bazzard: Leslie Heritage. Dick Datchery: Unnamed player (revealed in episode 7 as Bazzard). Mrs. Billikin: Rita Webb. Lieutenant Tartar: John Flint.

BARNABY RUDGE
BBC, UK, 1960, Serial 13x30 mins
D: Morris Barry. P: Douglas Allen. W: Michael Voysey. T: 30 Sep to 23 Dec 1960.
John Willet: Arthur Brough. Phil Parkes: John Atkinson. Tom Cobb: Tony Sympson. Solomon Daisy: John Gill. Mr. Edward Chester: Bernard Brown. The Stranger: Nigel Arkwright. Joe Willet: Alan Haywood. Gabriel Varden: Newton Blick. Mrs. Varden: Joan Hickson. Miss Miggs: Barbara Hicks. Dolly Varden: Jennifer Daniel. Barnaby Rudge: John Wood. Mrs. Rudge: Isabel Dean. Simon Tappertit: Timothy Bateson. Emma Haredale: Eira Heath. Betsy: Angela Crow. Mr. John Chester: Raymond Huntley. Stagg: Michael Hitchman. Benjamin: Malcolm Knight. Mark Gilbert: Ian Neill. Jonathan: Clive Marshall. George: Peter Blythe. Hugh: Neil McCarthy. Peak: Patrick Boxill. Lord George Gordon: Anthony Sharp. John Grueby: Richard Wordsworth. Dennis: Esmond Knight. Tom: Harold Reese. Squire: Michael Bird. Sir George Saville: John Moore. Mr. Burke: Brian Hayes. General Conway: Wilfred Grantham. Kennet, Lord Mayor: William Sherwood. Mr. Akerman: Jeffrey Segal. Mr. Dugdale: George Woodbridge. King George III: Allan McClelland. Mr. Haredale: Peter Williams.

Television and Video Productions 163

EBENEZER SCROOGE APPOPOLOUS
CBS, USA, 1960, 30 mins
T: 21 Dec 1960. In comedy series *My Sister Eileen*.
Ruth: Elaine Stritch. Eileen: Shirley Bonne. Mr. Appopolous (Scrooge): Leon Belasco. Also: Rose Marie, Mary Grace Canfield, George Kennedy. From *A Christmas Carol*.

THE CHARLIE DRAKE SHOW
BBC, UK, 1960, 30 mins
P: Ronald Marsh. W: Charlie Drake, Richard Waring. T: 23 Dec 1960. "A Christmas Carol, with acknowledgments to Charles Dickens."
Bob Cratchit: Charlie Drake. Scrooge: Philip Locke. Nancy: Jennifer Browne, Bill Sikes: Howard Lang. David Copperfield: Kenneth Gouge, Mr. Murdstone: Edwin Richfield. Mr. Pickwick: Lloyd Pearson. Miss Havisham: Marjorie Hawtrey. Nicholas Nickleby: Frazer Hines. Mr. Micawber: Austin Trevor. Fagin: Martin Benson. The Artful Dodger: Peter Delmer. Oliver Twist: Hennie Scott. Marley's Ghost: William Lyon Brown.

LA PETITE DORRIT (Little Dorrit)
RTF, France ?, 1961 103 mins
T: Belgium 16 Dec 1961.

OLIVER TWIST
BBC, UK, 1962, Serial 13x25 mins
P: Eric Tayler. W: Constance Cox. T: 7 Jan to 1 Apr 1962.
Oliver's mother: Jane Merrow. Old Sally: Aimee Delamain. Surgeon: Robert Mooney. Mrs. Mann: Mary Quinn. Susan: Jean Theobald. Bumble: Willoughby Goddard. Oliver Twist: Bruce Prochnik. Mr. Limbkins: Peter Stephens. Members of Workhouse Board: David King, Reginald Green, Eric Dodson. Workhouse Master: Henry McCarthy. Mr. Sowerberry: Donald Eccles. Mrs. Sowerberry: Barbara Hicks. Charlotte: Priscilla Morgan. Noah Claypole: Barry Wilsher. Artful Dodger: Melvyn Hayes. Fagin: Max Adrian. Charley Bates: Alan Rothwell. Nancy: Carmel McSharry. Bet: Margaret Wolfit. Mr. Brownlow: George Curzon. Monks: John Carson. Mrs. Bedwin: Madeleine Christie. Bill Sikes: Peter Vaughan. Mr. Grimwig: William Mervyn. Mrs. Corney: Peggy Thorpe-Bates. Toby Crackit: Harry Landis. Giles: Richard Caldicot. Tom Chitling: Peter Furnell. Rose Maylie: Gay Cameron. Dr. Losberne: Lloyd Pearson. Mrs. Maylie: Noel Hood. Harry Maylie: John Breslin.

AFFAIRE BARDELL CONTRE PICKWICK
RTF, France ?, 1962, 20 mins
W: Gerard Guilleumet. T: Belgium 14 Mar 1962. From *The Pickwick Papers*.

MR. CHOPS
RTF, France ?, 1962, 22 mins
W: Gerard Guilleumet. T: Belgium 2 July 1962. From *Going into Society*.

LE SIGNALEUR (The Signalman)
RTF, France ?, 1962, 18 mins
W: Gerard Guilleumet. T: Belgium 2 Jul 1962. From *Mugby Junction*.

SOUVENIRS D'ENFANCE DE DAVID COPPERFIELD
RTF, France, 1962, 15 mins
W: Gerard Guilleumet. T: Belgium 16 Jul 1962.

THE OLD CURIOSITY SHOP
BBC, UK, 1962, Serial 13x25 mins
D: Joan Craft. P: Douglas Allen. W: Constance Cox. T: 25 Nov 1962 to 17 Feb 1963.
Mrs. Jarley: Angela Baddeley. Nell Trent: Michele Dotrice. Grandfather Trent: Oliver Johnston. George: Victor Platt. Single gentleman: John Sharp. Sampson Brass: Bryan Pringle. Sally Brass: Patricia Jessel. Dick Swiveller: Anton Rodgers. Codlin: John Southworth. Short: Alan Hockey. Marchioness: Fiona Duncan. Miss Monflathers: Margaret Diamond. Miss Edwards: Patricia Pacy. Kit Nubbles: Ronald Cunliffe. Mrs. Nubbles: Megs Jenkins. Little Jacob: Robert Cook. Barbara: Lilian Grassom. Barbara's mother: Ruby Head. Jacob Jowl: John Rolfe. Isaac List: Douglas Blackwell. Gypsy: Ray Adamson. Quilp: Patrick Troughton. Mrs. Quilp: Sheila Shand Gibbs. Abel Garland: William Simons. Mr. Chuckster: Aubrey Woods. Mr. Witherden: Norman Pitt. Mr. Garland: Philip Ray. Mr. Slum: John Crocker. Mrs. Jiniwin: Peggyann Clifford. Tom Scott: Peter Hempson. Watchman: Terence de Marney. Mr. Marton: Clement McCallin. Fred Trent: Ian Thompson. Sophy Wackles: Margo Andrew. Jane Wackles: Anna Perry. Mr. Cheggs: Michael Wynne. Mrs. Garland: Helena McCarthy. Jemmy Groves: Noel Carey.

MR. MAGOO'S CHRISTMAS CAROL
NBC, USA, 1962, 52 mins
D: Abe Levitow. W: Barbara Chain. T: 18 Dec 1962. Animated color cartoon film, made by UPA Pictures.
Magoo/Scrooge: Voice of Jim Backus.
LOC record indicates a shorter version of 28 mins. Subsequently combined with *Mr. Magoo's Snow White* to form a 104-minute film entitled *Mr. Magoo's Holiday Festival*, released by Maron Films, 21 Nov. 1970. Includes six songs by Jule Styne and Bob Merrill.

Television and Video Productions

A CHRISTMAS CAROL
BBC, UK, 1962, 60 mins
P: Hal Burton. M: Edwin Coleman. W: Margaret Burns Harris. Opera, specially commissioned for BBC TV. T: 24 Dec 1962.
Scrooge: Stephen Manton. Bob Cratchit: Derick Davies. Scrooge's nephew: David Hillman. Woman canvasser/Charwoman: Marion Lowe. Ghosts of Jacob Marley/Christmas Present: Trevor Anthony. Christmas Past/Shopkeeper: Edmund Donlevy. Scrooge as boy: Andrew Clark. Scrooge's sister: Sheelagh Mulholland. Scrooge's fiancee: Brenda Marshall. Scrooge as young man: Rhys McConnochie. Mrs. Cratchit: Catherine Wilson. Cratchit daughters: Sylvia Eaves, Janette Lynn, Lynn Williams. Tiny Tim: Forrester Pyke. Nephew's friend: Gerwyn Morgan. Nephew's visitor/Laundress: Carole Rosen. Nephew's wife: Elizabeth Boyd. Christmas Future: Giles Havergal. Business man: Francis Egerton. Undertaker's man: Norman Lumsden. Errand boy: David Pinto.
Pro Arte Orchestra, conducted by William Reid.

A DICKENS CHRONICLE
CBS, USA, 1963, 60 mins
D: John J. Desmond. P & W: Don Kellerman. T: 13 Feb 1963.
A biographical program incorporating various characters from Dickens's stories; narrated by Clive Revill in the guise of Sam Weller.

A PASSION FOR JUSTICE
NBC, USA, 1963, 60 mins
T: 29 Sep 1963. Episode in the western series *Bonanza*.
Charles Dickens (Jonathan Harris) visits the Ponderosa.

MR. PICKWICK
Granada, UK, 1963, 90 mins.
D: Claude Whatham. P: Derek Granger. W: Stanley Young. T: 25 Dec 1963.
Mr. Pickwick: Arthur Lowe. Tupman: Jack May. Snodgrass: Philip Grout. Winkle: Trevor Danby. Mrs. Bardell: Susan Field. Sam Weller: James Bolam. Tony Weller: Patrick Newell. Betsy Cluppins: Jean Conroy. Tommy Bardell: Glen Slowther. Mary: Celestine Randell. Jingle: Gordon Rollings. Mrs. Leo Hunter: Betty Huntley Wright. Joe: Roy Bunter. Mr. Wardle: John Wentworth. Rachel Wardle: Eileen Kennally. Emily Wardle: Deborah Millington. Isabella Wardle: Harriett Harper. Dodson: Jack Austin. Fogg: Martin Dobson. Jackson: Allen Sykes. Wicks: Roy Minton. Sergeant Buzfuz: Roy Kinnear. Mr. Perker: Eric Longworth. Judge: Jack Woolgar. Sergeant Snubbin: Ray Gatenby.

IL GRILLO DEL FOCOLARE (The Cricket on the Hearth)
RAI, Italy, 1963, Length?

D: C. di Stefano. W: A. M. Romagnoli.

MARTIN CHUZZLEWIT
BBC, UK, 1964, Serial 13x25 mins
D: Joan Craft. P: Campbell Logan. W: Constance Cox. T: 19 Jan to 12 Apr 1964. R: 29 Jun to 14 Aug 1964. Martin Chuzzlewit: Gary Raymond. Martin Chuzzlewit, Sr.: Barry Jones. Pecksniff: Richard Pearson. Mary Graham: Ilona Rodgers. Mark Tapley: Tom Watson. Jonas Chuzzlewit: Alex Scott. Tom Pinch: John Quentin. Mercy: Anna Middleton. Charity: Rosalind Knight. John Westlock: Jeremy Burnham. Mrs. Lupin: Barbara Ogilvie. Montague Tigg: Peter Bayliss. Chevy Slime: Michael Bilton. Mr. Spottletoe: Arthur Spentelow. Mrs. Spottletoe: Betty Duncan. Anthony Chuzzlewit: Carl Bernard. Jane: Deborah Millington. Mrs. Todgers: Barbara Cavan. Bailey: Peter Craze. Ruth Pinch: Fern Warner. Mr. Jinkins: Peter Stephens. Mr. Moddle: Pearson Dodd: Mr. Gander: Clifford Parrish. Chuffey: Harold Scott. David Crimple: Tony Bronte. Lewsome: John Golightly. Dr. Jobling: John Bryans. Mrs. Gamp: Angela Baddeley. Colonel Diver: Hugh Cross. Captain: Murray Kash. Major Pawkins: Cal McCord. Jefferson Brick: Victor Henry. Mr. Bevan: Jon Farrell. Scadder: Esmond Bennett. General Choke: Derek Murcott. Mrs. Prig: Kathleen Harrison. Bullamy: Fred Hugh. Nadgett: Blake Butler. Mr. Fips: Ian Wilson.

LE MAGASIN D'ANTIQUITÉS (The Old Curiosity Shop)
RTF?, France, 1964, 90 mins
D: Rene Lucot. T: 3 May 1964.
With: Christine Simon, Georges Chamarat, Lucien Barjou, Daniel Janneau, Alfred Pasquali.

MR. SCROOGE
CBC, Canada, 1964, 60 mins
W: Richard Morris, Ted Woods. M: Doris Claman. T: 21 Dec 1964. A musical, originally created for the stage in Toronto in 1963.
Scrooge: Cyril Ritchard. Bob Cratchit: Alfie Bass. Mrs. Cratchit: Tessie O'Shea. Ghost of Christmas Past: Gillie Fenwick. Marley's Ghost: Eric Christmas.

A CAROL FOR ANOTHER CHRISTMAS
ABC, USA, 1964, 90 mins
D & P: Joseph L. Mankiewicz. W: Rod Serling. T: 22 Dec 1964.
Daniel Grudge (Scrooge): Sterling Hayden. Christmas Past: Steve Lawrence. Christmas Present: Pat Hingle. Christmas Future: Robert Shaw. Ben: Ben Gazzara. Imperial Me: Peter Sellers. Wave: Eve Marie Saint. Doctor: James Shigeta. Ruby: Barbara Ann Tear. Charles: Percy Rodriguez. Mother: Britt Ekland. Soldier: Gordon Spencer.

LES AVENTURES DE M. PICKWICK
RTF?, France, 1964, Serial? x25 mins
D: Rene Lucot. W: Michel Subiela. T: 24 Dec 1964 to? Pickwick: Andre Gilles. Snodgrass: Georges Audonbert. Winkle: Claude Nicot. Tupman: Hubert Deschamps. Rachel: Odette Pignet. Jingle: Jacques Gripel. Winkle, Sr.: Armand Bernard. Arabella: Daniele Girard. Miss Witherfield: Madeleine Barbulee. Le president: Pierre Risch. Le vice-president: Claude Mansard.

HUMBUG, MRS. BROWN
CBS, USA, 1964, 30 mins
D: Oscar Rudolph. W: Al Martin, Bill Kelsey. In series *My Favorite Martian*. Uncle Martin: Ray Walston. Mrs. Brown: Pamela Britton.
From *A Christmas Carol*.

DAVID COPPERFIELD
RTF?, France, 1965, 140 mins
D: Marcelle Cravenne. W: Claude Santelle. T: 1 Jan 1965.
David, enfant: Didier Hauperin. David, adulte: Bernard Verley. Steerforth: Michel Duchaussoy. Tante Betsy: Madeleine Clervanne. Mme. Peggotty: Germaine Michel. M. Peggotty: Jean Chevrier. Clara: France Descant. Rosa: Renee Faure. M. Murdstone: Robert Porty. Mlle Murdstone: Edith Perret. Petite Emily: Christine Simon. Emily: Michel Andre. Barkis: Lucien Raimbourg. Mme. Commindge: Madeleine Barbulee. M. Micawber: Michel Galabru. Mme. Micawber: Marguerite Cassan. Les enfants Micawber: Serge Bauchais, Christian Bernard. Ham: Jean Lescot. Docteur: Bruno Balp. Mell: Jean Martin. Creakle: Clement Harrari. Tungay: Marcel Peres. Traddles: Patrice Demongeot. Traddles Omer: Harry Max. Minnie: Paul Noel. Jeram: Renaud Verley. Dick: Armontel. Janet: Bernadette Onfroy. Mme. Steerforth: Luciene Lemarchand. Servante: May Chartrettes. Littimer: Michel Dacquin. Naine: Cacao. Les domestiques: Jean Peset, Georges Goudey. Caissiere: Andre Champeaux. Cocher de fiacre: Daniel de Rozeville. Garcon: Jean Tissier. Les creanciers: Michel Ferraud, Roger Bernard. Un agent: Henri Rondel.

MR. WHITE'S CHRISTMAS
NBC, USA, 1965, 60 mins
D: Don Taylor. T: 4 Apr 1965. Episode in series *The Rogues*.
(Scrooge): John McGiver. Also: Jill Haworth, Larry Hagman, Hedley Mattingly.

A TALE OF TWO CITIES
BBC, UK, 1965, Serial 10x25 mins

D: Joan Craft. P: Campbell Logan. W: Constance Cox. T: 11 Apr to 13 Jun 1965.
Marie: Pauline Munro. Jean: Peter Bourne. Chevalier St. Evremonde: Jerome Willis, Marquis St. Evremonde: Victor Winding. Dr. Manette: Patrick Troughton. Mme. Manette: Penelope Bartley. Defarge: George Selway. Marquise St. Evremonde: Sonia Graham. Charles St. Evremonde: Paul Brace. Jerry Cruncher: Ronnie Barker. Jarvis Lorry: Leslie French. Lucie Manette: Kika Markham. Miss Pross: Alison Leggatt. Gaspard: Wilfred Grove. Mme. Defarge: Rosalie Crutchley. Jacques 1, 2 and 3: Stephen Dartnell, Artro Morris, George Little. Charles Darnay: Nicholas Pennell. Gabelle: Rolf Lefebvre. Barsad: Peter Bayliss. Cly: Nicholas Smith. Sydney Carton: John Wood. Sergeant Stryver: Jack May. Mrs. Cruncher: Janet Henfrey. Master Cruncher: Darryl Read. The Vengeance: Diana King. Seamstress. Fiona Duncan.

TOO MANY CHRISTMAS TREES
ABC, UK, 1965, 30 mins
D: Rpy Baker. P: Julian Wintle. W: Tony Williamson. T: 23 Dec 1965; US 11 Aug 1966. Episode in the series *The Avengers*.
John Steed (Sydney Carton): Patrick McNee. Emma Peel (Oliver Twist): Diana Rigg.

DAVID COPPERFIELD
RAI, Italy, 1966, Serial 8x90 mins
D & W: Anton Guilio Majano. T: 16 Jan to 20 Feb 1966.
David as boy: Roberto Chevalier. David as man: Giancarlo Giannini. Aunt Betsy: Wanda Capodaglio. Peggotty: Elsa Vazzoler. Barkis: Luigi Pavese. Steerforth: Fabrizio Moroni. Micawber: Carlo Romano. Also: Anna Maria Guarnieri, Mario Geliciani, Stefano Sibaldi, Laura Efrikian, Alberto Terrani, Ubaldo Lay, Roldano Lupi.

DAVID COPPERFIELD
BBC, UK, 1966, Serial 13x25 mins
D: Joan Craft. P: Campbell Logan. W: Vincent Tilsley (A revised dramatization). T: 16 Jan to 10 Apr 1966.
David as boy: Christopher Guard. Peggotty: Lila Keys. Mr. Murdstone: Richard Leech. Mrs. Copperfield: Sheila Shand Gibbs. Barkis: Gordon Gostelow. Mr. Peggotty: Joss Ackland. Ham: Basil Moss. Mrs. Gummidge: Olga Lindo. Little Emily: Suzanne Togni. Miss Murdstone: Joan Peart. Traddles: Colin Huddy. Topsawyer: Frank Summers. Kemble: Ian Ellis. Peel: Michael Reynolds. Creakle: Barry Shawzin. Tungay: Tony Caunter. Steerforth: Barry Justice. Mr. Quinion: Robert Hartley. Mick Walker: Stewart Guidotti. Mealy Potatoes: Larry Hamilton. Mr. Micawber: Bill Fraser. Mrs. Micawber: Eleanor Summerfield. Betsey Trotwood: Flora Robson. Mr.

Dick: George Benson. Janet: Lynne White. Mr. Wickfield: Noel Johnson. Uriah Heep: Colin Jeavons. Agnes as girl: Sally Thomsett. Dr. Strong: Gordon Richardson. David as man: Ian McKellen. Agnes Wickfield: Hannah Gordon. Littimer: John Ringham. Mrs. Steerforth: Elizabeth Tyrrell. Rosa Dartle: Judy Parfitt. Emily: Angela Scoular. Mr. Spenlow: Andre van Gyseghem. Mr. Jorkins: Lionel Hamilton. Mrs. Crupp: Amelia Bayntun. Mr. Guppidge: Lloyd Pearson. Traddles: Clive Francis. Dora Spenlow: Tina Packer. Jip: Fleur. Clarissa Spenlow: Mary Hinton. Lavinia Spenlow: Nan Munro. Mary Anne: Barbara Hicks. Josh: Danny Rae. Mrs. Heep: Dorothy Frere. Mr. Bellstruther: John Byams. Sophy: Penelope Windows.

THE CASE OF THE TWICE-TOLD TWIST
CBS, USA, 1966, 60 mins
In series *Perry Mason*. T: 27 Feb 1966.
(Fagin): Victor Buono. From *Oliver Twist*.

GREAT EXPECTATIONS
BBC, UK, 1967, Serial 10x25 mins
D: Alan Bridges. P: Campbell Logan. W: Hugh Leonard. T: 22 Jan to 26 Mar 1967.
Pip as boy: Christopher Guard. Magwitch: John Tait. Mrs. Gargery: Shirley Cain. Compeyson: Kevin Stoney. Mr. Hubble: Sidney Vivian. Mrs. Hubble: Ursula Hirst. Wopsle: John Gill. Sergeant: John Caesar. Miss Havisham: Maxine Audley. Sarah Pocket: Elsie Wagstaff. Georgina: Marjorie Wilde. Camilla: Joan Geary. Raymond: Christopher Steele. Jaggers: Peter Vaughan. Herbert Pocket as boy: Derek Landen. Orlick: Ronald Lacey. Trabb: Redmond Phillips. Trabb's boy: Kenneth Nash. Bentley Drummle: John Lorrimore. Pip: Gary Bond. Herbert Pocket: Richard O'Sullivan. Wemmick: Bernard Hepton. Miss Skiffins: Hazel Bainbridge. Aged Parent: Frederick Piper. Joe Gargery: Neil McCarthy. Pumblechook: Norman Scase. Biddy: Hannah Gordon. Estella: Francesca Annis. Pip as youth: Douglas Mann.

THE MAGIC OF CHARLES DICKENS
CBS, USA, 1967, 60 mins
P: Chloe Gibson. T: 29 Jan 1967.
Emlyn Williams, in the guise of Charles Dickens, giving a selection of readings from the books, in the style of Dickens's own public readings.

CHARLES DICKENS
Rediffusion/Thames TV, UK, 1967, 30 mins
D: John Rhodes. P: Peter Hunt. W: K. J. Fielding. T: 8 Feb 1967. R: 20 Sep 1968. First in the series *Best Sellers*, devoted to celebrated British authors. Presented by Professor K. J. Fielding. Charles Dickens: Bernard Brown.

MR. DICKENS OF LONDON
ABC, USA, 1967, 60 mins
D: Barry Morse. P: Jules Power. W: Joseph Hurley. T: 12 Dec 1967.
Guide: Juliet Mills. Charles Dickens: Michael Redgrave.
Based in part on sections from *Sketches By Boz* and *The Seven Poor Travellers*.

THE CRICKET ON THE HEARTH
NBC, USA, 1967, 60 mins
T: 18 Dec 1967. In series *The Danny Thomas Hour*.
Animated film version, with the voice of Roddy McDowall.

(A CHRISTMAS CAROL)
CBS, USA, 1967, Length?
In series *The Smothers Brothers Show*.
Scrooge: Tom Smothers. Bob Cratchit: Jack Benny.

A TALE OF TWO CITIES
McGraw Hill, USA, 1967, 14 mins
Film or video?

NICHOLAS NICKLEBY
BBC, UK, 1968, Serial 13x25 mins
D: Joan Craft. P: Campbell Logan. W: Hugh Leonard. T: 11 Feb to 5 May 1968.
Ralph Nickleby: Derek Francis. Newman Noggs: Gordon Gostelow. Mr. Bonney: John Moore. Hannah: Valerie Newbold. Miss LaCreevy: Hazel Coppen. Mrs. Nickleby: Thea Holme. Nicholas Nickleby: Martin Jarvis. Kate Nickleby: Susan Brodrick. Wackford Squeers: Ronald Radd. Belling: Freddie Foote. Snawley: Allen Sykes. Mrs. Squeers: Sheila Keith. Wackford, Jr.: Malcolm Epstein. Cobbey: Alan Wade. Mobbs: Paul Bartlett. Graymarsh: Brent Oldfield. Bolder: John Gogulka. Mr. Mantalini: Maxwell Shaw. Mme. Mantalini: Thelma Ruby. Fanny Squeers: Karin MacCarthy. Smike: Hugh Walters. Miss Knag: Stella Tanner. John Browdie: David Richardson. Tilda Price: Mary Healey. Lord Frederick Verisopht: Raymond Clarke. Sir Mulberry Hawk: Terence Alexander. Pyke: Roland MacLeod. Pluck: Michael Waddon. Snobb: Roger Brierly. Col. Chowser: Darrol Richards. Mrs. Kenwigs: Brenda Cowling. Morleena Kenwigs: Maxine Taylor. Mr. Lillyvick: Tommy Godfrey. Miss Petowker: Maggie Jones. Scaley: Kevin Brennan. Tix: Sydney Bromley. Vincent Crummles: Dermot Tuohy. Crummles children: Christopher Witty, Malcolm Jones. Infant Phenomenon: Daphne Foreman. Folair: Bob Hornery. Mrs. Crummles: Marie Hopps. Lenville: Julian Curry. Mrs. Lenville: Rita Davies. Miss Snevellicci: Rosalind Knight. Mr. Snevellicci: Philip Morant. Mrs. Snevellicci: Vi Kane. Charles Cheeryble: Edward Palmer. Tim Linkinwater: Bartlett Mullins.

Ned Cheeryble: John Gill. Gentleman next door: Roy Kinnear. Madeline Bray: Sharon Gurney. Frank Cheeryble: Paul Shelley. Brooker: John Bailey. Bray: John Robinson. Arthur Gride: Geoffrey Bayldon. Peg Sliderskew: Daphne Heard. Westwood: Maurice Browning, Captain Adams: David Monico.

WHAT THE DICKENS?
BBC, UK, 1968, 55 mins
P: Darrol Blake. T: 15 Dec 1968. In series *Omnibus*. Professor Philip Collins, expert on the readings given by Charles Dickens, presented his own performance of extracts from Dickens's novels, letters, and short stories.

LES GRANDES ESPERANCES (Great Expectations)
RTF?, France, 1968, Length ?
D: Marcel Cravenne. P: Jean-Claude Dauphin.
Miss Havisham: Madeleine Renaud. Magwitch: Charles Vanel. Jaggers: Jean-Roger Caussimon.

IL CIRCOLO PICKWICK (The Pickwick Papers)
RAI, Italy, 1968, Serial 8x60 mins
D: Ugo Gregoretti. W: L. Codignola. T: 18 Feb to 7 Apr 1968.
Pickwick: Mario Pisu. Snodgrass: Leopoldo Trieste. Winkle: Gigi Ballista. Tupman: Guido Alberti. Jingle: Gigi Proietti. Also: Antonio Meshini, Maria Monti, Maria Teresa Bax, Piera Degli Espositi, Adolfo Fenoglio, Zoe Incrocci.

PICKWICK
BBC, UK, 1969, 90 mins
W: Wolf Mankowitz. M: Cyril Ornadel. Lyrics: Leslie Bricusse. Adapted from the stage musical (1963) for TV by James Gilbert and Jimmy Grafton. T: 11 Jun and 26 Dec 1969.
Mr. Pickwick: Harry Secombe. Sam Weller: Roy Castle. Mrs. Bardell: Hattie Jacques. Jingle: Aubrey Woods. Sergeant Buzfuz: Bill Fraser. Snodgrass: Julian Orchard. Tupman: Robert Dorning. Winkle: Ian Trigger. Mary: Sheila White. Wardle: Michael Logan. Rachel: Joyce Grant. Isabella: Julia Sutton, Emily: Cheryl Kennedy. Fat boy: Robert Yetzes. Master Bardell: Christopher Reynolds. Judge: Erik Chitty. Dodson: Michael Darbyshire. Fogg: Tony Sympson. Sergeant Snubbin: Ian Gray.

DOMBEY AND SON
BBC, UK, 1969, Serial 13x25 mins
D: Joan Craft. P: Campbell Logan. W: Hugh Leonard. T: 17 Aug to 9 Nov 1969.

Mr. Dombey: John Carson. Mrs. Dombey: Maude Foster. Mrs. Blockitt: Phillada Sewell. Young Florence: Vicky Williams. Dr. Parker Peps: Peter Stephens. Dr.Pilkins: Lionel Hamilton. Louisa Chick: Hilda Braid. Lucretia Tox: Pat Coombs. Polly Toodle: Charlotte Mitchell. Mr. Toodle: Davyd Harries. Young Rob Toodle: Robert Smith. Solomon Gills: Meadows White. Walter Gay: Derek Seaton. Captain Cuttle: William Moore. Susan Nipper: Helen Fraser. Mrs. Brown: Fay Compton. Mrs. Wickam: Dorothy Frere. Florence Dombey: Kara Wilson. Paul Dombey: Roland Pickering. Mrs. Pipchin: Joan Haythorne. Bitherstone: Robert Fountain. Mr. Brogley: Will Stampe. Towlinson: Edward Topps. Dr. Blimber: John Sharp. Mrs. Blimber: Joan Gray. Cornelia Blimber: Gillian Webb. Mr. Toots: Christopher Sandford. John Carker: David Garth. James Carker: Gary Raymond. Mr. Feeder: Pitt Wilkinson. Johnson: Dominic Guard. Mrs. MacStinger: Barbara Mitchell. Mr. Perch: John Rudling. Major Bagstock: Clive Swift. The Hon. Mrs. Skewton: Marian Spencer. Edith Granger: Sally Home. Rob Toodle: Douglas Mann. Cousin Feenix: Geoffrey Edwards. Game Chicken: Milton Reid. Harriet Carker: Diana Scougall. Captain Bunsby: Barry Linehan.

MR. GUPPY'S TALE
BBC, UK, 1969, 50 mins
D: James MacTaggart. P: Jordan Lawrence. W: Hugh Whitemore. T: 9 Nov 1969. In series *Detective*.
Reverend Clarence Purefoy: Geoffrey Rose. William Guppy: Bill Fraser. William Knottage: Charles Adey-Grey. Mildred Knottage: Josie Bradley. Ernest Guppy: Esmond Knight. Beatrice Lidwill: Geraldine Newman. Ethel Guppy: Sheila Burrell. Samuel Lidwill: Hamilton Dyce. Albert Guppy: Jeremy Wilkin. George Lidwill: Russell Brown. Jemima Lidwill: Jenny McCracken. Alfred Knottage: Aubrey Morris. Charles Knottage: Michael Craze. From *Bleak House*.

CARRY ON CHRISTMAS
Thames TV, UK, 1969, 55 mins
D: Ronnie Baxter. P: Peter Eton W: Talbot Rothwell. T: 24 Dec 1969.
Scrooge: Sidney James. Spirit of Christmas Past: Charles Hawtrey. A spoof, starring Peter Rogers' *Carry On* team; other characters included Elizabeth Barrett, Robert Browning, Dracula, Frankenstein, and Cinderella.

THE GHOST AND CHRISTMAS PAST
ABC, USA, 1969, 30 mins
T: 25 Dec 1969. In series *The Ghost and Mrs. Muir*. From *A Christmas Carol*.

A CHRISTMAS CAROL
Air Programs Intl., Australia, 1969, 50 mins

Television and Video Productions   173

D: Zoran Janjic. P: Walter J. Hucker. W: Michael Robinson. T: US Dec 1970. Animated color film.

THE HERO OF MY LIFE
Thames TV, UK, 1970, 90 mins
D: Michael Darlow. W: Bruce Norman. P: Darlow and Norman. T: 9 Jun 1970; US 2 Mar 1972.
Charles Dickens: Michael Jayston. Maria Beadnell: Amanda Reiss. Ellen Ternan: Isla Blair. Eleanor P: Jo Rowbottom. Catherine Hogarth: Sheila Grant. Mary Hogarth: Ciaran Madden. George Hogarth: Maureen Beck. Mr. Hogarth: Anthony Higginson. Mrs. Hogarth: Dorothea Phillips. Dickens's father: Ken Wynne. Dickens's mother: Joan Haythorne. Nurse: Esme Church. Dickens as boy: Johnny Butler. John Forster: Jonathan Drew. Wilkie Collins: Colin Jeavons. Acting teacher: James Grout. Narrator: David March.

CLOSED DOORS
Thames TV, UK, 1970, 20 mins
D: Richard Gilbert. P: Charles Warren. W: Christopher Woodland. T: 3 & 6 Nov 1970. In schools program series *Ways With Words*, for 12 to 13 years. The theme was the outsider, interpreted through poems, and a scene from *Great Expectations*.
Miss Havisham: Joan Haythorne. Mr. Pumblechook: Billy Milton. Estella: Lynette Erving. Pip: Len Jones. Also: Bari Johnson, Patsy Crowther, Robert Efford.

SCROOGE GETS AN OSCAR
ABC, USA, 1970, 30 mins
D: George Tyne. P: Gerry Marshall. W: Ron Friedman. T: Dec 1970. In series *The Odd Couple*.
Oscar Madison (Scrooge): Tony Randall. Felix Unger: Jack Klugman.

THE GREAT INIMITABLE MR. DICKENS
BBC, UK, 1970, 90 mins
D: Ned Sherrin. W: Caryl Brahms, Ned Sherrin. T: 25 Dec 1970. A biography of Dickens based on scenes from his novels.
Charles Dickens: Anthony Hopkins. John Dickens: Arthur Lowe. Mrs. Dickens: Vivian Pickles. Elizabeth Ball Dickens: Sybil Thorndike. Rosa Emma Drummond: Nora Nicholson. Mr. Vuffin: Stanley Holloway. Mrs. Jarley: Mona Washbourne. Mrs. Gamp: Dandy Nichols. William Shaw: Freddie Jones. Macready: Patrick Cargill. Maria Beadnell: Joan Greenwood. Mrs. Ternan: Gladys Cooper. Dolby: Michael Wilding. Narrator: Gordon Jackson.

A CHRISTMAS CAROL
Anglia TV, UK, 1970, 50 mins
D: John Salway. P, W, and Narrator: Paul Honeyman. Drawings: John Worsley. T: 25 Dec 1970 (Anglia), 26 Dec 1970 (London).

LA PEQUENA DORRIT (Little Dorrit)
TVE, Spain, 1970, Serial 10x48 mins

EL DUELO (The Duel)
TVE, Spain, 1970, 42 mins
From *The Pickwick Papers?*

THE CRICKET ON THE HEARTH
CBS, USA, 1971, Length?
T: 25 Nov 1971. Animated film.

A CHRISTMAS CAROL
Richard Williams Studio, UK, 1971, 25 mins
D: Richard Williams. P: Chuck Jones. T: ABC US 21 Dec 1971; BBC 24 Dec 1972 & 25 Dec 1973. An animated color film in the style of the Phiz illustrations, made for the Foundation of Full Service Banks, USA.
Voices of: Michael Redgrave (Narrator), Alastair Sim (Scrooge), Michael Hordern (Marley's Ghost). Also: Melvyn Hayes, Joan Sims, Paul Whitsun-Jones, David Tate, Diana Quick, Felix Felton, Annie West, Mary Ellen Ray, Alexander Williams.

A CHRISTMAS TREE
?, USA, 1972, Length?
Rankin/Bass animation studio production.

MARCEL MARCEAU'S CHRISTMAS CAROL
BBC, UK, 1973, 40 mins
P: Tristram Powell. T: 23 Dec 1973.
The story narrated by Michael Hordern and mimed by the world-famous Marceau.

SMIKE!
BBC, UK, 1973, 55 mins
P: Paul Ciani. W: Roger Holman, Simon May. A pop stage musical adapted for TV by John Morley, Paul Ciani. T: 26 Dec 1973.
Smike: Ian Sharrock. Mrs. Steele/Mrs. Squeers: Beryl Reid. Mr. Steele/Mr. Squeers: Andrew Keir. Mr. Nicholls/Nicholas Nickleby: Leonard Whiting. Miss Grant/Fanny Squeers: Christine McKenna. Graymarsh: John Cooper.

Wackforth: Romeo Stavrou. Cobbey: Perry Clayton. Bolder: Andrew Rinous. Also: Pupils of the Kingston Grammar School.

DICKENS AND GREAT EXPECTATIONS
BBC & OU, UK, 1973, 25 mins
In series *The Nineteenth Century Novel and its Legacy*. Distributed by The Open University Film Library.

CHARLES DICKENS: CHILDHOOD IN VICTORIAN FICTION
BBC & OU, UK, 1973, 25 mins
In series *The Nineteenth Century Novel and its Legacy*. Distributed by The Open University Film Library.

TRIAL FOR MURDER
Anglia TV, UK, 1974, 30 mins
D: Peter Sykes. P: John Jacobs. W: C. A. Collins. T: 30 Apr 1976. US 13 Mar 1974. In series *Orson Welles Great Mysteries*.
Charles Stubbs: Ian Holm. Alice Stubbs: Jennie Linden. Higgins: Keith Buckley. Judge: Wallas Eaton. Sir Richard Muir, QC: John Savident. Vachell, QC: Hugh Dickson. Clerk of the Court: Tony Bateman. Warder: Barry Stanton. Masters: William Moore. Maria Perkins: Lindsay Ingram. Ghost of Venables: Edwin Finn. From *Doctor Marigold*.

DAVID COPPERFIELD
BBC, UK, 1974, Serial 6x55 mins
D: Joan Craft. P: John McRae. W: Hugh Whitemore. T: 1 Dec 1974 to 5 Jan 1975. R: 25 Apr to 30 May 1976. US 1977.
Betsey Trotwood: Patience Collier. Clara Copperfield: Colette O'Neil. Peggotty: Pat Keen. Mr. Chillip: John Gill. Davy: Jonathan Kahn. Mr. Murdstone: Gareth Thomas. Quinion: Oscar Quitak. Barkis: Edward Sinclair. Ham Peggotty: David Troughton. Little Emily: Katharine Levy. Dan Peggotty: Ian Hogg. Mrs. Gummidge: Lala Lloyd. Jane Murdstone: Anne Ridler. Mr. Mell: Laurence Carter. Mr. Creakle: Clifford Kershaw. Tungay: Victor Langley. Young Traddles: Richard Baxell. Steerforth: Anthony Andrews. Mr. Micawber: Arthur Lowe. Mick Walker: Michael Troughton. Mealy Potatoes: David Seath. Mrs. Micawber: Patricia Routledge. Mr. Dick: Timothy Bateson. Uriah Heep: Martin Jarvis. Mr. Wickfield: Godfrey Kenton. Mrs. Steerforth: Sheila Keith. Rosa Dartle: Jacqueline Pearce. Emily: Melanie Hughes. Mr. Spenlow: Anthony Sharp. Mrs. Crupp: Madeline Orr. Agnes Wickfield: Gail Harrison. Dora: Beth Morris. Clarissa: Hazel Bainbridge. Lavinia: Eileen Erskine. Traddles: Peter Bourke. Mr. Suckling; Stuart Latham.

THE CHARLES DICKENS SHOW
?, UK, 1974, 27 mins
D: Piers Jessop. P: John Seabourne.
With: Victor Spinetti, Roy McArthur, Paula Jacobs.
In series *Great Authors*. Intended for children aged 12 and up. Included dramatized excerpts from *Oliver Twist*, *Martin Chuzzlewit*, *David Copperfield*, and *A Christmas Carol*.

THE PARISH BOY'S PROGRESS
BBC, UK, 1975, 75 mins
P: Ben Rea. W: Nigel Williams. T: 13 Dec 1975. In series *2nd House*.
An examination of working class lives in Dickens's time, compared with those of characters in *Oliver Twist*. The title of the program is the subtitle of the novel.

THE ENERGY CAROL
NFB, Canada, 1975, 11 mins
D: Les Drew. P: Sidney Goldsmith. T: CBC 26 Dec 1975.
An animated educational film, depicting a wasteful Scrooge transformed by the spirits of energy past, present, and future. From *A Christmas Carol*.

OLIVER TWIST
Warner Bros, USA, 1975, 90 mins
An animated cartoon version. Same as below?

OLIVER AND THE ARTFUL DODGER
Warner Bros, USA, 1975, 90 mins?
R: US 7 Mar 1985, 10 Oct 1985. A cartoon sequel in the *Animated Classics* series, by the Hanna and Barbera partnership. From *Oliver Twist*.

SCROOGE
RCA, UK, 1975, 20 mins
D & W: Norman Stone. T: BBC ? In *First Picture Show*.
Scrooge: Ron Moody. Marley: Richard Caldecott. Cratchit: Graham Stark. TV reporter: John Benson. Citizen One: John Dryden. Citizen Two: Jonathan Burn.

OUR MUTUAL FRIEND
BBC, UK, 1976, Serial 7X55 mins
D: Peter Hammond. P: Martin Lisemore. W: Julia Jones. T: 1 Mar to 12 Apr 1976. R: 13 Jun to 25 Jul 1978. US 9 Apr to 21 May 1978.
Inspector: Brian Wilde. Juryman: Stuart Latham. Blight: Sean Clarke. Mr. Boffin: Leo McKern. Silas Wegg: Alfie Bass. Mrs. Boffin: Kathleen Harrison. Mrs. Wilfer: Patricia Lawrence. Bella: Jane Seymour. Lavinia: Debbie Ash.

Television and Video Productions

Mr. Wilfer: Ray Mort. Jenny Wren: Polly James. Riah: Harold Goldblatt. Bradley Headstone: Warren Clarke. Mr. Dolls: Edmond Bennett. Betty Higden: Hilda Barry. Gaffer Hexam: Duncan Lamont. Lizzie Hexam: Lesley Dunlop. Rogue Riderhood: John Colin. Retainer: John Baker. Twemlow: Jeffrey Gardiner. Mortimer Lightwood: Andrew Ray. Mr. Veneering: John Golightly. Lady Tippins: Agnes Lauchlan. Mrs. Veneering: Liza Ross. Mr. Podsnap: John Savident. Mrs. Podsnap: Jo Warne. Mr. Boots: Richard Stilgoe. Eugene Wrayburn: Nicholas Jones. Charley Hexam: Jack Wild. Julius Handford/John Harman/John Rokesmith: John McEnery. Sloppy: David Troughton. Mr. Venus: Ronald Lacey. Abbey Potterson: Joan Hickson. Bob Gliddery: Alan Collins. Tom Tootle: James Appleby. George Radfoot: James Kelly. Pleasant Riderhood: Lois Baxter.

DICKENS OF LONDON
Yorkshire TV, UK, 1976, Series 13x60 mins
D & P: Marc Miller. W: Wolf Mankowitz. T: 28 Sep to 21 Dec 1976. US 28 Aug to 30 Oct 1977 (10 episodes).
Charles Dickens (boy): Simon Bell. Charles Dickens (young man): Gene Foad. Charles Dickens (later ages): Roy Dotrice. John Dickens: Roy Dotrice. Mrs. Dickens: Diana Coupland. Pickwick: Bill Reimbold. Maria Beadnell: Karen Dotrice. Fanny Dickens: Henrietta Baynes. W. H. Ainsworth: David Ashford. John Macrone: John Nettles. Fred Dickens: Graham Faulkner. Catherine Hogarth: Adrienne Burgess. Georgina Hogarth: Christine McKenna. Chapman: John Ringham. Hall: Richard Kay. John Forster: Trevor Bowen. Hablot Browne: Robert Longden. Richard Bentley: John Baddeley. Quilp: Roy Dotrice. Fagin: Paul Nelson. Daniel Maclise: Richard Hampton. Poe: Seymour Matthews.
(On Christmas Day 1976, four days after the series ended in UK, Roy Dotrice appeared as Charles Dickens in *Carols From Durham Cathedral*, reading passages from Dickens's *Life of Our Lord*.)

THE SIGNALMAN
BBC, UK, 1976, 40 mins
D: Lawrence Gordon. P: Rosemary Hill. W: Andrew Davies. T: 22 Dec 1976. R: 21 Dec 1991.
Signalman: Denholm Elliott. Traveller: Bernard Lloyd. Bride: Carina Wyeth. Engine driver: Reginald Jessup. From *Mugby Junction*.

SCROOGE
BBC, UK, 1976, 50 mins
P: Alan Russell. M: Larry Ashmore, Johnny Coleman, Johnny Pearson, Derek Warne. T: 24 Dec 1976.
A musical performance by The All Star Record Breakers.
Scrooge: Roy Castle. From *A Christmas Carol*.

NICHOLAS NICKLEBY
BBC, UK, 1977, Serial 6x55 mins
D: Christopher Barry. P: Barry Letts. W: Hugh Leonard. T: 27 Mar to 1 May 1977. R: 1 Aug to 5 Sep 1978.
Ralph Nickleby: Derek Godfrey. Newman Noggs: Robert James. Mr. Bonney: Alec Linstead. Hannah: Jayne Lester. Miss LaCreevy: Patsy Smart. Mrs. Nickleby: Hilary Mason. Nicholas Nickleby: Nigel Havers. Kate Nickleby: Kate Nicholls. Wackford Squeers: Derek Francis. Belling: Mark Teal. Mr. Snawley: Ron Pember. Smike: Peter Bourke. Mrs. Squeers: Anne Ridler. Wackford, Jr.: Denis Gilmore. Cobbey: Roger Pope. Mobbs: Paul Pender. Graymarsh: Mark Rogers. Bolder: Paul Ellison. Alfred Mantalini: Malcolm Reid. Mme. Mantalini: Patricia Routledge. Fanny Squeers: Isabelle Aymes. Miss Knag: Gretchen Franklin. Matilda Price: Henrietta Baynes. John Browdie: Andrew McCulloch. Lord Frederick Verisopht: Nigel Hughes. Sir Mulberry Hawk: Anthony Ainley. Pyke: David Whitworth. Pluck: John Owens. Mrs. Kenwigs: Maureen Morris. Mr. Lillyvick: Edward Burnham. Miss Petowker: Pauline Moran. Morleena Kenwigs: Pia Martinus. Vincent Crummles: Freddie Jones. Mrs. Crummles: Pauline Letts. The Infant Phenomenon: Ann Hasson. Mr. Folair: Peter Forbes-Robertson. Mr. Lenville: Tom Durham. Miss Snevellicci: Joolia Cappleman. Mrs. Lenville: Gloria Walker. Mr. Snevellicci: Raymond Young. Charles Cheeryble: Raymond Mason. Tim Linkinwater: Preston Lockwood. Edwin Cheeryble: John Hewer. Madeline Bray: Patricia Brake. Brooker: Alan Collins. Walter Bray: Dennis Edwards. Arthur Gride: Paul Curran. Peg Sliderskew: Liz Smith. Mr. Westood: Roger Ostime. Captain Adams: Roger Leach. Frank Cheeryble: David Griffin.

HARD TIMES
Granada TV, UK, 1977, Serial 4x60 mins
D: John Irvin. P: Peter Eckersley. W: Arthur Hopcraft. T: 25 Oct to 15 Nov 1977. R: (Cut to 3x60 mins) 7 to 21 Jul 1979. R: (4 episodes) 11 Sep to 2 Oct 1983. US 18 May to 8 Jun 1976. R: US 1 to 22 Oct 1983.
Gradgrind: Patrick Allen. Bounderby: Timothy West. Stephen Blackpool: Alan Dobie. Rachel: Barbara Ewing. Mrs. Sparsit: Rosalie Crutchley. Mrs. Gradgrind: Ursula Howells. Louisa: Jacqueline Tong. Tom: Richard Wren. Sleary: Harry Markham. Sissy Jupe: Michelle Dibnah. Bitzer: Sean Flanagan. Childers: Tony Heath. Kidderminster: Michael Deeks. McChoakumchild: Paul Ridley. Mrs. Blackpool: Brenda Elder. James Harthouse: Edward Fox. Slackbridge: Patrick Durkin.

THE HONEYMOONERS' CHRISTMAS SPECIAL
ABC, USA, 1977, 60 mins
D: Jackie Gleason. P: Ed Waglin. W: Walter Stone, Robert Hilliard. T: 28 Nov 1977.

Ralph Cramden: Jackie Gleason. Ed Norton (Scrooge and Tiny Tim): Art Carney. Also: Audrey Meadows, Jane Kean, Johnny Owen. From *A Christmas Carol*.

BING CROSBY'S MERRIE OLDE CHRISTMAS
CBS, USA, 1977, 60 mins
D: Dwight Hemion. P: Gary Smith, Dwight Hemion. T: 30 Nov 1977. UK 24 Dec 1977.
Charles Dickens/Scrooge/Fagin/Quilp: Ron Moody. Tiny Tim/Artful Dodger/Little Nell: Twiggy.

A CHRISTMAS CAROL
BBC, UK, 1977, 60 mins
D: Moira Armstrong. P: Jonathan Powell. W: Elaine Morgan. T: 24 Dec 1977. R: 25 Dec 1979.
N: Alvar Liddell. Scrooge: Michael Hordern. Marley: John Le Mesurier. Bob Cratchit: Clive Merrison. Fred: Paul Copley. Christmas Past: Patricia Quinn. Scrooge as boy: Dorian Healy. Fan: Tracey Childs. Fezziwig: Will Stampe. Scrooge as young man: John Salthouse. Dick Wilkins: Nicholas John. Belle: Zoe Wanamaker. John: Stephen Churchett. Mrs. Cratchit: Carol MacReady. Peter Cratchit: David Ronder. Belinda Cratchit: Claire McLellan. Martha Cratchit: Zelah Clarke. Tiny Tim: Timothy Chasin. Christmas Future: Michael Mulcaster. Mrs. Dilber: June Brown. Christmas Present: Bernard Lee.

THE STINGIEST MAN IN TOWN
NBC, USA, 1978, 60 mins
D & P: Arthur Rankin, Jules Bass. W: Romeo Muller. M: Fred Spielman. Book and lyrics: Janice Torre. T: 23 Dec 1978.
Animated musical. With voices of Walter Matthau (Scrooge), Tom Bosley, Theodore Bikel, Robert Morse, Dennis Day, Paul Frees, Sonny Melendez, and others. From *A Christmas Carol*.

RICH LITTLE'S CHRISTMAS CAROL
CBC, Canada, 1978, 60 mins
D: Trevor Evans. T: 24 Dec 1978.
The impressionist Rich Little has, since 1963, been presenting and developing his *Scrooge and the Stars* version of the story, in which he plays the various characters as portrayed by Hollywood personalities and political celebrities. Thus W. C. Fields as Scrooge, Paul Linde as Cratchit, Richard Nixon as Marley, Johnny Carson as Fred, Truman Capote as Tiny Tim, Humphrey Bogart as the Ghost of Christmas Past, Columbo (Peter Falk) as Christmas Present, and Inspector Clouzot (Peter Sellers) as Christmas Future.

The show, also known as *The Merriest Christmas Yet*, has been repeated on TV in the USA and UK; e.g., US 2 Dec 1983.

A CHRISTMAS CAROL
HTV, UK, 1978, 55 mins
D & P: Michael Hayes. M: Norman Kay. W: John Morgan. T: 25 Dec 1978.
Scrooge: Geraint Evans. Bob Cratchit: Ryland Davies. Mrs. Cratchit: Elizabeth Gale. Also: Gwynne Howell.
A specially commissioned operatic version.

THE OLD CURIOSITY SHOP
BBC, UK, 1979, Serial 9x30 mins
D: Julian Amyes. P: Barry Letts. W: William Trevor. T: 9 Dec 1979 to 3 Feb 1980.
Grandfather Trent: Sebastian Shaw. Daniel Quilp: Trevor Peacock. Sampson Brass: Colin Jeavons. Mrs. Jiniwin: Freda Jackson. Little Nell: Natalie Ogle. Dick Swiveller: Granville Saxton. Kit Nubbles: Chris Fairbank. Mrs. Quilp Sandra Payne. Mrs. George: Daphne Anderson. Tom Scott: Colin Mayes. Mrs. Nubbles: Patsy Byrne. Little Jacob: Simon Garstang. Sally Brass: Freda Dowie. Mr. Witherden: Laurence Hardy. Mr. Garland: Donald Bissett. Mrs. Garland: Pauline Winter. Abel Garland: Keith Hazemore. Short: Bernard Stone. Codlin: Anthony Pedley. Jerry: Jerrold Wells. Grinder: Richard Merson. Vuffin: Tom Mennard. George: James Marcus. Mr. Slum: Peter Bland. Miss Monflathers: Pauline Letts. Single gentleman: Wensley Pithey. Mrs. Jarley: Margaret Courtenay. Marchioness: Annabelle Lanyon. Schoolmaster: Brian Oulton.

A CHRISTMAS CAROL AT FORD'S THEATRE
PBS, USA, 1979, 90 mins
D: Kirk Browning. P: Ron Bishop. W: Timothy Near, Rae Allen. T: 15 Dec 1979.
Scrooge: Ron Bishop.

AN AMERICAN CHRISTMAS CAROL
ABC, USA, 1979, 120 mins
D: Eric Till. W: Jerome Coopersmith. T: 16 Dec 1979.
Benedict Slade (Scrooge): Henry Winkler. Slade's employee: R. H. Thomson. Bookseller: David Wayne. Orphanage director: Gerard Parkes. Farmer: Dorian Harewood. Slade's fiancée: Susan Hogan.

THE SKINFLINT
?, USA, 1979, Length?
Cyrus Flint (Scrooge): Hoyt Axton. Ghost of Christmas Past: Martha Raye. Also: Barbara Mandrell, Larry Gatlin, Tom T. Hall, Lynn Anderson, Dottie

West, the Statler Brothers. A country and western style musical. From *A Christmas Carol*.

THE FURTHER ADVENTURES OF OLIVER TWIST
ATV, UK, 1980, Serial 13x30 mins
D: Ian Fordyce, Paul Harrison. P: Ian Fordyce. W: David Butler. T: 2 Mar to 1 Jun 1980. R: 28 Jul to 8 Sep 1981.
Oliver Twist: Daniel Murray. Rose Maylie: Mary Chilton. Harry Maylie: Derek Smith. Mrs. Bedwin: Dorothea Phillips. Fagin: David Swift. Artful Dodger: John Fowler. Ned Fingers: Gary Shail. Mr. Bumble: Harold Innocent. Noah Claypole: Leonard Preston. Mr. Stalker: Robert James. Monks: Geoffrey Larder. Charlotte: Pauline Quirke. Mr. Fang: William Fox.

A TALE OF TWO CITIES
BBC, UK, 1980, Serial 8x30 mins
D: Michael E. Briant. P: Barry Letts. W: Pieter Harding. T: 5 Oct to 23 Nov 1980. R: 4 Jul to 22 Aug 1982. US 28 Sep to 16 Nov 1980.
Sydney Carton/Charles Darnay: Paul Shelley. Jarvis Lorry: Nigel Stock. Dr. Manette: Ralph Michael. Lucie Manette: Sally Osborn. Miss Pross: Vivien Merchant. Mme. Defarge: Judy Parfitt. Defarge: Stephen Yardley. Jerry Cruncher: Peter Cleall. Young Cruncher: Dennis Savage. John Barsad: David Collings. Roger Cly: Frank Tregear. Jacques 1, 2, and 3: Michael Halsey, Brian Grellis, Eric Mason. Gabelle: David Webb. Stryver: Harold Innocent. Marquis St. Evremonde: Morris Perry. Gaspard: Michael Gothard. Attorney General: John Ringham. Roadmender: John Abineri. Doorkeeper: Royston Tickner.

A TALE OF TWO CITIES
ABC, USA, 1980, 120 mins
D: Jim Goddard. P: Norman Rosemount. W: John Gay. T: 2 Dec 1980. UK 7 Jan 1989.
Sydney Carton/Charles Darnay: Christopher Sarandon. Dr. Manette: Peter Cushing. Jarvis Lorry: Kenneth More. Miss Pross: Flora Robson. Mme. Defarge: Billie Whitelaw. Marquis St. Evremonde: Barry Morse. Lucie Manette: Alice Krige. Defarge: Norman Jones. Sergeant Stryver: Nigel Hawthorne. Jerry Cruncher: George Innes. Attorney General: Robert Urquhart. Lord Chief Justice: Kevin Stoney. Clerk of Court: Martin Carroll. Foreman: Wally Thomas. Barsad: David Suchet.

THE SECRET OF CHARLES DICKENS
? USA 1981 60 mins
T: 10 Aug 1981
Based on revelations by Dickens's daughter.

GREAT EXPECTATIONS
BBC, UK, 1981, Serial 12x30 mins
D: Julian Amyes. P: Barry Letts. W: James Andrew Hall. T: 4 Oct to 20 Dec 1981.
Pip, aged 9: Graham McGrath. Magwitch: Stratford Johns. Miss Havisham: Joan Hickson. Joe Gargery: Phillip Joseph. Uncle Pumblechook: John Stratton. Mrs. Joe: Marjorie Yates. Compeyson: Peter Whitbread. Mr. Wopsle: Peter Benson. Mr. Hubble: Walter Sparrow. Mrs. Hubble: Christine Ozanne. Orlick: Lionel Haft. Pip, aged 12: Paul Davies-Prowles. Estella as girl: Patsy Kensit. Sarah Pocket: Mollie Maureen. Herbert Pocket as boy: Jason Smart. Biddy: Christine Absalom. Mr. Jaggers: Derek Francis. Wemmick: Colin Jeavons. Herbert Pocket: Tim Munro. Pip: Gerry Sundquist. Trabb: James Belchamber. Trabb's boy: Colin Mayes. Mr. Pocket: Timothy Bateson. Mrs. Pocket: Elizabeth Morgan. Bentley Drummle: Iain Ormsby-Knox. Startop: Kevin Hart. Aged Parent: Tony Sympson. Estella: Sarah-Jane Varley. Miss Skiffins: Charlotte West-Orm. Clara Barley: Melanie Hughes. Bill Barley: Roger Bizley. Molly: Judith Buckingham.

ORPHANS, WAIFS AND WARDS
CBS, USA, 1981, 60 mins
T: 26 Nov 1981.
Fagin: John Schmuck. Extracts from 3 Dickens stories.

LE GRILLON DU FOYER (THE CRICKET ON THE HEARTH)
CBC, Canada, 1981, 120 mins
D: Florent Forget. W: Gerard Robert. T: 20 Dec 1981.
In series *Les Beaux Dimanches* by Societé Radio-Canada.
Dot: JoAnn Querel. John: Jacques Thisdele. Bertha: Roseline Hoffmann. Caleb: Guy Hoffmann. Madame Fielding: Olivette Thibaud. Tackleton: Paul Hebert. May: Denise Tessier. Edouard: Denis Mercier. La servante: Diane Cardinal. Le choeur: Toulouse.

MEL'S CHRISTMAS CAROL
CBS, USA, 1981, 30 mins
D: Marc Daniels. W: Vic Ranseo, Linda Morris. T: 20 Dec 1981. In comedy series *Alice*.
Mel Sharples (Scrooge): Vic Tayback. Ghosts of Christmas Past, Present, and Future: Jack Gilford.

BAH, HUMBUG!
CBS, USA, 1981, 30 mins
D: Rod Daniel. W: Lissa Levin. T: 23 Dec 1981. In comedy series *WKRP in Cincinnati*.

Arthur Carlson (Scrooge): Gordon Jump. Jennifer Marlowe (Ghost of Christmas Past): Loni Anderson. Venus Flytrap (Ghost of Christmas Present): Tim Reed. Johnny Fever (Ghost of Christmas Future): Howard Hesseman.
From *A Christmas Carol.*

THE OLD CURIOSITY SHOP
Burbank, Australia, 1981, Length?
Animated color film.

NICKLEBY & CO.
London Weekend TV, UK, 1982, 120 mins
D & P: Andrew Snell. Editor: Melvyn Bragg. T: 2 Aug 1982.
In series *The South Bank Show.* A special documentary showing the preparation and rehearsals of the Royal Shakespeare Company's landmark stage production of *Nicholas Nickleby.* For cast details, see below.

THE LIFE AND ADVENTURES OF NICHOLAS NICKLEBY
Primetime TV, UK, 1982, Serial 3x120 mins and 1x180 mins
D: Jim Doddard. P: Colin Callender. W: David Edgar.
A television record of the Royal Shakespeare Company's stage production. T: 7 to 28 Nov 1982 (weekly). R: 29 Dec 1987 to 1 Jan 1988 (daily). US 10 to 13 Jan 1983 (daily) on *Mobil Oil Showcase;* introduced by Peter Ustinov.
Nicholas Nickleby: Roger Rees. Kate Nickleby: Emily Richard. Ralph Nickleby: John Woodvine. Mrs. Nickleby: Jane Downs. Newman Noggs: Edward Petherbridge. Hannah: Hilary Townley. Miss LaCreevy: Rose Hill. Sir Matthew Pupker: David Lloyd Meredith. Mr. Bonney: Andrew Hawkins. Irate gentleman: Patrick Godfrey. Flunkey: Timothy Kightley. Mr. Snawley: William Maxwell. Snawley major: Janet Dale. Snawley minor: Hilary Townley. Belling: Stephen Rashbrook. William: John McEnery. Waitresses: Sharon Bower, Sally Nesbitt. Coachman: Clyde Pollit. Mr. Mantalini: John McEnery. Mme. Mantalini: Thelma Whiteley. Flunkey: Griffith Jones. Miss Knag: Janet Dale. Rich ladies: Sharon Bower, Shirley King. Mr. Squeers: Alun Armstrong. Mrs. Squeers: Lila Kaye. Smike: David Threlfall. Phib: Sally Nesbitt. Milliners: Suzanne Bertish, Sharon Bower, Ian East, Lucy Gutteridge, Cathryn Harrison, William Maxwell, Sally Nesbitt, Stephen Rashbrook, Hilary Townley. Fanny Squeers: Suzanne Bertish. Young Wackford Squeers: Ian McNeice. John Browdie: Bob Peck. Tilda Price: Cathryn Harrison. Tomkins: William Maxwell. Coates: Andrew Hawkins. Graymarsh: Alan Gill. Jennings: Patrick Godfrey. Mobbs: Christopher Ravenscroft. Bolder: Mark Tandy. Pitcher: Sharon Bower. Jackson: Nicholas Gecks. Cobbey: John McEnery. Peters: Teddy Kempner. Sprouter: Lucy Gutteridge. Roberts: Ian East. Brooker: Clyde Pollit. Walter Bray: Christopher Benjamin. Mr. Kenwigs: Patrick Godfrey. Mrs. Kenwigs:

Shirley King. Morleena Kenwigs: Hilary Townley. Mr. Lillyvick: Timothy Kightley. Miss Petowker: Cathryn Harrison. Mr. Crowl: Ian East. George: Alan Gill. Mr. Cutler: Jeffery Dench. Mrs. Cutler: Janet Dale. Mrs. Kenwigs' sister: Sharon Bower. Lady downstairs: Rose Hill. Miss Green: Jane Downs. Benjamin: Teddy Kempner. Pugstyles: Roderick Horn. Old Lord: Griffith Jones. Young Fiancee: Lucy Gutteridge. Landlord: Jeffery Dench. Vincent Crummles: Christopher Benjamin. Mrs. Crummles: Lila Kaye. Infant Phenomenon: Hilary Townley. Percy Crummles: Teddy Kempner. Master Crummles: Mark Tandy. Mrs. Grudden: Rose Hill. Miss Snevellicci: Suzanne Bertish. Mr. Folair: Clyde Pollitt. Mr. Lenville: Christopher Ravenscroft. Miss Ledrock: Lucy Gutteridge. Miss Bravassa: Sharon Bower. Mr. Wagstaff: Alun Armstrong. Miss Belvawney: Janet Dale. Miss Gazingi: Sally Nesbitt. Mr. Pailey: William Maxwell. Mr. Hetherington: Andrew Hawkins. Mr. Bane: Stephen Rashbrook. Mr. Fluggers: Griffith Jones. Mrs. Lenville: Shirley King. Mr. Curdle: Hubert Rees. Mrs. Curdle: Emily Richard. Sir Mulberry Hawk: Bob Peck. Lord Frederick Verisopht: Nicholas Gecks. Pluck: Teddy Kempner. Pyke: Mark Tandy. Mr. Snob: Christopher Ravenscroft. Col. Chowser: Timothy Kightley. Mr. Snevellicci: John McEnery. Mrs. Snevellicci: Thelma Whiteley. Scaley: Ian McNeice. Tix: Teddy Kempner. Mr. Wititterly: Roderick Horn. Mrs. Wititterly: Janet Dale. Opera singers: Sharon Bower, Andrew Hawkins, John Woodvine. Charles Cheeryble: David Lloyd Meredith. Ned Cheeryble: Hubert Rees. Tim Linkinwater: Griffith Jones. Nurse: Thelma Whiteley. Madeline Bray: Lucy Gutteridge. Frank Cheeryble: Christopher Ravenscroft. Arthur Gride: Jeffery Dench. Peg Sliderskew: Suzanne Bertish. Hawk's rival: Edward Petherbridge. Captain Adams: Andrew Hawkins. Westwood: Alan Gill. Croupier: Ian McNeice. Casino proprietor: Patrick Godfrey. Surgeon: Timothy Kightley. Umpire: Roderick Horn. Policemen: Andrew Hawkins, Mark Tandy. Mrs. Snawley: Janet Dale. Young woman: Hilary Townley.

THE DAY THE REBS TOOK LINCOLN
NBC, USA, 1982, 60 mins
D: Bernard McEveety. P: Robert Bennett Feinhauser. W: Robert Janes. T: 21 Nov 1982. In series *Voyagers*.
Phineas Bogg: John Eric Hexum. Jeffrey Jones: Meeno Peluce. Charles Dickens: Gerald Hichen. Abraham Lincoln: John Anderson. Also: Karen Dotrice.

A CHRISTMAS CAROL
BBC, UK, 1982, Serial 4x15 mins
D: Christine Secombe. P: Angela Beeching. W: Janie Grace. T: 21 to 24 Dec 1982.
Michael Bryant narrated the story, with illustrations by Paul Birkbeck.

A CHRISTMAS CAROL
Granada TV, UK, 1982, 120 mins
D: Dave Heather. P: Steve Hawes. T: 24 Dec 1982. Operatic version by Thea Musgrave, in the Royal Opera House Covent Garden production first given on the stage in the UK in 1981.
Scrooge: Frederick Burchinal. Spirit of Christmas: Murray Melvin. Fan/Belinda Cratchit/Liza Fezziwig/Lucy: Sandra Dugdale. Belle Fezziwig/Rosie: Eiddwen Harrby. Martha Cratchit: Vivien Townley. Mrs. Fezziwig/Aunt Louise: Elizabeth Bainbridge. Mrs. Cratchit: Phyllis Cannan. Bob Cratchit: Robin Leggate. Mr. Dorrit: Terry Jenkins. Ben: Philip Gelling. Fred: William Shimell. Mr. Fezziwig: Forbes Robinson. Marley's ghost: Philip Locke. Mr. Grubb: Howard Bell. Tiny Tim: Ivo Martinez.

A CHRISTMAS CAROL
Burbank Films, Australia, 1982, 72 mins
D: Jean Tych. P: Eddy Graham. W: Alex Budo.
Animated color film.

OLIVER TWIST
Burbank Films, Australia, 1982, 90 mins
D: Richard Slapczinski. P: George Stephenson. Animated color film. T: US 15 May 1984.

DAVID COPPERFIELD
Burbank Films, Australia, 1982, 90 mins
D: George Stephenson. Animated color film. T: US 2 Oct 1984.

GREAT EXPECTATIONS
Burbank Films, Australia, 1982, 72 mins
P: Eddy Graham. Animated color film.

THE MAGIC FISHBONE
Kratky Film Studios, Czechoslovakia, 1982, 11 mins
D: Marie Satrapova. Animated film ? From *A Holiday Romance*.

HARD TIMES
RCA, UK, 1982, 55 mins
D & P: Iain Bruce, Nick Dubrule, Ross Keith. With: Andrew de la Tour, Clare McIntyre, Alfred Molina, John Surman. Video. Includes dramatized excerpts from the novel. A 20-minute version appears to have been available in 1983.

DOMBEY AND SON
BBC, UK, 1983, Serial 10x30 mins

D: Rodney Bennett. P: Barry Letts. W: James Andrew Hall. T: 16 Jan to 20 Mar 1983.
Mr. Dombey: Julian Glover. Louisa Chick: Rhoda Lewis. Miss Tox: Shirley Cain. Young Florence: Romyanna Wood. Susan Nipper: Zelah Clarke. Dr. Parker Peps: Paul Imbusch. Towlinson: Kenton More. Mr. Chick: Ivor Roberts. Polly Toodle: Jenny McCracken. Young Biler: Bradley Hardiman. Jemima: Hetty Baynes. Toodle: Anthony Dutton. Carker: Paul Darrow. Captain Cuttle: Emrys James. Solomon Gills: Roger Milner. Perch: Ronald Herdman. Young Walter Gay: Finn Fordham. Florence: Lysette Anthony. Walter Gay: Max Gold. Paul Dombey: Barnaby Buik. Mrs. Pipchin: Barbara Hicks. Toots: Neal Swettenham. Bitherstone: Justin Salmon. Berinthia: Theresa Watson. Major Bagstock: James Cossins. Mr. Brogley: John Quarmby. The Hon. Mrs. Skewton: Diana King. Edith Granger: Sharon Maughan. Withers: Andrew Dunford. Biler: Steve Fletcher. Mrs. Parker Peps: Nancy Mansfield. Lord Feenix: Roger Ostime.

A CHRISTMAS CAROL
CBS, USA, 1983, 30 mins
T: 4 Dec 1983. In series *Kenner Family Classics*.
Animated color film.

A CHRISTMAS CAROL
NBC, USA, 1983, Length ?
T: 14 Dec 1983. In comedy series *Family Ties*.

THE GOSPEL ACCORDING TO SCROOGE
CBN, USA, 1983, 120 mins
W & M: James P. Schumacher. N: Dean Jones. T: 23 Dec 1983. Fundamentalist musical, on the Christian Broadcasting Network. From *A Christmas Carol*.

THE GREAT SANTA CLAUS CHASE
CBS, USA, 1983, 60 mins
D: Denver Pyle. W: Martin Roth. T: 23 Dec 1983. In comedy series *The Dukes of Hazzard*.
Boss Hogg (Scrooge): Sorrell Brookes. From *A Christmas Carol*.

A CHRISTMAS CAROL
Burbank Films, Australia, 1983, 90 mins?
Animated color film.

A DIFFERENT TWIST
ABC, USA, 1984, 30 mins
T: 10 Mar 1984.

Drama concerning a girl auditioning for the role of the Artful Dodger in the musical *Oliver!* From *Oliver Twist*.

A CHRISTMAS CAROL
WNEO, USA, 1984, 90 mins
T: 22 Dec 1984. Dramatization performed at the F. Turner Stump Theatre, Kent State University.

CHRISTMAS CAROL
TF1, France, 1984, 90 mins
D & W: Pierre Boutron. T: 25 Dec 1984.
Scrooge: Michel Bouquet. Spirit of Christmas Past: Pierre Clementi. Christmas Present: Georges Wilson. Christmas Future: Lisette Malidor. Bob Cratchit: Pierre Olaf. Scrooge's nephew: Manuel Bonnet. Also: Bernard Bauguli, Phillipe Brizart, Serge Calic, Bernard Cazassus, Phillipe Cousin, Pierre Devilder, Arnaud-Didier Fuchs, David Gabison, Jeanne Herivale, Franck Personne.

A TALE OF TWO CITIES
Burbank Films, Australia, 1984, 55 mins
D: George Stephenson. Animated color film.

GREAT EXPECTATIONS AND CHARLES DICKENS
Penguin Books, UK?, 1984, 90 mins
D & P: Noel Hardy. W: Julia Jones.
A Penguin Study video, which includes dramatizations of parts of the book and a reenactment of one of Dickens's public readings.

THE PICKWICK PAPERS
BBC, UK, 1985, Serial 12x30 mins
D: Brian Lighthill. P: Barry Letts. W: Jack Davies. T: 6 Jan to 24 Mar 1985. Mr. Pickwick: Nigel Stock. Tupman: Clive Swift. Winkle: Jeremy Nicholas. Snodgrass: Alan Parnaby. Jingle: Patrick Malahide. Sam Weller: Phil Daniels. Mr. Wardle: Colin Douglas. Rachel Wardle: Freda Dowie. Mrs. Wardle: Patience Collier. Arabella Allen: Sarah Finch. Isabella Wardle: Dione Inman. Emily Wardle: Valerie Whittington. Joe: David Nunn. Dr. Slammer: Gerald James. Lt. Tapperton: John Patrick. Dr. Payne: David Webb. Sergeant Buzfuz: David Waller. Sergeant Snubbin: John Woodnutt. Mr. Perker: Milton Johns. Mr. Justice Stareleigh: Leslie Glazer. Fogg: Kenneth Waller. Phunky: Michael Ripper. Mrs. Bardell: Jo Kendall. Mrs. Sanders: June Ellis. Mrs. Cluppins: Deddie Davies. Master Bardell: Ned Williams. Mr. Roker: Dallas Cavell. Tony Weller: Howard Lang. Peter Magnus: George Little. Miss Witherfield: Shirley Cain. Mr. Winkle, Sr.: Geoffrey Edwards. Mary: Tamsin Heatley. Mrs. Budger: Mary Maxted. Mr. Trundle: Nicholas Jeune.

BLEAK HOUSE
BBC, UK, 1985, Serial 8x55 mins
D: Ross Devenish. P: John Harris, Betty Willingale. W: Arthur Hopcraft. T: 10 Apr to 29 May 1985. R: 3 Jan to 21 Feb 1991. US: 1 Dec 1985 to 19 Jan 1986.
Young Esther: Rebecca Sebborn. Miss Barbary: Fiona Walker. Esther Summerson: Suzanne Burden. Jo: Chris Pitt. Nemo: Donald Sumpter. William Guppy: Jonathan Moore. Lord Chancellor: Graham Crowden. Ada Clare: Lucy Hornak. Richard Carstone: Philip Franks. Miss Flite: Sylvia Coleridge. Krook: Bernard Hepton. Tulkinghorn: Peter Vaughan. Sir Leicester Dedlock: Robin Bailey. Lady Dedlock: Diana Rigg. Gridley: Frank Windsor. Guster: Kathy Burke. Snagsby: Sam Kelly. John Jarndyce: Denholm Elliott. Harold Skimpole: T. P. McKenna. Beadle: Christopher Whitehouse. Coroner: Gerald Flood. Allan Woodcourt: Brian Deacon. Neckett: Bill Wallis. Hortense: Pamela Merrick. Boythorn: Robert Urquhart. Mrs. Pardiggle: Rosemary McHale. Brickmaker: Jack Carr. Brickmaker's wife: Heather Tobias. Mrs. Blinder: Patsy Byrne. Tom Neckett: James Holland. Charley Neckett: Samantha Holland. Mrs. Smallweed: Katharine Page. Smallweed: Charlie Drake. Judy Smallweed: Eileen Davies. Rosa: Felicity Finch. Sergeant George: Dave King. Phil Squod: Harry Jones. Mrs. Snagsby: Hilary Crane. The Reverend Chadband: Malcolm Terris. Mrs. Chadband: Stella Tanner. Inspector Bucket: Ian Hogg. Watt Rouncewell: Paul Venables. Ironmaster Rouncewell: George Sewell. Mrs. Rouncewell: Gabrielle Daye. Mrs. Guppy: Pat Coombs. Jenny: Heather Tobias. Mrs. Bagnet: Anne Reid. Bagnet: Guy Standeven. Vholes: Colin Jeavons. Kenge: Anthony Raye.

OLIVER TWIST
BBC, UK, 1985, Serial 12x30 mins
D: Gareth Davies. P: Terrance Dicks. W: Alexander Baron. T: 13 Oct to 29 Dec 1985. R: 4 Apr to 27 Jun 1987. US: 7 Jan to 8 Feb 1986. R: 2 Dec 1986 to 6 Jan 1987.
Young Oliver Twist: Scott Funnell. Agnes Fleming: Lysette Anthony. Mr. Bumble: Godfrey James. Old Sally: Betty Turner. Mrs. Mann: June Brown. Oliver Twist: Ben Rodska. Monks: Pip Donaghy. Mr. Sowerberry: Raymond Witch. Mrs. Sowerberry: Elizabeth Proud. Charlotte: Carys Llewelyn. Noah Claypole: Julian Firth. Fagin: Eric Porter. Mr. Brownlow: Frank Middlemass. Artful Dodger: David Garlick. Charley Bates: Nicholas Bond-Owen. Bill Sikes: Michael Attwell. Bookseller: Jeffrey Segal. Fang: Henry Stamper. Nancy: Amanda Harris. Mrs. Bedwin: Hilda Braid. Mr. Grimwig: Edward Burnham. Mrs. Corney: Miriam Margoyles. Toby Crackit: Christopher Driscoll. Martha: Janet Henfrey. Susan: Margaret Ainley. Mrs. Maylie: Gillian Martell. Dr. Losberne: David McKail. Rose

Maylie: Lysette Anthony. Harry Maylie: Dominic Jephcott. Giles: David King.

CHRISTMAS CAROL II: THE SEQUEL
CBS, USA, 1985, 30 mins
In *George Burns' Comedy Week*. T: 11 Dec 1985. Scrooge: James Whitmore.

(TITLE UNKNOWN)
? USA 1985 Length ?
W: Carl Gottlieb, David Axelrod. T: 14 Dec 1985. In series *Fame*.
From *A Christmas Carol*. Quentin Morlock (Scrooge): Ken Swofford.

CHRISTMAS PRESENT
Telekation Intl., UK, 1985, 80 mins
D & W: Tony Bicat. P: Barry Hanson. T: 19 Dec 1985.
Nigel Playfayre (Scrooge): Peter Chelsom. From *A Christmas Carol*.

OLIVER TWIST
Burbank Films, Australia, 1985, 75 mins
D: Richard Slapczynski. P: Jean Tych. W: John Palmer. Animated color film.

THE PICKWICK PAPERS
Burbank Films, Australia, 1985, 75 mins
D: Warwick Gilbert. Animated color film.

DAVID COPPERFIELD
BBC, UK, 1986, Serial 10x30 mins
D: Barry Letts. P: Terrance Dicks. W: James Andrew Hall. T: 10 Oct to 21 Dec 1986. US: 27 Mar to 1 May 1988 (@ 60 mins).
Young David: David Dexter. Betsey Trotwood: Brenda Bruce. Mr. Murdstone: Oliver Cotton. Peggotty: Jenny McCracken. David Copperfield: Colin Hurley. Clara: Francesca Hall. Dr. Chillip: Giles Oldershaw. Barkis: Ronald Herdman. Ham: Owen Teale. Mrs. Gummidge: Hilary Mason. Young Emily: Lee-Emma Blakemore. Daniel Peggotty: Stephen Thorne. Jane Murdstone: Sarah Crowden. Mr. Mell: Reggie Oliver. Demple: Jonathan Lacey. Young Traddles: Dylan Dolan. Steerforth: Jeremy Brudenell. Boys: Nicholas Bond-Owen, Chris Chandler. Mr. Creakle: John Savident. Mr. Sharp: Leon Eagles. Micawber: Simon Callow. David (older boy): Nolan Hemmings. Mrs. Micawber: Sandra Payne. Mr. Dick: Thorley Walters. Janet: Jenny Funnell. Uriah Heep: Paul Brightwell. Mr. Wickfield: Artro Morris. Young Agnes: Sophie Green. Agnes Wickfield: Natalie Ogle. Mrs. Steerforth: Nyree Dawn Porter. Rosa Dartle: Alison Fiske. Emily: Valerie Gogan. Mr. Spenlow: Terence Lodge. Tiffey: John Baker. Dora: Francesca Hall. Mrs. Crupp: Fanny Carby. Captain Trigger: Mark Bassen-

senger. Julia Mills: Irene Richard. Markham: Mark Strickson. Grainger: Philip Wright. Traddles: Neal Swettenham. Mrs. Heep: Ann Way.

THE OLD CURIOSITY SHOP
Rikini Ltd, Australia, 1986, 75 mins
D: Warwick Gilbert. P: Eddy Graham. Animated color film. T: US 6 Apr 1986. R: 4 Feb 1989.

JOHN GRIN'S CHRISTMAS
ABC, USA, 1986, 60 mins
D: Robert Guillaume. W: Charles Eric Johnson. T: 6 Dec 1986.
John Grin: Robert Guillaume. Also: Roscoe Lee Browne, Ted Lange, Geoffrey Holder, Alonso Robeiro. From *A Christmas Carol*.

IT'S A WONDERFUL JOB
ABC, USA, 1986, 60 mins
D: Ed Sherin. W: Debra Frank, Carl Sautter. T: 16 Dec 1986. UK 22 Dec 1988. Episode in detective series *Moonlighting*.
Maddie Hayes (Scrooge): Cybill Shepherd. Agnes Dipesto (Cratchit): Allyce Beasley. From *A Christmas Carol*.

OLIVER TWIST
Emerald City Prodns., USA, 1986, 60 mins
D, P, & W: Al Guest, Jean Mathieson. Animated color film.

GREAT EXPECTATIONS - THE UNTOLD STORY
ABC, Australia, 1987, Serial 6x60 mins
D & W: Tim Burstall. P: Ray Alchin, Tom Burstall. T: 7 Feb to 14 Mar 1987. Magwitch: John Stanton. Pip: Todd Boyce. Estella: Anne Louise Lambert. Jaggers: Noel Ferrier. Bridget: Sigrid Thornton. Joe Gargery: Bruce Spence. Solomon Tooth: Gerard Kennedy. Miss Havisham: Jill Forster. Pip as child: Danny Simmonds. Estella as child: Leah Richardson. Bentley Drummle: Leigh Biolis. Herbert Pocket: David Sandford. Molly: Jennifer Hagan. Biddy: Nell Schofield. Wemmick: Alan Tobin. Uncle Pumblechook: Brian Moll. Mr. Wopsle: Tony Taylor. Mrs. Joe: Annie Byron. Startop: John Linton. Sergeant: Anthony Wager. Mr. Trabb: Ron Hackett. Sarah Pocket: Philomena Lonergan.

GHOST STORIES FROM PICKWICK PAPERS
Emerald City Prodns., USA, 1987, 50 mins
D, P, & W: Al Guest, Jean Mathieson. T: US 11 Oct 1990. Animated color film.

Television and Video Productions 191

SCENES FROM GREAT EXPECTATIONS
Dickens Project, USA, 1987, 35 mins
W: Kate Rickman. M: Gene Lewis.
With: Robert Fenwick, Gene Lewis, Simon Kelly, Kate Rickman. Issued as video cassette.

BLACKADDER'S CHRISTMAS CAROL
BBC, UK, 1988, 45 mins
D: Richard Boden. P: John Lloyd. W: Richard Curtis, Ben Elton. T: 23 Dec 1988. R: 23 May 1989.
Ebenezer Blackadder: Rowan Atkinson. Baldrick: Tony Robinson. Spirit of Christmas: Robbie Coltrane. Queen Elizabeth I: Miranda Richardson. Lord Melchet: Stephen Fry. Prince Regent: Hugh Laurie. Queen Victoria: Miriam Margoyles. Prince Albert: Jim Broadbent. King Bernard: Patsy Byrne. Mrs. Scratchit: Pauline Melille.

SEE, HEAR
BBC, UK, 1988, Length ?
A Christmas special in a series for the deaf, which included a special adaptation, with subtitles and sign language, of *A Christmas Carol*.

SCENES FROM HARD TIMES
Dickens Project, USA, 1988, 45 mins
D: Andrew Doe, Becca King. W: Kate Rickman.
With: Robert Fenwick, Claire-Marie Ghelardi, Simon Kelly, Gene Lewis, Kate Rickman, Richard Salzberg. Issued as video cassette.

A TALE OF TWO CITIES
Granada TV/Dune AT2, UK/France, 1989, 120 and 105 mins
D: Philippe Mounier. P: Roy Roberts. W: Arthur Hopcraft. T: 21 & 22 May 1989. US 19 Nov & 3 Dec 1989.
Sydney Carton: James Wilby. Charles Darnay: Xavier Deluc. Lucie Manette: Serena Gordon. Jarvis Lorry: John Mills. Dr. Manette: Jean-Pierre Aumont. Miss Pross: Anna Massey. Jerry Cruncher: Alfred Lynch. Mme. Defarge: Kathie Kriegel. Defarge: Gerard Klein. Marquis St. Evremonde: Jean-Marc Bory. Gaspard: Jean-Paul Tribout. Mrs. Cruncher: Mary Healey. Young Jerry: James Patten. Old chemist: John Serret. Judge: John Moffatt. Attorney General: John Woodvine. Public Prosecutor: Jean-Pierre Stewart. Sergeant Stryver: Jonathan Adams. Cly: Derek Deadman. Barsad: Karl Johnson. Roadmender: Gilles Gaston-Dreyfus. Gabelle: Francois Lalande. Undertaker: Anthony Benson. Clergyman: Ron McCormick. Vengeance: Zoe Zag.

HUNTED DOWN
Thames TV, UK, 1989, 60 mins
D: Michael Simpson. P: Michael Chapman. W: Hugh Leonard. T: 30 May 1989. In series *Storyboard*.
Aeneas Sampson: Alec McCowen. Vicar: Philip Dunbar. Skipton: Stephen Moore. Margaret Winer: Polly Walker. Adams: John Southworth. Hewes: Clive Swift. Landlady: Maggie McCarthy. Alfred Beckwith: Nicholas Gecks. Krane: Richard Beale. Lady: Jo Abercrombie. Man: Jim Holmes.

GREAT EXPECTATIONS
Primetime et al, UK, 1989, Serial 3x120 mins or 6x60 mins
D: Kevin Connor. P: Greg Smith. W: John Goldsmith. T: US 24 to 26 Jul 1989. UK 21 Jul to 25 Aug 1991. A coproduction by Primetime, Disney Channel, HTV, and Tesauro TV (Spain).
Miss Havisham: Jean Simmons. Joe Gargery: John Rhys Davies. Pip: Anthony Calf. Mr. Jaggers: Ray McAnally. Estella: Kim Thomson. Magwitch: Anthony Hopkins. Herbert Pocket: Adam Blackwood. Compeyson: Sean Arnold. Orlick: Niven Boyd. Biddy: Susan Franklyn. Young Pip: Martin Harvey. Mr. Wemmick: Charles Lewsen. Mrs. Joe: Rosemary McHale. Uncle Pumblechook: Frank Middlemass. Mr. Wopsle: John Quentin. Bentley Drummle: Owen Teale. Trabb: Frank Thornton. Hoddle: Preston Lockwood. Mrs. Hoddle: Eve Pearce. Sergeant: P. J. Davidson. Sarah Pocket: Maria Charles. Georgina Pocket: Madaleine Moffatt. Mr. Raymond: Gerald Campion. Mrs. Pegge: Hilary Mason. Mrs. Camilla: Shirley Stelfox. Young Herbert Pocket: Henry Power. Urchin: John Savage. Jaggers' client: Desmond Barrit. Sarak: Martino Lazzeri. Startop: Simon Warwick. Philbean: Charles Pemberton. Molly: Carolyn Jones. Mrs. Pocket: Angela Ellis. Aged Parent: Arthur Hewlet. Matthew Pocket: Jonathan Newth. The Avenger: Paul Reynolds. Finch: Jonathan Stevens. Miss Skiffins: Sarah Crowden. Vicar: Jeffrey Gardiner. Ophelia: Christine Moore. Fat partygoer: John Quarmby. Clara: Stephanie Schonfeld. Doctor: Frank Moody. Judge: John Sharp. Clerk of Court: Peter Gorey. Customs Officer: Peter Spraggon.

ERASMUS MICROMAN
Granada TV, UK, 1989, 25 mins
D: David Richards. P: Stephen Trombley. T: 24 Nov 1989.
Charles Dickens: Steve Steen. Jane Austen: Amanda Swift.

MR. DICKENS PRESENTS
BBC, UK, 1989, 35 mins
W: John Kassman. T: 1 Dec 1989. In school series *English File*.
Charles Dickens: Paul Beech.

DAVID COPPERFIELD
Dickens Project, USA, 1989, 50 mins
D: Dan Bessie. W: Kate Rickman. With: Robert Fenwick, Kate Rickman, Simon Kelly, Gene Lewis, Claire-Marie Ghelardi, Elizabeth Shipley, Sheffield Chastain, James Rickman. Issued as video cassette.

A TALE OF TWO CITIES
Emerald City Prodns., USA, 1989, 60 mins
D, P, & W: Al Guest, Jean Mathieson. Animated color film.

ACKROYD'S DICKENS
London Weekend TV, UK, 1990, 75 mins
D & P: David Thomas. W: Melvyn Bragg. T: 9 Sep 1990. In series *South Bank Show*. Charles Dickens: John Sessions. A documentary to coincide with Peter Ackroyd's massive biography of Dickens.

FAMOUS AUTHORS: CHARLES DICKENS
Skon Productions, UK, 1991, 30 mins
D & P: Malcolm Hossick. A concise pictorial biography. Issued as video cassette.

UNDERSTANDING NARRATIVE: DICKENS'S HARD TIMES
BBC OUPC, UK, 1993, 25 mins
T: 20 and 24 Mar 1993. A program in the Arts Foundation course, with extracts from Chapter 3 of *Hard Times*. Bounderby/Gradgrind: Stephen Ley. Mrs. Gradgrind/Louisa: Kate Binchy. N: Stephen Earle.

THE NEW ADVENTURES OF OLIVER TWIST
?, Mexico, ?, 92 mins
T: UK 7 Oct 1993 onward.
Animated film.

BRER RABBIT'S CHRISTMAS CAROL
?, USA, ?, 58 mins
D: Al Guest. T: UK 17 Dec 1993
Animated film.

A CHRISTMAS CAROL
BBC, UK, 1993, 90 mins
D: Kriss Rumanis. P: Christopher Gable. M: Carl Davis.
W: Davis and Gable. T: 25 Dec 1993
Performed by the Northern Ballet Theatre.
Scrooge: Jeremy Kerridge. Bob Cratchit: William Walker. Mrs. Cratchit: Polly Benge. Cratchit children: Katherine Fletcher, Claire Rowland, Chris-

topher Akrill. Tiny Tim: Ryan Ward. Marley's Ghost: Matthew Madsen. Christmas Past: Lorena Vidal. Christmas Present: Royce Neagle. Christmas Future: Steven Wheeler. Fezziwig: Graham Fletcher. Mrs. Fezziwig: Victoria Westall. Young Scrooge: Fergus Logan. Fiancee: Jayne Regan. Scrooge's nephew: Peter Parker. His wife: Graciela Kaplan. BBC Philharmonic Orchestra, conductor John Pryce-Jones. Recorded at the Victoria Theatre, Halifax, Yorkshire. A BBC/Arts & Entertainment Network/RPTA Primetime coproduction.

HARD TIMES
BBC, UK, 1994, Serial 4x30 mins
D & W: Peter Barnes. P: Richard Langridge. T: 29 Apr to 29 May 1994. R: 30 Sep to 21 Oct 1994.
Mrs. Sparsit: Dilys Laye. Bounderby: Alan Bates. Gradgrind: Bob Peck. Rachel: Harriet Walter. Tom: Christien Anholt. Bitzer: Alex Jennings. Louisa: Beatie Edney. Sissy: Emma Lewis. Bounderby's mother: Patsy Byrne. Blackpool: Bill Paterson. Miner: Christopher Ettridge. Sleary: Peter Bayliss. Kidderminster: Jonathan Butterell. Childers: Timothy Bateson. Young Louisa: Elizabeth Cornfield. Young Tom: Damian Hunt. Coproduction with WGBH/Boston.

MARTIN CHUZZLEWIT
BBC, UK, 1994, Serial 1x90 mins, 5x60 mins
D: Pedr James. P: Chris Parr. W: David Lodge. T: 7 Nov to 12 Dec 1994.
Old Martin/Anthony Chuzzlewit: Paul Scofield. Seth Pecksniff: Tom Wilkinson. Montague Tigg: Pete Postlethwaite. Jonas Chuzzlewit: Keith Allen. Tom Pinch: Philip Franks. Mercy Pecksniff: Julia Sawalha. Charity Pecksniff: Emma Chambers. Young Martin: Ben Walden. Mrs. Lupin: Lynda Bellingham. Mary Graham: Pauline Turner. Mark Tapley: Steve Nicolson. Mrs. Todgers: Maggie Steed. Chevy Slime: Peter-Hugo Daly. Bailey: Paul Francis. John Westlock: Peter Wingfield. Ruth Pinch: Cornelia Hayes O'Herlihy. Augustus Moddle: John Padden. Mr. Jinkins: Robin Hooper. Chuffey: John Mills. Mrs. Gamp: Elizabeth Spriggs. Betsy Prig: Joan Sims.

Bibliography

American Film Institute Catalog, *Feature Films 1911-1920*. Berkeley: University of California Press, 1988.
American Film Institute Catalog, *Feature Films 1921-1930*, New York: R. R. Bowker, 1971.
American Film Institute Catalog, *Feature Films 1931-1940*. Berkeley: University of California Press, 1993).
American Film Institute Catalog, *Feature Films 1961-1970*. New York: R. R. Bowker, 1976.
Arvidson, Linda, *When the Movies Were Young*. New York: E. P. Dutton, 1925.
Behlmer, Rudy, *Memo From David O. Selznick*. New York: Macmillan, 1973.
Blount, Trevor, *Charles Dickens: The Early Novels*. London: British Council, 1968.
Bluestone, George, *Novels Into Film*. Berkeley: University of California Press, 1966.
Bolton, H. Philip, *Dickens Dramatized*. London: Mansell, 1987.
Brownlow, Kevin, *The Parade's Gone By*. London: Secker and Warburg, 1968.
Catalog of Copyright Entries, *Motion Pictures 1894-1912, 1912-1939, 1940-1949, 1950-1959*. Washington, DC: Library of Congress, 1951 onward.
Chirat, Raymond, *Catalogue des films français de long metrage 1919-1929*.Toulouse: Cinémathèque de Toulouse, 1984. *Catalogue des films français de long metrage 1929-1939*. Brussels: Cinémathèque Royale de Belge, 1975.
Clarens, Carlos, *George Cukor*. London: Secker and Warburg, 1976.
Cooke, Alistair, *Garbo and the Night Watchmen*. London: Jonathan Cape, 1937.
_____. *Masterpieces*. London: Bodley Head, 1981.
Daisne, Johan, *Dictionnaire Filmographique de la Litterature Mondiale*. Ghent: Editions Scientifiques, 1971.

Davis, Paul, *The Lives and Times of Ebenezer Scrooge*. New Haven, CT: Yale University Press, 1990.

Davy, Charles, *Footnotes to the Film*. London: Lovat Dickson, 1938.

Eisner, Joel, and Krinsky, David, *Television Comedy Series*. Jefferson, NC: McFarland, 1984.

Fielding, K. J., *Charles Dickens*. London: British Council, 1953.

Garis, Robert, *The Dickens Theatre*, London: Oxford University Press, 1965.

Gianakos, Larry James, *Television Drama Series Programming 1947-1959, 1959-1975, 1975-1980, 1980-1982, 1982-1984, 1984-1986*. Metuchen, NJ: Scarecrow Press, 1978 onward.

Gifford, Denis, *British Film Catalogue 1895-1970*. Newton Abbot: David & Charles, 1973.

Hardy, Barbara, *Charles Dickens: The Later Novels*. London: British Council, 1977.

Haver, Ronald, *David O. Selznick's Hollywood*. New York: Alfred A. Knopf, 1980.

Hepworth, Cecil M., *Came the Dawn*. London: Phoenix House, 1951.

Hicks, Seymour, *Between Ourselves*. London: Cassell, 1930.

Klein, Michael, and Parker, Gillian, *The English Novel and the Movies*. New York: Frederick Ungar, 1981.

Koszarski, Richard, *Hollywood Directors 1914-1920*. New York: Oxford University Press, 1976.

Lambert, Gavin, *On Cukor*. London: W. H. Allen, 1973.

Lanchester, Elsa, *Charles Laughton and I*. London: Faber, 1938.

Lauritzen, Einar and Lundquist, Gunnar, *American Film Index 1908-1915*. Stockholm: Film-Index, 1976.

_____. *American Film Index 1916-1920*. Stockholm: Film-Index, 1984.

Lean, David, *Great Expectations: Article in The Cinema 1952*. London: Penguin Books, 1952.

Leese, Betty, Unpublished typescript: Dickens filmography. London: BFI Library.

Limbacher, James, *Haven't I Seen You Somewhere Before?* Ann Arbor, MI: Pierian Press, 1980.

Low, Rachael, *The History of the British Film 1906-1914, 1914-1918, 1918-1929*. London: Allen and Unwin, 1949 onward.

Pearson, George, *Flashback*. London: Allen and Unwin, 1957.

Philip, Alex J., and Gadd, Laurence, *The Dickens Dictionary*. London: Simpkin Marshall, 1928.

Pratley, Gerald, *The Cinema of David Lean*. Cranbury, NJ: A. S. Barnes, 1974.
Richardson, Robert, *Literature and Film*. Bloomington: Indiana University Press, 1969.
Rosenberg, Bernard, and Silverstein, Harry, *The Real Tinsel*. New York: Macmillan, 1970.
Rubin, Leon, *The Nicholas Nickleby Story*. London: Heinemann, 1981.
Silver, Alan, and Ursini, James, *David Lean and his Films*. London: Leslie Frewin, 1974.
Silverman, Stephen M., *David Lean*. New York: Harry N. Abrams, 1989.
Sinyard, Neil, *Filming Literature*. London: Croom Helm, 1986.
Slide, Anthony, *The Big V*. Metuchen, NJ: Scarecrow Press, 1976.
Wagenknecht, Edward, *The Movies in the Age of Innocence*. Norman: University of Oklahoma Press, 1962.
Wagner, Geoffrey, *The Novel and the Cinema*. London: A. S. Barnes, 1975.
Williams, Bransby, *By Himself*. London: Hutchinson, 1954.
York, Michael, *Travelling Player*. London: Headline, 1991.

Periodicals Consulted

Bianco e Nero
The Bioscope
The Dickensian
The Era
Films in Review
Focus on Film
Hollywood Reporter
Journal of the Society of Film and Television Arts
Der Kinematograph
Kinematograph Weekly
Monthly Film Bulletin

The Moving Picture World
The New York Times
Radio Times
Screen
Screen International
Sight and Sound
The Stage
Telerama
The Times

TV France
TV Times
Variety

Index

Abelow, S. I. 80
Ackland, Joss 88
Ackroyd's Dickens 193
The Adventures of Mr. Pickwick 45, 130
Affaire Bardell contre Pickwick 163
Alice 101, 182
Allan Elizabeth 59
Allen, Patrick 85
An American Christmas Carol 101, 180
American Mutoscope Co. 7, 15
American Notes 28
Anderson, G.M. 20
Angel, Heather 62
Anthony, Lysette 96
Arden, Eve 99
Arvidson, Linda 23
Atkinson, G. A. 44
Attwell, Michael 97
Aumont, Jean-Pierre 110
The Avengers 102-103, 168
Les Aventures de M. Pickwick 167
Le Avventure di Nicola Nickleby 79, 157

Bah, Humbug! 182
Balderston, John L. 62
Bancroft, George 50
Baragrey, John 76
Bardell Against Pickwick 74, 145
Bardell versus Pickwick 77, 80, 151, 158
Barnaby Rudge 19, 25, 38, 112, 118, 123-124, 126, 162
Bart, Lionel 85, 86

Bartholomew, Freddie 56
Beaumont, Richard 87
Behrman, S.N. 59
Belasco, Leon 99
Bell, Karina 44
Benjamin, Arthur 78, 102
Bennett, Jill 89
Benny, Jack 100
Benson, Elaine 52
Bentley, Thomas 31-32, 37, 38, 39, 44-45, 52-53
Betjeman, John 52
Bevan, Billy 60
Bing Crosby's Merrie Olde Christmas 179
Biograph 7, 20, 38
The Birth of a Soul 128
Blaché, Herbert 37, 38
Blackadder's Christmas Carol 101, 191
Bleak House 41-42, 50, 79, 83, 96-97, 100, 110, 113, 119, 128, 129, 131, 133, 157-158, 172, 188
Bogarde, Dirk 71
Bonanza 102
Bond, Derek 69
Bonne, Shirley 99
The Boots at the Holly Tree Inn 153
Botelho, João 107-108
La Bottega dell'Antiquario 131
The Boy and the Convict 119
Boyd, William Stage 50
Braithwaite, Lillian 40
Bransby Williams 150, 151
Breakston, Georgie 51
Brer Rabbit's Christmas Carol 193

Bricusse, Leslie 86-87
Briers, Richard 80
British Internatinoal Pictures 51-52
British Sound Film Productions 49-50
Brough, Mary 45
Brownlow, Kevin 26
Buckstone, J. C. 13, 34
Buik, Barnaby 96
Bunny, John 27, 34
Burns, Vinnie 30
Bush, W. Stephen 25

Cain, Shirley 96
Calthrop, Donald 61
Camp, Agnes 40
Carney, Art 101
A Carol for Another Christmas 102, 166
Carr, J. Comyns 29
Carr, John Dickson 80
Carradine, John 75
Carry on Christmas 100, 172
The Case of the Twice-Told Twist 169
Cavalcanti, Alberto 65, 69
Cenedella, Robert 80
Chaney, Lon 46
Chaplin, Charles 39, 45
Characters from Bleak House 74
Charles Dickens 169
Charles Dickens: Childhood in Victorian Fiction 175
A Charles Dickens Christmas 71, 139
The Charles Dickens Show 176
The Charlie Drake Show 100, 163
Chesterton, G. K. 3
The Chimes 37, 125
Christmas at Dingley Dell 158
A Christmas Carol 13, 16, 20, 21, 25, 34-35, 40, 60-62, 74, 75, 76, 79, 80, 92, 99, 100, 101, 102, 103, 105, 108, 112, 117, 118, 119, 124, 126, 127-128, 131, 132, 133, 134, 136, 137, 138, 139, 140, 141, 142, 143, 145, 146, 147, 149, 150, 152, 153, 154, 155, 161, 163, 164, 165, 166, 167, 170, 172-173, 174, 177, 179, 180, 182, 184, 185, 186, 187, 189, 190, 191, 193-194
A Christmas Carol at Ford's Theatre 180
Christmas Carol II: The Sequel 189
Christmas Eve with Charles Laughton 152
Christmas Present 189
A Christmas Tree 174
Chronophone sound-on-disc system 19-20
Cilento, Diane 80
Il Circolo Pickwick 79, 171
Clarendon Speaking Pictures 33
Cliffe, Cedric 78, 102
Closed Doors 173
Coates, Albert 73, 74
Collier, Constance 42
Collings, David 87
Colman, Ronald 59
Compton, Fay 70
Conway, Jack 59
Coogan, Jackie 44, 45-46
Cooke, Alistair 23, 76
Cooper, Jackie 56
Cooper, Melville 76, 77
Corey, Wendell 76
Cossins, James 96
Costello, Maurice 26
Coward, Noel 31
Cox, Constance 83
The Cricket on the Hearth 20, 22, 37, 38, 44, 75, 76, 79, 118, 125, 126, 131, 132, 134, 146, 148, 153, 165-166, 170, 174, 182
Crosby, Bing 75
Cross, John Keir 80
Crowther, Bosley 70
Crutchley, Rosalie 71
Crystal Film Co. 29
Cukor, George 56-58

Index

Cushing, Peter 93

Danger 76, 147
David and Betsey Trotwood 160
David and Dora 160
David and Dora Married 160
David and his Mother 159
David and Mr. Micawber 160
David Copperfield 22, 25, 28, 31-32, 43, 44, 49, 55-58, 77, 78, 79, 87, 103, 112, 119, 120, 121, 123, 132, 135, 140, 150, 152-153, 155, 159-161, 164, 167, 168-169, 175, 176, 185, 189-190, 193
Davies, John Howard 69
Davis, Paul 60
The Day The Rebs Took Lincoln 184
Death of Nancy Sykes 7, 117
Delaney, Leo 26
de Mille, William 55
Dent, Alan 66
Desmond, Eric 32
Dickens and Great Expectations 175
Dickens, Charles: first color movie from 71-72, 139; first film from 7, 117; first talkie from 19, 49-50, 133; first television from 73, 145; first TV serial from 76; illustrations in his books 4; interest in drama 2; multitude of characters 2
A Dickens Chronicle 165
Dickens' London 133
Dickens, Mamie 2
Dickens of London 91, 177
Dickens Up-to-Date 132
A Dickensian Fantasy 134
Dickens' Christmas Carol 146
A Different Twist 186
Dobie, Alan 85
Doctor Marigold 175
Dolly Varden 19, 25, 118, 123
Dombey and Son 40, 50, 96, 127, 133-134, 171-172, 185-186

Donaldson, Geoffrey 41
Donner, Clive 105
Donner, Richard 108
Doro, Marie 30, 39
Dotheboys Hall; Or Nicholas Nickleby 15, 117
Dotrice, Roy 91
Drake, Charlie 100
Drayton, Alfred 70
Dream of Old Scrooge 119
El Duelo 174
The Dukes of Hazzard 186
Dunlop, Lesley 84

Ealing Studios 64, 70
The Early Life of David Copperfield 28, 120
Ebenezer Scrooge Appopolous 100, 163
Edison Manufacturing Co. 25, 28, 33
Edzard, Christine 106, 107
Eisenstein, Sergei 1, 22
Eklund, Britt 102
Eldridge, Florence 79
Elliott, Denholm 97
Elvey, Maurice 42
Emlyn Williams as Charles Dickens 147
Encyclopedia Britannica Films 71
The Energy Carol 103, 176
Erasmus Microman 192
Essanay Film Manufacturing Co. 20
Eugene Wrayburn 25, 120
Evans, Edith 86, 87
Evans, Fred 41
Evans, Geraint 103
Evans, Joe 41

Fagin 131
Fame 189
Family Ties 186

Famous Authors: Charles Dickens 193
The Fancy Ball 149
Farnum, William 41
Fenton, Mabel 7
Fields, W. C. 56-57
Finney, Albert 86-87
Flying A 38
Fowler, Harry 70, 80
Fox, William 41
Fox Film Corporation 41
Francis, Derek 91, 94
Francis, Raymond 80
The Further Adventures of Oliver Twist 93, 181

Gabriel Grub the Surly Sexton 15, 117
Gaumont Co. 15, 16, 19, 20, 50
Die Geheimnisse von London 42, 129
Gellardi, Bertha 42
The Ghost and Christmas Past 100, 172
The Ghost and Mrs. Muir 100, 172
Ghost Stories from Pickwick Papers 190
Gianakos, Larry James 95
Gillette, William 39
Gleason, Jackie 101
Glover, Julian 96
Going Into Society 164
Goodwin, Nat C. 29-30, 39
Gordon, Serena 110
The Gospel According to Scrooge 186
Gould, Jack 76
Les Grandes Esperances 171
Grandfather Smallweed 133
Great Expectations 40, 43, 51, 52, 65-68, 77, 79, 80, 87, 92, 94, 102, 110, 119, 127, 128, 135, 137, 138, 140-141, 150, 157, 161, 162, 171, 173, 182, 185, 190, 191, 192
Great Expectations and Charles Dickens 187

Great Expectations—The Untold Story 109, 190
The Great Inimitable Mr. Dickens 103, 173
The Great Santa Claus Chase 186
Greene, Graham 59
Greenwood, Joan 106
Griffith, D. W. 20, 21-23, 38
Il Grillo del Focolare 79, 165-166
Le Grillon du Foyer 131, 134, 153, 182
Guers, Paul 71
Guinness, Alec 66, 68, 69, 86, 88, 105, 106

Hale, Alan 51
Hall, James Andrew 83
Hall, Mordaunt 50
Hard Times 39, 49, 84, 107-108, 110, 113, 126, 142-143, 178, 185, 191, 193, 194
Hardwicke, Cedric 70, 76
Hardy, Robert 78
Harrison, Louis Reeves 28
Harvey, John Martin 47
Harvey, Laurence 80
Havelock-Allan, Anthony 66
Havers, Nigel 91
Hayden, Sterling 102
Hayter, James 70
Helsengreen, Emil 43
Hemmings, David 89
Hepworth, Cecil 27, 30-32, 37, 38, 39
The Hero of My Life 103, 173
Herzberg, Martin 44
Hicks, Seymour 13, 14, 34, 45, 60-61
Hickson, Joan 80, 94
Hobson, Valerie 51, 62, 67
A Holiday Romance 155-156, 185
The Holly Tree 153, 158
Holmes, Phillips 51
The Honeymooners' Christmas Special 101, 178-179
The Honourable Event 123

Index

Hopcraft, Arthur 83, 97, 100
Hopkins, Anthony 10
Hordern, Michael 89, 92, 100
How Bella Was Won 25, 120
Howes, Sally Ann 69
Hughes, Roddy 71
Humbug, Mrs. Brown 100, 167
The Humour of Dickens 148
Hunt, Martita 66, 67, 79-80
Hunted Down 76, 148, 192

Ingram, Rex 27
It's a Wonderful Job 190

Jacobi, Derek 106
James, Sidney 100
Jensen, Frederick 44
Jo the Crossing Sweeper 119, 128
John Grin's Christmas 190
Julian, Rupert 40

Keen, Malcolm 76
Kelly, Grace 76
Kenner Family Classics 186
Kent, Charles 27
King, Dennis 75
Klein Doortje 41, 127
Klein Dorrit 134
A Knight for a Night 119
Kriegel, Kathie 110

Laemmle, Carl 52
Lanchester, Elsa 56-57
Langley, Noel 70
Lasky, Jesse L. 30, 39
Laughton, Charles 56-57
Lean, David 51, 65, 80, 86, 110
Leaves from the Books of Charles Dickens 121
Lee, Christopher 71
Leighton, Margaret 88
Leonard, Hugh 83, 92
Lesser, Sol L. 46
Lester, Mark 85

Letts, Barry 78
Levin, Bernard 94
Lewton, Val 60
Leyenda de Navidad 137
Library of Congress 15
The Life and Adventures of Nicholas Nickleby 94-96, 183-184
Lille Dorrit 132-133
Lilli Palmer Theatre 77
Literature—adaptation for the screen 3-6
Little Dorrit 28, 29, 41, 43, 106-107, 123, 127, 129, 132-133, 134, 142, 163, 174
Little Emily 121
Little Em'ly and David Copperfield 28, 121
Little Nell 19-20, 118
Little, Rich 101
The Lives and Times of Ebenezer Scrooge 60
Lloyd, Frank 41, 46
Loader, Kevin 97
Lockhart, Gene 61-62
Love and the Law 25, 119
The Loves of David Copperfield 28, 121
Lowe, Arthur 103

M-G-M 55-62, 71, 112
McDowall, Roddy 77
McGiver, John 102
McNee, Patrick 70
Le Magasin d'Antiquities 166
The Magic Fishbone 155, 185
The Magic of Charles Dickens 169
Malberg, Peter 44
The Man From the Moors 78, 151
Mancini, Henry 102
Mankiewicz, Joseph L. 102
Mankowitz, Wolf 86, 91
Manvell, Roger 49
Marcel Marceau's Christmas Carol 174

March, Frederic 79, 102
Margolyes, Miriam 107
Marley's Ghost 76, 147
Marsh, Ngaio 80
Martin Chuzzlewit 28, 29, 83, 112, 113, 121, 125, 166, 176, 194
Martin, Buddy 44
The Mating of Watkins Tottle 152
Matz, B.W. 43
Mayer, Louis B. 55, 56, 58
Meet Mr. Dickens 79, 158
Méliès, Georges 8
Mel's Christmas Carol 101, 182
The Merriest Christmas Yet 186
The Merry Christmas 102, 152, 156-157
Mickey's Christmas Carol 105, 109, 141-142
Miles, Bernard 67, 70
Miles, Sarah 88
Mills, John 67
Mills, Juliet 103
Miss Havisham 79, 161
Mister Quilp 88-89, 92, 141
Mitchell Boys Choir 75
The Modern Oliver Twist 16-19, 117
Monogram Pictures Corporation 50
Montgomery, Douglass 62, 63
Moody, Ron 86, 109
Moonlighting 101
Moore, Dickie 50-51
More, Kenneth 93
Morley, Robert 80
Morrison, James 26-27
Mr. Bumble the Beadle 8, 117
Mr. Chops 164
Mr. Dickens of London 103, 170
Mr. Dickens Presents 192
Mr. Guppy's Tale 172
Mr. Horatio Sparkins 123
Mr. Magoo's Christmas Carol 100, 164
Mr. Pickwick 73, 145, 165

Mr. Pickwick in a Double Bedded Room 124
Mr. Pickwick's Christmas at Wardle's 8, 117
Mr. Pickwick's Dilemma 159
Mr. Pickwick's Predicament 25, 33, 122
Mr. Scrooge 102, 166
Mr. White's Christmas 102, 167
Mrs. Corney Makes Tea 124
Mrs. Lirriper's Legacy 29, 123
Mrs. Lirriper's Lodgers 29, 122
Mrs. Lirriper's Lodgings 158
Mugby Junction 158, 164, 177
The Muppet Christmas Carol 143
Musgrave, Thea 103
Music Review 153
My Favorite Martian 100
My Little Boy 127-128
My Sister Eileen 99
The Mystery of Edwin Drood 20, 38, 62, 76, 80, 111, 118, 122, 125, 135-136, 143-144, 147-148, 162

Nancy 130
Neame, Ronald 66, 86
The New Adventures of Oliver Twist 193
Newley, Anthony 69, 88, 89
Newton, Robert 69
Nicholas Nickleby 6, 15, 25, 28, 41, 65, 69, 78, 79, 91-92, 94-96, 103, 117, 119, 121, 137, 154, 155, 157, 170-171, 174-175, 178, 183-184
Nickleby & Co. 183
Nielsen, Peter 43
Nordisk Films Co. 43
Nye, Thomas 20

The Odd Couple 101, 173
Old Scrooge 119
The Old Curiosity Shop 2, 19, 20, 28, 44, 51-52, 80, 83, 88, 92, 112, 113, 118, 120, 121, 124, 130, 131, 134-

Index

135, 141, 151, 161-162, 164, 166, 180, 183, 190
The Old Soldier 160-161
Oliver! 85-86, 87, 139
Oliver and Company 109, 143
Oliver, Edna May 60
Oliver Twist 7, 8, 16, 20, 21, 29, 30, 31, 42, 46, 50, 65, 66, 67, 68-69, 70, 78, 80, 83, 85, 86, 92, 96, 97, 109, 112, 117, 118, 119, 120, 122, 124, 126, 127, 128, 129, 130, 134, 138, 139, 141, 143, 158, 163, 176, 181, 185, 186, 188-189, 190, 193
Oliver Twist Jr. 42-43, 129
Oliver Twist Sadly Twisted 126
Oliver Twisted 41, 127
Omnibus 76, 149
The Only Way 47, 75, 133, 146
Orphans of the Storm 22
Orphans, Waifs and Wards 182
Orson Welles' Great Mysteries 175
O'Shea, Tessie 102
Osward, Richard 42
Otis, Elita 20
Our Miss Brooks 99, 153
Our Mutual Friend 25, 43, 79, 84, 92, 120, 129-130, 155, 156, 176-177
Owen, Reginald 60, 61

Paramount Publix Corporation 40, 50
Parfitt, Judy 93
The Parish Boy's Progress 176
Pasco, Richard 80
A Passion for Justice 102, 165
The Passions of Carol 89, 141
Patrick, Nigel 71
Paul, Robert W. 8, 13, 14, 15, 27
Pearson, George 44
La Pequeña Dorrit 174
Perry Mason 169
La Petite Dorrit 163
Petrie, Hay 52
Pichel, Irving 50

Pickering, Sarah 107
Pickford, Jack 40
Pickford, Mary 40
Pickwick 86, 91, 171
The Pickwick Papers 15, 25, 33-34, 45, 49, 70, 71, 76, 77, 79, 80, 86, 96, 112, 117, 119, 122, 123, 124, 130, 131, 138-139, 140, 145, 148-149, 151, 152, 158-159, 163, 165, 167, 171, 174, 187, 189, 190
Pickwick versus Bardell 124
Pip! 87
Porter, Eric 97
Powell, Dilys 87
Powell, Robert 111

Quayle, Anthony 88

Rains, Claude 62, 111
Rank Films 71
Rathbone, Basil 59, 80, 102
Ray, Andrew 88
Readers Digest Films 89
Redgrave, Michael 87, 100, 103
Reed, Carol 85
Rees, Roger 95
Renown Pictures 70
Rescued by Rover 30
Reynolds, Stanley 92
Rich Little's Christmas Carol 101, 179-180
Rich Man's Folly 50, 133-134
Richard, Emily 95
Richards, Jeffrey 47
Richardson, Ralph 76, 87
Rigg, Diana 97
The Right to be Happy 40, 126
Ritchard, Cyril 102
Roberts, Rachel 88
Robey, George 70
Rogers, Peter 100
The Rogues 102
Ross, Charles 7
Royal College of Art 108

Royal Shakespeare Company 94
Rufus Rose Marionettes 75
The Runaways 79, 158

Saint, Eve Marie 102
Sam Weller and his Father 159
Sandberg, A.W. 43, 44
Sarandon, Christopher 93
Scenes from Great Expectations 191
Scenes from Hard Times 191
Schenk, Nicholas 57, 59
Scott, George C. 105
Scrooge 13, 34, 50, 60, 70 86, 88, 92, 105, 108-109, 113, 124, 131, 132, 133, 136, 138, 140, 176, 177
Scrooge and the Stars 101
Scrooge Gets An Oscar 101, 173
Scrooge McDuck and Money 106
Scrooge: Or Marley's Ghost 8-13, 117
Scrooged 108, 143
Secombe, Harry 85, 86
The Secret of Charles Dickens 181
See, Hear 191
Selig 20
Sellers, Peter 102
Selznick, David O. 55-60, 87, 112
Serling, Rod 102
The Seven Poor Travellers 170
Seyler, Athene 45, 70, 80
Shaw, Robert 102
Sheffield, Reggie 31
Shelley, Paul 93
Shirley Temple's Storybook 155
The Shooting Party 123
Le Signaleur 164
The Signalman 149, 151, 164, 177
Silverman, Stephen 86
Sim, Alastair 70, 100, 105
Simmons, Jean 67, 100
Sketches by Boz 123, 152, 170
The Skinflint 180-181
The Small Servant 80, 151, 161-162
Smike! 103, 174-175
Smothers Brothers 100

Smothers, Tom 100
Il Sogno del Vecchio Usuraio 119
The South Bank Show 193
Souvenirs d'Enfance de David Copperfield 164
Spanuth, H. A. 29-30
Stannard, Eliot 41
Stark, Graham 109
The Stingiest Man in Town 102, 153, 179
Stock, Nigel 93, 96
Stone, Norman 108
Store Forventninger 128
The Story of the Christmas Carol 152
Storyboard 192
The Strange Christmas Dinner 75
Stritch, Elaine 99
Styne, Jule 99, 100
Sullivan, Francis L. 51, 62, 67, 76
Susskind, David 78
Sverchok Na Pechi 126

A Tale of Two Cities 20, 26-27, 28, 34, 41, 47, 59, 71, 75, 76-77, 78, 83, 93, 102, 109-110, 112, 118, 120, 127, 128, 131, 136, 139, 146, 149, 154, 155, 156, 167-168, 170, 181, 187, 191, 193
Tales From Dickens 79-80, 158-161
Talmadge, Norma 27
Taylor, John Russell 65
Tempos Dificeis, Este Tempo 142-143
Terriss, Ellaline 14
Terriss, Tom 14, 37, 38
Thalberg, Irving 58
Thanhouser, Edwin 27-28
Thanhouser Film Co. 28
Thesiger, Ernest 45
Thomas, Ralph 71
Thorndike, Sybil 70
Threlfall, David 95
The Tom Tuckett Story 102, 162
Too Many Christmas Trees 102-103, 168

Index

Topper 99
Tourneur, Jacques 60
Towers, Harry Alan 79
Trail to Christmas 154-155
Trans-Atlantic Film Co. 39
Trevor, William 92
Trial for Murder 175
The Trial of Mr. Pickwick 76, 149
True Heart Susie 22
Turner, Florence 26
Tutin, Dorothy 71
Twist Oliver 128
The Two Orphans 22

Understanding Narrative: Dickens' Hard Times 193
Uneasy Dreams: The Life of Mr. Pickwick 140
Unger, Gladys 51
Universal Pictures 39, 51, 52, 62
Uriah Heep 161
Ustinov, Peter 95

Varley, Sarah Jane 89, 94
Vaughan, Peter 97
Veness, Amy 52
Vitagraph Co. 16, 19, 20, 26-27, 34
Volpe, Frederick 45
Vor Faelles Ven 129-130
Voyagers 184

Wagenknecht, Edward 22
Wagon Train 102
Walker, Stuart 51

Wall, Max 106
Wallis, Shani 85
Walpole, Hugh 56, 68
Walt Disney Productions 105
Walthall, Henry B. 60
Warner, David 89
Webster, Ben 52
Welsh-Pearson Film Co. 44
West, Timothy 85
The Westgate Seminary 123
What the Dickens? 171
Whitelaw, Billie 93
Whitemore, Hugh 83
Wilby, James 110
Wilcox, Herbert 47, 75
Wild, Jack 84, 85
Williams, Bransby 14, 31, 45, 49-50, 75, 150, 151
Williams, Emlyn 75, 76, 87
Williams, Richard 92, 100
Williams, Vaughan 75
Williamson, James 15
Winkler, Henry 101
WKRP in Cincinnati 101, 182
Wolfit, Donald 70-71, 77, 80
Woods, Aubrey 70
Wyatt, Jane 51

York, Michael 88
A Yorkshire School 25, 119

Zanuck, Darryl F. 59
Zenith Film Co. 34

About the Author

MICHAEL POINTER is a retired businessman living in Lincolnshire, England, where he has been a Justice of the Peace for 30 years. He is the author of *The Public Life of Sherlock Holmes* (1975), which was the first detailed survey of all the dramatizations featuring the famous detective on stage, film, TV, radio, and records. As well as *The Sherlock Holmes File* (1976) and *The Pictorial History of Sherlock Holmes* (1991), he has written 10 books dealing with various aspects of the history of his home town of Grantham, and edited 6 similar works.

His long-held interest in the dramatizations of famous literature has been the subject of articles he has contributed to *American Film*, *The Times*, *The New York Times* and *Plays and Players*. He is also active as a lecturer on the above topics.